CONSCIENCE
and
OTHER
VIRTUES

THE PENNSYLVANIA STATE UNIVERSITY PRESS
UNIVERSITY PARK, PENNSYLVANIA

FROM BONAVENTURE TO MACINTYRE

. . . .

CONSCIENCE
and
OTHER
VIRTUES

DOUGLAS C. LANGSTON

Library of Congress Cataloging-in-Publication Data

Langston, Douglas C.
    Conscience and other virtues : from Bonaventure to MacIntyre /
Douglas C. Langston.
        p.   cm.
    Includes bibliographical references (p.   ) and index.
    ISBN 0-271-02789-4 (cloth : alk. paper)
    1. Conscience.   2. Virtues.   3. Conscience—History.   I. Title.
BJ1471.L36 2001
171'.6—dc21
                                                            00-027430

CONTENTS

Acknowledgments   vii
Introduction   1

PART I: HISTORICAL BACKGROUND

1   Classical Background to Discussions of Conscience   7
2   Bonaventure's View of Conscience and Synderesis   21
3   Aquinas on Conscience, the Virtues, and Weakness of Will   39
4   Scotus and Ockham on Synderesis and Conscience   53
5   Luther and the Rise of Conscience as a Faculty   71

PART II: THE CONTEMPORARY DISMISSAL OF CONSCIENCE

6   Freud and Ryle on Conscience   87
7   Conscience as Something Other Than a Faculty   99
8   More Traditional Views of Conscience   109
9   The Existence of Conscience   121

PART III: CONSCIENCE AS A KEY TO VIRTUE ETHICS

10   Conscience Among the Virtue Ethicists   135
11   Conscience and Virtue Ethics   151
12   Conscience and Other Virtues   173

Appendix: MacIntyre's Project   179
Bibliography   185
Index   189

. . . .

ACKNOWLEDGMENTS

Both Plato and Aristotle wrote on friendship, and they spent a considerable amount of time extolling its importance. In their works, an idyllic picture of friends discussing important ideas in restful circumstances emerges. In the midst of familial and professional duties, my friends and I discuss important and unimportant issues in whatever locale can be found, whether real or virtual. And there are many friends I need to thank for helping me bring this book to completion.

Russ Sizemore, former colleague at New College, receives the greatest thanks. He interested me in the ethics of virtue and, in a course on the virtues that we co-taught, he led me to appreciate many subtleties I might otherwise have missed about the tradition. While I am happy for his success in his new profession, I still miss his energy and intelligence.

Simo Knuuttila and other friends in Finland (Lilli Alanen and Olli Hallamaa, to mention only two) hosted me during my Fulbright stay at the University of Helsinki and gave me an opportunity to discuss my ideas with a group of sophisticated students of philosophy and religion. Simo's help in opening for me a new line of research on the passions and emotions affected the present book in many ways. I will always be honored that several of my friends there bestowed on me the title of "Honorary Finn."

Jeff Stout graciously read the manuscript and offered important suggestions for improving it. Our friendship has become a virtual one over the years given the distance between Princeton and Sarasota. But it is one that I cherish in a number of ways. Luckily, Mike Michalson, another friend from graduate school, works with me at New College. Now that we have both escaped the stresses of college governance, we are able to fish and discuss our intellectual projects with greater frequency. His advice on refocusing parts of this book made for a tighter structure, and I am in his debt. I have also benefited from many conversations over the years with Sayers Brenner, another denizen of Sarasota.

Rega Wood and Robert Andrews encouraged me to submit an essay on Bonaventure's view of conscience and synderesis to *Franciscan Studies*. Their comments on the material helped me get a clearer idea of Bonaventure's importance for views about conscience. I learned much from Rega's *Ockham on the Virtues* and continually learn from our embodied and virtual conversations. As readers will see, I have also learned a great amount from reading, re-reading, and teaching Martha Nussbaum's *The Fragility of Goodness* and Alasdair MacIntyre's *After Virtue*. Here I can only claim a friendship of ideas.

A special note of thanks to Philip Winsor and Sandy Thatcher of The Pennsylvania State University Press. Philip, now retired from the Press, encouraged me to produce another book, and I am happy that I was finally able to send it to him for consideration. I was delighted that Sandy immediately took on the project on Philip's retirement and shepherded it through the various paths leading to its publication. Michael Baylor and another unidentified reader read the manuscript for the Press and offered many important comments.

I owe much to my wife, Connie Whitesell, and our son, Nat. It is hard to live with someone who loves the intellectual life but feels drawn to the practical. I have learned about virtues and wisdom in living with them. I am afraid that much of this learning comes from my failures of virtue and their loving forgiveness. It is perhaps small consolation that I dedicate this book to them.

INTRODUCTION

Conscience has been ignored. Although we use it to guide our actions and we appeal to freedom of conscience in a variety of situations, in the last twenty-five years little has been written about conscience as a useful analytical concept. Why?

It is easy to point to the atrocities of this century as reason to abandon the notion of conscience. Writers like Elie Wiesel and Primo Levi have chronicled the horrors of the Holocaust. Apartheid in South Africa, racial slaughter in Rwanda, and ethnic cleansing in the Balkans all seem to indicate that there is not the guiding force in human behavior that conscience was thought to provide. But beyond the failure of conscience in this century, there are reasons in the philosophical community for abandoning the analytical usefulness of conscience. It is, for example, clear that discussions of conscience after the seventeenth century regard it as a faculty distinct from, but on a par with, the intellect, will, and memory. And recent theoretical discussions have abandoned the notion of faculties as useful. It is thus obvious why the faculty of conscience has passed into disfavor over the last three decades. Yet, we still use the concepts of intellect, memory, and will as useful analytical tools even though we no longer regard them as faculties. Why, then, should conscience be ignored?

Perhaps the long-standing identification of conscience with some set of rules for behavior undercuts its importance. We follow the rules we formulate or are given and try to deduce even more. This reasoning seems much like ordinary moral discussion and need not be put under the notion of conscience.

Once we remove moral reasoning from conscience, it appears that the only function of conscience is to goad us to proper behavior by making us feel uncomfortable when we do other than we should. Yet, this reduction of conscience to an emotional buzzer hardly preserves a notion of conscience.

The discomfort can be explained in terms of emotional dissonance; there is little need to assume that a conscience is the source for feeling ill at ease.

So we do not write much about conscience because we seem to be able to dispense with it as an analytical tool. But we still talk about conscience. Why?

The quick answer is that conscience is still an extremely useful concept even in the face of the failures of conscience witnessed this century. In fact, I shall argue in Part III, Conscience as a Key to Virtue Ethics, that it is an important part of any good theory of the virtues. Before presenting this argument, however, I hope in Part I, Historical Background, to tell the story (or at least present the highlights of a certain story) of the concept of conscience in the Western intellectual tradition. Given our contemporary understanding of conscience, it is a surprising story.

We presently live in an era when most discussions of ethics are framed in utilitarian or deontological terms. But this approach to ethics is a recent development. Classical thinkers—especially Plato and Aristotle—propounded what has been called an ethics of virtue. Instead of emphasizing acts and rules, a virtue ethics discusses the development of the moral agent and argues that his or her development is best achieved by the cultivation of moral virtues like prudence, justice, fortitude, and temperance as well as the intellectual virtues. A moral agent armed with the virtues will be able to make the proper decisions that lead to a life of fulfillment. The classical view of virtue ethics was also dominant in the Middle Ages, but in a somewhat Christianized form. Medieval thinkers added an intentional element to the views of Plato and Aristotle, which made the aim of fulfilling God's loving commands crucial to the development of all virtues.

The Middle Ages also witnessed a sophisticated discussion of the nature and function of conscience. Although the notion of conscience can be found in some classical and biblical sources, what should be regarded as the source for our present understanding of conscience comes most directly from these medieval discussions. As it turns out, the tradition of virtue ethics in the Middle Ages provided an essential context to these discussions. Unfortunately, subsequent discussions of conscience lost this context as a result of the increasing dominance of the belief that conscience is a faculty. This problematic development has caused the modern concept of conscience to be relegated to the realm of fiction and has cut off any significant discussion of conscience among the recent proponents of a modern virtue ethics. This fact is regrettable.

There has been a dearth of philosophical material on conscience in the last quarter century, but most of what has been written seems to assume that conscience is a faculty with merely personal authority and fairly circumscribed functions. My aim in Part II, The Contemporary Dismissal of Conscience, is to discuss this contemporary view particularly in light of the story I offer in Part I. I argue that many of the contemporary criticisms of conscience can be met by a return to key aspects of conscience as it was articulated in the Middle Ages. Once we cease to regard conscience as a faculty whose judgments are infallible but merely personal and purely punitive, a more fruitful contemporary understanding of conscience can be developed. I sketch such a view of conscience in Chapter 9. This view is informed both by the history I present and by the work of certain contemporary theorists (discussed in Chapter 8) who discuss the nature of a "mature conscience."

The three parts of this book have different emphases and thus have various appeals to diverse audiences. Part I will be of most interest to those who are concerned with historical issues. Because I do not present an exhaustive survey of the history of conscience, I choose what I deem to be the most important periods and figures in this (unwritten) history. As I have indicated, and as I hope to demonstrate in the work itself, I focus on the discussions of conscience and the virtue tradition in the Middle Ages. This period, and the figures I concentrate on, presents aspects of the relation between conscience and the virtues that have been lost in contemporary discussion of conscience. Part II will interest those who look for an analysis of concepts. I have tried in this part to look at both philosophical and theological sources. While this is not an exhaustive treatment of all the issues and concepts surrounding conscience, I address key issues and questions that contemporary theorists have raised about conscience. Finally, Part III will be of interest to those concerned with virtue ethics or theories of moral development. I have tried to survey much of the recent material on virtue ethics but have focused on two important presentations of it.

The three parts, although somewhat independent of one another, are not meant to be read in isolation from one another. To understand fully, for example, my discussion in Part III of the concept of the morally good person so important to virtue ethicists, one must understand my discussion of Aquinas's notions of *eubulia* and *synesis* in Part I and my discussion in Part II of Freud and the advocates of what is called a mature conscience. In talking about conscience, as is true for so many things, the whole is greater than the sum of the parts.

PART ONE

HISTORICAL BACKGROUND

CLASSICAL BACKGROUND TO
DISCUSSIONS OF CONSCIENCE

Our modern notion of conscience has had an unfortunate development. To-day, most people regard conscience as a judging and punishing faculty. It judges the worth of a person's actions and influences how a person behaves by making the person experience guilt when wrong is done. As an internal judge, its pronouncements and punishments are limited to the person whose conscience it is. But this modern notion of conscience developed from con-siderably different views.

The modern term *conscience* derives most immediately from the Latin term *conscientia*. This term in turn derives from the Greek term *suneidesis*. Both the Latin and Greek terms carry a double meaning of "either the state (or act) of sharing knowledge or else simply knowledge, awareness, apprehension—

even something like mind or thought."[1] The double meaning is preserved in the French term *conscience*. In modern English, however, the double meaning is broken up. 'Consciousness' carries the notion of awareness or apprehension. 'Conscience' is connected with a type of knowledge: typically the knowledge of what an individual should do. Except in the trivial sense that moral language itself is a shared discourse among human beings, the idea that conscience involves a sharing of knowledge with others has been lost. Why should our modern notion of conscience differ so markedly from the notions from which it developed? The answer to the question involves several historical departures from the medieval view of conscience.

In the Middle Ages, conscience was not seen as a faculty; on the contrary, it was viewed as an aspect of practical reason. After Aquinas, discussions about conscience were integrally linked with issues concerning the development and cultivation of the virtues. With the Protestant Reformation, conscience became increasingly viewed as an entity that functioned as an internal (God-given) judge. Its tie with the virtues became more and more remote as did its connection to practical reason. In concert with the rise of faculty psychology, conscience became regarded as a faculty of the human mind on a par with the intellect, will, and memory. Its principal functions were to represent to the individual the universal laws of moral behavior, apply them in specific cases, and punish the individual for going against them. As attacks on belief in universal laws of moral behavior grew, the emphasis on conscience as a personal faculty increased. If there are no universal laws of behavior, each person must have an individual faculty for determining how he or she should act. Although an individual may listen to the others' viewpoints, the individual's faculty of conscience is the final judge for the individual. With the downfall of faculty psychology, however, the very idea that there could be such a judging faculty has been challenged.

It is unfortunate that conscience has attained a dubious status, for it is clear that ordinary discourse indicates the continued importance of the roles conscience has played for moral discussion. This suggests that instead of rejecting the existence of conscience we should formulate a proper understanding of it. Rediscovering the historical roots of the notion of conscience is one way to formulate a proper view for modern audiences because these

1. C. S. Lewis, *Studies in Words* (Cambridge: Cambridge University Press, 1967), 181. Those interested in the nature of conscience in other cultures can consult Jayne Hoose, ed., *Conscience in World Religions* (South Bend: University of Notre Dame Press, 2000).

roots offer important considerations for any viable theory of conscience. I believe that a proper view of conscience involves interweaving the notion of conscience with issues about the development of the virtues, the nature of practical reason, and the puzzle of weakness of will. These issues were discussed by Bonaventure (d. 1274), Aquinas (d. 1274), Scotus (d. 1308), and Ockham (d. 1349), and I devote considerable time (Chapters 3, 4, and 5) to their views. But some important background is necessary first.

Late medieval discussions of conscience derived most immediately from Peter Lombard's presentation of the concepts of conscience and synderesis in his *Sentences*. Lombard (d. 1160) cites a passage from Saint Jerome (d. 419), interpreting Ezekiel's vision of four living creatures coming out of a cloud.[2] Each creature was shaped like a man, but each had four faces: The front face was human; the right was that of a lion; the left was that of an ox; and the back was that of an eagle (Ezekiel 1.4–14). Jerome identifies the human face as representing the rational part of humans, the lion as the emotional, the ox as the appetitive, and the eagle as that "which the Greeks call synteresis: that spark of conscience which was not even extinguished in the breast of Cain after he was turned out of paradise, and by which we discern that we sin, when we are overcome by pleasures or frenzy and meanwhile are misled by an imitation of reason" (689). Jerome's comment that synteresis (alternatively, synderesis) is never extinguished in human beings and his remarks elsewhere to the effect that wicked people cease to have any conscience led Lombard and subsequent thinkers to distinguish synderesis from conscience. It is unclear that Jerome meant to distinguish the two, but the distinction plays a major role in late medieval discussions of conscience.[3]

In these discussions of conscience and synderesis, constant reference was made to certain works by Plato and Aristotle. Neither Plato nor Aristotle explicitly mentions conscience, however. It is their discussions of the virtues, practical wisdom, and weakness of will that form the critical backdrop to medieval discussions of conscience and their contributions to a viable view of conscience. For Plato (d. 347 B.C.E.), it is clear that his concern with the question of whether virtue can be taught influenced medieval discussions of conscience. In the *Protagoras*, for example, Plato pits Protagoras, the sophist, against Socrates on the question. At the beginning of the dialogue,

2. Timothy Potts, "Conscience," in N. Kretzmann, A. Kenny, and J. Pinborg, eds., *The Cambridge History of Later Medieval Philosophy* (Cambridge: Cambridge University Press, 1980), 688–89. (Hereafter Potts, "Conscience.")

3. Ibid., 690. The distinction between conscience and synderesis is explored in Chapter 2.

Protagoras maintains that virtue can be taught, and he teaches it. Socrates opposes this view and argues that, if virtue were teachable, virtuous men would instruct their children in it and so there would be no unvirtuous children of virtuous men. Yet, there are many examples to the contrary (319e–320b). Protagoras's first long speech is given, in part, to answer this argument, and his explanation that children may have natural talents different from their fathers' (327a–c) and not learn virtue seems plausible enough. It is of surprise to readers that Socrates responds to the speech by asking an apparently irrelevant question: "Now I want you to tell me truly whether virtue is one whole of which justice and temperance and holiness are parts or whether all these are only the names of one and the same thing" (329c–d). As it turns out, this unexpected question introduces a topic that occupies Plato throughout the dialogues: the unity of the virtues.[4] It is also a topic that influenced medieval discussions of conscience.

Protagoras answers Socrates' question by saying that the qualities Socrates mentions are parts of Virtue, which is one. Elaborating further, he suggests that the virtues are a part of Virtue in the same way that the parts of a face are part of the face: They are different from one another but united by being part of a whole of which the others are also part. In line with this analogy, Protagoras claims that it makes sense to think that one can possess one of the virtues without possessing the others. So the unity he proposes among the virtues allows for considerable diversity among them.

In response to Protagoras's view about the unity of the virtues, Socrates seems to defend the claim that the virtues are unified by their all being mere names for the same thing; that is, courage, temperance, justice, and wisdom all name the same thing—Virtue. Needless to say, it follows from this view that no one can possess any one virtue in isolation from the others, for if all the virtues name the same thing and someone possesses courage, the person also possesses the other virtues. In fact, Socrates uses the virtue of courage to show Protagoras the unity of the virtues by demonstrating that one who possesses courage must also possess knowledge, namely the knowledge of what is and is not dangerous. Protagoras's capitulation to Socrates on this issue is, however, short sighted from Socrates' viewpoint. For at the end of the dialogue, he realizes that he has shown that Virtue is Knowledge. And if this is true, Virtue must be teachable because Knowledge is teachable. But

---

4. Gregory Vlastos analyzes the unity in "The Unity of the Virtues in the *Protagoras*," in his *Platonic Studies* (Princeton: Princeton University Press, 1981). (Hereafter Vlastos, "The Unity of the Virtues in the *Protagoras*.")

the view that Virtue is teachable was the very view of Protagoras that Socrates was trying to defeat at the beginning of the dialogue. Socrates' puzzlement at having defeated himself causes the dialogue to end on an incomplete note. Yet, this incompleteness is fitting, for the teachability of virtue is discussed once again in the *Meno*.

Although many people focus on this dialogue for its famous presentation of the Doctrine of Recollection, the dialogue mostly concerns virtue. In fact, the dialogue begins with a quest for the essential definition of 'virtue,' and the failure to find it leads to the Eristic Paradox and the story of the slave boy that is used to present the Doctrine of Recollection. This doctrine with its message that truth is already within the soul is, as a matter of fact, intended to give hope that we can look for Virtue and discuss it even if we cannot define it, because its definition is in us, waiting to be brought out.

On this hopeful note, the dialogue continues with a discussion of whether virtue can be taught. We are once again faced with the problem of the *Protagoras*: If it is a form of knowledge it can be taught, but if it can be taught surely the children of virtuous men would have been taught it and themselves be virtuous; yet many children of virtuous men are not virtuous. Although the *Protagoras* ends with the view that, despite the problem of unvirtuous children of virtuous men, virtue seems to be a form of knowledge, the *Meno* ends on the opposite note. Virtue seems to be god given: "If all we have said in this discussion, and the questions we have asked, have been right, virtue will be acquired neither by nature nor by teaching. Whoever has it gets it by divine dispensation without taking thought, unless he be the kind of statesman who can create another like himself" (99e–100). Socrates seems to reach this conclusion in part by arguing that there are neither teachers nor students of Virtue, and so Virtue is not teachable and is not knowledge. But there are two important discussions in the dialogue that should not be overlooked.

Immediately after the story of the slave boy, Socrates repeats the familiar point, "If on the other hand virtue is some sort of knowledge, clearly it could be taught" (89c). He moves on to suggest that Virtue, whatever it is, makes us good, and all good things are advantageous. So Virtue must be advantageous. As it turns out, what makes things advantageous is "right use" of them (88a). In particular, the "right use" of temperance and quickness involves wisdom, and "everything that the human spirit undertakes or suffers will lead to happiness when it is guided by wisdom but to the opposite, when guided by folly" (88c). Socrates then draws the following conclusion: "If then virtue is an attribute of the spirit, and one which cannot fail to be beneficial, it must be wisdom, for all spiritual qualities in and by themselves are neither advantageous nor harmful, but become advantageous or harmful by the presence with them of wisdom or folly. If we accept this argument, then virtue, to be something advantageous, must be a sort of wisdom" (88c–d).

The claim that virtue is a form of wisdom is repeated a few lines later: "So we may say in general that the goodness of nonspiritual assets depends on our spiritual character, and the goodness of that on wisdom. This argument shows that the advantageous element must be wisdom, and virtue, we agree, is advantageous; so that amounts to saying that virtue, either in whole or in part, is wisdom" (88e–89a). What is added in this passage is that the spiritual character of an individual, which determines the goodness of nonspiritual assets, depends on the individual's wisdom. Socrates then goes on to discuss whether the spiritual quality of an individual is "by nature" or "by learning." Needless to say, this inquiry is really the inquiry whether wisdom is achieved through nature or learning. Clearly, wisdom is not from nature, because it is not possessed by all human beings. But is it from learning? Meno attacks this question by once again asking the familiar question of whether it is a form of knowledge and thus teachable. This issue becomes connected with the issue of whether there are teachers and students of Virtue. Anytus picks up this concern, and it quickly becomes a discussion of the merits of the sophists, supposed teachers of Virtue. This discussion, unfortunately, obscures the second important discussion I wish to bring attention to, for it figures prominently in medieval discussions of conscience.

After Anytus has had his say, Meno and Socrates reach agreement that Sophists are not teachers of knowledge. But instead of offering a wholesale condemnation of the sophists, Socrates says:

> I have a suspicion, Meno, that you and I are not much good. Our masters Gorgias and Prodicus have not trained us properly. We must certainly take ourselves in hand, and try to find someone who will improve us by hook or crook. I say this with our recent discussion in mind, for absurdly enough we failed to perceive that it is not only under the guidance of knowledge that human action is well and rightly conducted. I believe that may be what prevents us from seeing how it is that men are made good. (96d–e)

What follows is a brief discussion of the difference between knowledge and true opinion. This discussion ends with the surprising conclusion: "Therefore true opinion is as good a guide as knowledge for the purpose of acting rightly" (97b). It is important to notice the qualification "for the purpose of acting rightly," for Socrates immediately indicates that, in general, knowledge is superior to true opinion because it is tethered by recollection to the Forms and true opinion is not. Yet, when it comes to the affairs of the state, right opinion is as useful as knowledge, and both of them are not from nature but are acquired (98d).

If we link this second discussion on knowledge and true opinion with the first discussion on Virtue as a form of wisdom, a position seems to emerge. Although Virtue is a form of wisdom, wisdom is not to be seen as knowledge. Knowledge can lead to Virtue (Plato thinks that knowledge of the Forms in fact gives it), but Virtue is usually achieved through right opinion about the affairs of the state. Thus wisdom as Socrates uses it in the *Meno* seems to be a form of right opinion. And it seems to be linked to the experience of statesmen who by activity learn what is good for the state even if they cannot teach their wisdom (99b–c). The dialogue concludes by stating that right opinion is not teachable; nor is it given through nature. It is by "divine dispensation." That is to say, it is a mystery why some (the few) have it but others do not. There is thus a recognition in Plato's writings that cultivation of the virtues requires activity in the world and is tied to experience. It is not to be learned by purely speculative means or discourse alone. Experience seems to matter even if experience alone will not yield virtue.

Aristotle (d. 322 B.C.E.) is also concerned with the acquiring of right opinion and the virtues. He discusses these issues in his *Nicomachean Ethics* and emphasizes the importance of developing practical wisdom. His discussion had tremendous influence on medieval discussions of practical knowledge as well as conscience and offers considerations that any contemporary theory of conscience needs to take into account.

The discussion in Book I of the *Nicomachean Ethics* is paradigmatic of the overall argument of the work. At the beginning of the book, in an obvious echo of certain Platonic views, Aristotle claims that all things aim at the good. Because human beings are a part of "all things," they also aim at the good. But what is "the good" for them? Noting that the good must be that for which all other activities are done, Aristotle argues that the good for human beings must be happiness. Of course, there are many different views about what constitutes human happiness. To decide what human happiness is, Aristotle suggests that, whatever it is, it must be unique to human beings and must be something that cannot easily be taken away. Using these two criteria, he easily disposes of the views that happiness consists in pleasure, honor, or wealth. Although he does not argue in Book I that human happiness is the contemplative life, it becomes clear later in *Nicomachean Ethics* that the contemplative life is an important component of happiness.[5]

But Aristotle's real concern in Book I is not so much to explain what human happiness is as to indicate how it may be achieved. His answer is very clear: We can achieve human happiness through the practice of the virtues. In fact, in Book I he defines human happiness in relation to the virtues: "[H]uman good turns out to be activity of soul in accordance with virtue, and if there are more than one virtue, in accordance with the best and most complete" (1098a15f.). Given his view that the virtues are the means to achieve happiness, it is not surprising that a considerable portion of *Nicomachean Ethics* is devoted to issues about the virtues.

There are two types of virtues for Aristotle: the intellectual and the moral. The intellectual virtues are five in number: scientific knowledge, intuitive wisdom, art, practical wisdom, and philosophical wisdom. Aristotle says that these virtues may be taught, but the moral virtues must be achieved through practice (1103a15f.). Among the moral virtues he treats in Books III to V are courage, temperance, liberality, magnificence, pride, good temper, friendliness, truthfulness, shame, and justice. Although it is clear that he thinks there are only five intellectual virtues, it is not as clear that the virtues he treats constitute an exhaustive list of the moral virtues.

In Book II, Aristotle emphasizes that moral virtue is formed by repeated acts of a certain type that give rise to a habit. But it is a habit of a particular type: a state of character. He clearly wishes to emphasize by this notion that a virtue is something that is both long lasting in a person and also forms a critical aspect of the person. A virtue transforms a person in the sense that not only does he or she act in appropriate ways but also he or she acts and feels in a certain way when performing the appropriate action. The actions of a just person, for example, are qualitatively different from the actions of a person who simply acts justly: The just person acts with the proper feeling state associated with justice.[6] Aristotle is not clear (nor can he be) about

5. Book 10 of the *Nicomachean Ethics* has presented difficulties for commentators on Aristotle. Chapters 6 through 8 seem to present an account of the happy life that regards it as purely contemplative. This account seems at odds with the account of the happy life throughout the rest of the work as involving friendship and the moral virtues. See Nussbaum's discussion of the difficulty in the Appendix to Part III in *The Fragility of Goodness* (Cambridge: Cambridge University Press, 1986). It is worth remarking that in Book 10 Aristotle indicates that in Book 1 he has argued that the best life is the contemplative one. An examination of Book 1 does not seem to support this claim, however.

6. An excellent discussion of this point can be found in L. A. Kosman's "Being Properly Affected:

how the habits of virtue become virtues, but he offers a useful contrast with the arts:

> Again, the case of the arts and that of the virtues are not similar; for the products of the arts have their goodness in themselves, as that it is enough that they should have a certain character, but if the acts that are in accordance with the virtues have themselves a certain character, it does not follow that they are done justly or temperately. The agent also must be in a certain condition when he does them; in the first place, he must have knowledge, secondly he must choose the acts, and choose them for their own sakes, and thirdly his action must proceed from a firm and unchangeable character. (1105a27f.)

Aristotle portrays virtues as means between excesses and deficiencies. For example, the virtue of good temper is a mean between the excess, irascibility, and the deficiency, inirascibility. What is for one person an excess, however, might well be a deficiency for another, and Aristotle acknowledges that there are no hard and fast rules for any individual to develop the virtues. At best, one can start with rough rules of thumb like "avoid pleasure" or "pattern yourself after a man exemplifying the particular virtue you are interested in developing." Ultimately, what constitutes a virtue is what gets one to the state of practical wisdom: "Virtue, then, is a state of character concerned with choice, lying in a mean, i.e. the mean relative to us, this being determined by a rational principle, and by that principle by which the man of practical wisdom would determine it" (1107a1f.).

Practical wisdom is treated throughout Book VII, and it is presented in contrast with the other intellectual virtues. It is different from scientific knowledge because its first principles are variable. It is not an art because it is a doing and not a making. Moreover, it is a doing that involves actions that could be done in another way. It involves the part of the soul that forms opinions (the calculative part), and it is particularly concerned with opinions about the good for human beings. In general, the mark of the person of practical wisdom is that he can deliberate well about that which leads to the good life in general.

Virtues and Feelings in Aristotle's Ethics," in Amelie Rorty, ed., *Essays on Aristotle's Ethics* (Berkeley and Los Angeles: University of California Press, 1980).

In Chapter 13 of Book VII, Aristotle relates practical wisdom to the platonic problem of the Unity of the Virtues:

> This is why some say that all the virtues are forms of practical wisdom, and why Socrates in one respect was on the right track while in another he went astray; in thinking that all the virtues were forms of practical wisdom he was wrong, but in saying they implied practical wisdom he was right. This is confirmed by the fact that even now all men, when they define virtue, after naming the state of character and its objects add "that (state) which is in accordance with the right rule"; now the right rule is that which is in accordance with practical wisdom. (1144b15f.)

Although one might easily dispute Aristotle's interpretation of Plato here and question whether it is wisdom or practical wisdom that provides unity to the virtues for Plato, it is critical to note that Aristotle suggests in this passage that there is some type of unity to the virtues and that practical wisdom in some way provides it. Aristotle sheds more light on these two points a few lines later in the text:

> It is clear, then, from what has been said, that it is not possible to be good in the strict sense without practical wisdom, nor practically wise without moral virtue. But in this way we may also refute the dialectical argument whereby it might be contended that the virtues exist in separation from each other; the same man, it might be said, is not best equipped by nature for all the virtues, so that he will have already acquired one when he has not yet acquired another. This is possible in respect of the natural virtues, but not in respect of those in respect of which a man is called without qualification good; for with the presence of the one quality, practical wisdom, will be given all the virtues. And it is plain that, even if it were of no practical value, we should have needed it because it is the virtue of the part of us in question; plain too that the choice will not be right without practical wisdom any more than without virtue; for the one determines the end and the other makes us do the things that lead to the end. (1144b30f.)

Practical wisdom seems to consist, in large part, of the right rules for each of the moral virtues. The person of practical wisdom knows in a rough and ready way what it means to act justly, and the person acts in accordance with this wisdom. But it is important to stress that the knowledge of the right rules can be achieved only through the experience of the practice of the moral virtues. Without the experience of performing just acts in the world, the just person will not formulate the rough and ready right rule about what it is to act justly. There is an obvious circularity here, for one needs knowledge of the right rule to act in a virtuous way, but one must have acted in a virtuous way to achieve the knowledge. Moreover, it is also clear that Aristotle thinks that the moral virtues are not developed one by one; rather, they are developed all together, and with the proper development of them all comes practical wisdom. So there is, as it were, a de facto unity to the virtues in the sense that one cannot be developed without developing all the others. This understanding of the unity of the virtues underlies many medieval discussions of conscience and the virtues.

Aristotle's views about practical wisdom seem to be the crux of his differences with Plato over the nature of ethics.[7] While Plato suggests that there can be universal rules of behavior that can be taught and, if followed, lead one to the end of human activity—contemplation of the Forms—Aristotle thinks there are no such rules. The contingencies of the world, luck, fate, and even individual differences among human beings make it impossible to establish such certain guides to the end of human activity. In recognition of these difficulties, Aristotle suggests that the best human beings can do is to prepare themselves for contingencies by developing practical wisdom, which seems to be more of a learned skill than a science. Practical wisdom itself is developed from the cultivation of the virtues. But how can one cultivate the virtues? Although there can be no certain guide to their cultivation, Aristotle seems to suggest the following path.

Every human being is born into a society and is raised in an atmosphere of certain values and goals. These values and goals are communicated directly, through literature and the arts, and through examples. People beginning the development of the virtues do well by surrounding themselves with a good group of friends and by imitating the heroes of society. Imitation must, however, give way to conscious variation. One soon discovers that what is appropriate for, say, Pericles or Priam might not be appropriate for oneself because the strengths and natural dispositions of Pericles and Priam are different from one's own. So seekers of virtue must learn to modify behavior in accord with what they are. They must also learn through experi-

---

7. This is one of the central theses of Nussbaum's *The Fragility of Goodness*.

ence what actions and rules of thumb work well and which work poorly. Although people have some successes, they must learn from their failures. At a certain point, with luck and effort, people will have developed the skill of acting correctly in a variety of circumstances. Along with this skill comes a transformation of character so that people not only act correctly but also feel in the ways proper to the various virtues. At this point, we can talk of the achievement of practical wisdom. In fact, this description of the development of the virtues is widely accepted in medieval discussions of the virtues.

The pitfalls of not achieving practical wisdom are displayed clearly in the problem of *akrasia* (weakness of will) that Aristotle discusses in Book VII. The problem is presented in the context of Plato's view that evil is done only through ignorance:

> Now we may ask (1) how a man who judges rightly can behave incontinently. That he should behave so when he has knowledge, some say is impossible; for it would be strange—so Socrates thought—if when knowledge was in a man something else could master it and drag it about like a slave. For Socrates was entirely opposed to the view in question, holding that there is no such thing as incontinence; no one, he said, when he judges acts against what he judges best—people act so only by reason of ignorance. Now this view plainly contradicts the observed facts. (1145b23f.)

It is clear from the passage that Aristotle believes that one can know what one should do (have knowledge about what is right) and not do it. He thus puts himself in opposition to Plato's views. But it is difficult to understand Aristotle's explanation of how one who knows what is to be done does otherwise.[8]

8. There are many discussions of weakness of will in Aristotle's thought. In addition to Nussbaum's *The Fragility of Goodness* and Rorty's *Essays on Aristotle's Ethics*, other discussions include James J. Walsh, *Aristotle's Conception of Moral Weakness* (New York: Columbia University Press, 1963); Norman O. Dahl, *Practical Reason, Aristotle, and Weakness of Will* (Minneapolis: University of Minnesota Press, 1984); Donald Davidson, "How Is Weakness of Will Possible?" in *Moral Concepts*, ed. Joel Feinberg (Oxford: Oxford University Press, 1969); W. Charlton, *Weakness of Will: A Philosophical Introduction* (Oxford: Blackwell's, 1988). Useful accounts of Aristotle's views are also in Bonnie Kent's "Transitory Vice: Thomas Aquinas on Incontinence," *Journal of the History of Philosophy* 27 (1989): 199–223, and in Risto Saarinen's *Weakness of the Will in Medieval Thought from Augustine to Buridan* (Leiden: E. J. Brill, 1994). (Hereafter Kent, "Transitory Vice," and Saarinen, *Weakness of Will in Medieval Thought*.)

Chapter 3 of Book VII seems to contain Aristotle's analysis. In the chapter, he offers four explanations of how one acts incontinently. The first explanation presents only a schema that the other three follow: "Since we use the word 'know' in two senses (for both the man who has knowledge but is not using it and he who is using it are said to know), it will make a difference whether, when a man does what he should not, he has the knowledge but is not exercising it, or is exercising it; for the latter seems strange, but not the former" (1146b30–35). Aristotle deems it impossible for one to know actively that something ought to be done and yet not do it. Incontinence must then be a situation in which someone has knowledge but does not exercise it.

The second explanation follows this schema but seems to accord with Plato's view that evil is done through ignorance: "Further, since there are two kinds of premisses, there is nothing to prevent a man's having both premisses and acting against his knowledge, provided that he is using only the universal premiss and not the particular; for it is particular acts that have to be done" (1146b35–1147a4). One might have knowledge of a universal like "dry food is good for every man" but not know whether a particular food is dry or not. People would not act in the best way in such circumstances because they would not eat the food, but their so acting incontinently would be a result of ignorance. The knowledge of the universal might be active knowledge, but without also knowing the particular fact, people would not behave properly.

The third explanation seems to be a direct expansion on the schema of the first explanation. Aristotle distinguishes between people who have knowledge in a normal state and those who have it when asleep, mad, or drunk. Such people have knowledge, for example, of scientific truths or the verses of Empedocles, but cannot use it. Their abnormal state has made their knowledge inactive even though it is not lost. Aristotle then claims that "incontinent people must be said to be in a similar condition to men asleep, mad, or drunk" (1147a16f.).

The fourth explanation describes a conflict. One may hold a principle such as "one should not eat sweet things" but also hold a rule based on appetite that "everything sweet is pleasant." When faced with a sweet thing and the knowledge that it is sweet, a person may act based on appetite. In so acting, he or she acts from a rule and an opinion; he or she also acts incidentally in conflict with the principle because the act he or she performs is in conflict with the principle but the rule he or she follows is not directly contrary to the principle. Aristotle talks about this case as a situation in which the person has or does not have a certain opinion about a perceptible object. The correct opinion about the object—it is a thing not to be eaten because it is sweet—is not actively held by the person. (Aristotle, in fact, draws a comparison with a man in a drunken state where knowledge is present but not active.) The opinion of the object according to which he acts—it is a pleasant object—is what causes his action.

One may easily describe all four of these cases as cases of ignorance. So seen, the cases do not show that Aristotle's analysis is other than Plato's view that evil doing comes from ignorance. But this conclusion misses the point of Aristotle's discussion. The people in explanations three and four have put themselves into a situation of ignorance. They have either cultivated a state (drunkenness, madness, passion) that renders their knowledge inactive, or they have allowed their perception of an object to be informed by appetite rather than the appropriate principle. Effectively, they have failed to put themselves in the requisite state to meet the situation properly. In other words, they have failed to cultivate the virtues that would allow them to exercise the proper knowledge correctly. There is a failure of training that occurred long before the particular case arose.

Aristotle's linking of weakness of will to the lack of cultivation of the virtues has been overlooked by most contemporary scholars.[9] Yet, it is an obvious link, given the general emphasis on the virtues in the *Nicomachean Ethics,* and it helps to explain why Aristotle saw himself as diverging from Plato's views about the source for doing evil. Moreover, contemporary discussions of conscience also overlook this link and the role conscience plays in it. As we shall see, the link between the virtues and weakness of will did not escape Thomas Aquinas, and his emphasis on issues about the source for doing evil is a critical moment in medieval discussions of conscience and the virtues. To view Aquinas's contributions adequately, however, it is crucial to discuss Augustine's adaptation of the virtue tradition. It is also important to understand Bonaventure's views about conscience and synderesis.

---

9. In his first chapter of *Weakness of Will in Medieval Thought,* Saarinen provides a useful summary of ways that Aristotle's notion of weakness of will has been treated in the literature.

BONAVENTURE'S VIEW OF CONSCIENCE *and* SYNDERESIS

Medieval Background to Bonaventure's Views

In their treatment of the virtues and conscience, the medieval schoolmen drew on the works of both Plato and Aristotle; but they were heavily influenced by Augustine's modification of the classical tradition. While acknowledging his debt to Plato and Aristotle, Augustine (d. 430) constantly criticized their views for failing to take into account the critical role of God in any human activity. In fact, Augustine went so far as to claim that what the Greeks consider virtues Christians should view as vices: "No, the virtues on which the mind preens itself as giving control over the body and its urges, and which aim at any other purpose or possession than God, are in point of fact vices rather than virtues" (*City of God,* Book XIX, chapter 25). Augustine says this principally because he adds a new component to the Greek view of virtue. In addition to claiming (in agreement with Aristotle in Book II, chapter 4, of the *Nicomachean Ethics*) that a virtue is developed by a person who knows what he is doing, chooses to perform the relevant acts, chooses these acts for their own sakes, and performs his actions from a firm and unchangeable character, Augustine claims that a virtue has to be developed "for the love of God."[1] In fact, Augustine, in Book I, chapter 15, of *On the Morals of the Catholic Church*, defines the four cardinal virtues of prudence, justice, fortitude, and temperance as differing expressions of love of God. If a person lacks love of God and fails to develop the virtues with the explicit intention of developing them for the love of God, the person cannot develop the virtues according to Augustine.

The addition of this intentional element in the development of the virtues has a tremendous impact on later discussions of the virtues in the medieval period and the Reformation. Moreover, the linking of the virtues to love of God also bears on the issue of the unity of the virtues.[2] Because the virtues are identified with "the love of God" for Augustine, if one has love of God, one has all the virtues. Likewise one can possess a virtue only if one has love of God, and with this love one possesses them all. Yet, Augustine allows that there are degrees of the possession of love of God and, consequently, degrees of possession of the virtues. In fact, until one perfects the love of God, one can possess certain virtues while displaying the vices of other virtues.[3] Apparently, it is only in a life "found in no one as long as he lives the life of man" that there is perfect love of God and a complete unity of the virtues. Augustine's notion that possession of the virtues comes in degrees that culminate in a perfect possession of all of the virtues also receives great attention among the late scholastics.

Although Augustine was not familiar with the seventh book of the *Nicomachean Ethics* and its discussion of weakness of will, his views on why evil is done also deeply influence subsequent discussion of the problem.[4] Risto Saarinen has recently argued that Augustine should be viewed as subscribing to the following model of choice:

> In the first model (3a.), choice is connected with the traditional Greek view of man as a rational being who always aims at acting

1. G. Scott Davis makes this point in his "The Structure and Functions of the Virtues," in *Acta Congressa Augustiana, 1986* (Rome: Institutum Patristicum Augustinianum, 1987), 9–18.

2. John P. Langan treats the unity of the virtues in Augustine's thought in his "Augustine on the Unity and Interconnection of the Virtues," *Harvard Theological Review* 72 (1979).

3. Ibid., 91–93.

4. Saarinen, *Weakness of Will in Medieval Thought*, 87.

virtuously. If the agent is free, he tries to make optimal decisions. Freedom, accordingly, is always connected with the virtues: blameworthy actions indicate that the agent is either ignorant of the true virtue or prevented from doing what he considers best. Under this understanding of freedom, the free will always tries to choose the optimal alternative, although it can in principle choose something else. (18–19)

Saarinen labels this view "indirect voluntarism" and summarizes this as meaning "that human agents sometimes consciously choose to act against better judgment, but do so only because of serious defections and ignorance within the agent's mind" (42). Augustine's view of the will thus appears to be one in which the will, capable of choosing other options, follows the dictates of the intellect. The will's failure in the doing of evil thus appears to be principally a failure of the intellect. Through some form of ignorance, the intellect directs the will to a path of evil. Even though Augustine's view of the will was not developed in response to Aristotle's views about weakness of will, his view formed the background to subsequent medieval discussions of weakness of will as well as discussions of conscience and synderesis.

As I indicated at the beginning of the first chapter, medieval interpreters of Jerome (c. 347–419) distinguished synderesis from conscience. Although it is unclear that Jerome meant to distinguish the two, the distinction is critical for understanding late medieval discussions of conscience. But what is the difference between them? To a large extent, various thinkers disagree, identifying a variety of differences. In general, however, two distinct views of the difference between the two emerged: one voluntaristic and one intellectualistic.[5] The former can be identified with Franciscan thinkers, chief among whom is Bonaventure, whereas the latter has its clearest exponent in Thomas Aquinas. As Potts suggests, both of these traditions seem to derive from a treatise on conscience by Philip the Chancellor (d. 1236).

In the third article of Philip's treatise, "Can one sin by following synderesis?" Philip distinguishes conscience and synderesis in this way:

> To the objection that conscientia can be now right, now mistaken, and if mistaken is undeserving but if right deserving, it should be said that conscientia comes from the conjunction of synderesis with free choice and is not synderesis itself, and is related as knowledge in

5. Eric D'Arcy identifies these two trends in *Conscience and Its Right to Freedom* (New York: Sheed and Ward, 1961), 29.

action is related to knowledge in general and to knowledge from reason proper, as being between them. For example, suppose that it is written in synderesis that everyone who makes himself out to be the son of God, should die the death; but that this man (pointing to Christ) makes himself out to be the son of God, yet is not; it is then supposed: therefore he should die the death. What was contributed by synderesis was unchangeable and dictated only good, but this conjoined with what was contributed by reason dictated sin. So, therefore, synderesis plus the reason for a free choice makes conscientia right or mistaken, and conscientia sticks more to the side of reason; synderesis itself, however, which is the spark of conscientia, as blessed Gregory says, is not mistaken.[6]

Philip here describes synderesis as an unerring intellectual dispositional potentiality. It is related to general truths that free choice leads one to act in accordance with or against, while conscience is the specific applications of the general truths comprehended by synderesis. Philip's view seems to fall in direct line with the intellectualistic understanding of synderesis, which sees it as either a set of practical first principles or as the power for determining such principles.[7]

Yet, elsewhere in his treatise on conscience, Philip states: "I say that synderesis affects free choice by telling it to do good and restraining it from evil, and moves us to the general good which is found in this or that good deed. Hence it is not in itself directed to particular good deeds, but to the general [good] which is present in them" (101–2). In this passage, he describes synderesis as the drive toward good we find in ourselves. Elsewhere in the treatise he links synderesis with displeasure over evil[8] and guilt.[9] These passages connect synderesis with a desire for the good in general as

6. Timothy Potts, *Conscience in Medieval Philosophy* (Cambridge: Cambridge University Press, 1980), 104. (Hereafter Potts, *Conscience*.)

7. D'Arcy, however, believes that Philip puts the synderesis in the affective order (*Conscience and Its Right to Freedom*, 27).

8. Ibid., 107. "Moreover, synderesis is not extinguished in such a person [one who does evil] because, although he may be mistaken about the particular matter, evil in general still displeases him, mistakes [in general] still displease him, and this is in accordance with synderesis."

9. Ibid., 108. "To the objection about the rich man and Lazarus, the effects of synderesis in impelling to good are to be distinguished, either in connection with guilt or outside this context. It should be said, therefore, that synderesis, as impelling to good and as making us displeased without qualification about evil faults, is extinguished in the devil and the damned. But in the third way, it is not extinguished, and this remains as guilt."

well as with emotional reactions, for instance, guilt, when one follows evil instead of good. As we shall see, these emphases are in line with the voluntaristic view of synderesis that Bonaventure emphasizes in his analysis. It thus appears that, for Philip, synderesis is both part of the intellectual order and connected to the affective order (the volitional and the emotional).

Bonaventure on Conscience

Bonaventure (1221–74) discusses both conscience and synderesis in his *Commentary on the Sentences*, Book II, distinction 39. He places conscience squarely within the rational faculty, specifying that it is part of practical reason because it is connected to the performance of actions. It is thus also connected to both the will and the emotions.[10] On the other hand, he places synderesis in the affective part of human beings, for he regards synderesis as that which stimulates us to the good.[11]

It is important to note that Bonaventure's prefatory remarks at the beginning of the distinction discuss how Lombard's (d. 1160) treatment of conscience and synderesis is guided by a key question: How does the will become depraved when it is the case that men naturally will and desire good? In particular, how can human wills become depraved when conscience always dictates good and synderesis inclines toward good and turns away from evil?[12] Because human beings are directed toward good by conscience and synderesis, their performance of evil requires an explanation. Lombard's presentation of his discussion of conscience and synderesis obviously influenced Bonaventure. In addition to discussing the nature of conscience and synderesis, Bonaventure constantly returns to the question of how men can commit evil despite their orientation to good from both conscience and synderesis.

Conscience is divided into two general parts by Bonaventure. The first part seems to be a power for discovering the truth of very general practical principles like "obey God," "honor your parents," and "do not harm your

10. Bonaventure, *Commentary on the Sentences*, in *Opera Theologica Selecta* (Florence: Ad Claras Aquas, 1934), 2:934a and b. (Hereafter Bonaventure, *Commentary*.)

11. Ibid., 945a.

12. Ibid., 932a. According to J. Guy Bougerol in his *Introduction to the Works of Bonaventure* (New York: Desclee, 1964), 57f., Bonaventure always offers a commentary on Lombard's text before offering his own analysis. The commentary perhaps came from his *cursorie* reading of the *Sentences*, and it is closely connected with the *dubia* discussed at the end of each question.

neighbors" (934a). He talks about this power as a light on a par with the power of the intellect to discover the truth of first principles of theoretical reason (938a and b). Bonaventure regards this part of conscience as unerring as well as innate. Not only does it never make a mistake about the truth of very general practical principles, but also it can never be lost to any person, no matter how morally corrupt that person may become. For ease of reference, let us label this part of conscience "the potential conscience."[13]

The second part of conscience is the application of the very general principles to situations that may be either general or particular. A general situation is one that covers a variety of cases, for example the Jewish prohibition against eating pork. On Bonaventure's analysis, the Jews have correctly realized the truth of the very general practical principle that "God is to be obeyed," and they have applied this very general principle to the general prohibition against eating pork, which covers a variety of actions. Whenever anyone is faced with the specific choice of eating or not eating pork, he is presented with a particular application of the very general principle ("God is to be obeyed") obviously connected to the general application of this principle ("Do not eat pork"). Again, for ease of reference, let us call this part of conscience—whether it is general or particular—the "applied conscience."

According to Bonaventure, the applied conscience is also innate, for we naturally apply the very general practical principles to situations. It can, however, be mistaken, and a very general principle may be misapplied through ignorance or faulty reasoning. For example, Jews, according to Bonaventure, misapply the very general principle "God is to be obeyed" when they incorrectly hold that God now commands the circumcision of male children and abstinence from certain foods. For God does not now command these actions, even though they were commanded in earlier ages. Moreover, a person who is ignorant that a situation fits a general practical principle also suffers from a mistaken applied conscience. For example, although a person might know that "God is to be obeyed," he or she might not obey Christ and, in fact, might harm Christ because he or she is ignorant of the fact that Christ is God.[14]

Clearly, Bonaventure's distinction between the "potential conscience" and the "applied conscience" helps to explain how human beings, who are natu-

13. This, as well as "applied conscience," is my term, and it is not to be found in Bonaventure's writings.
14. The example comes from Philip the Chancellor. Compare Potts, *Conscience*, 104.

rally oriented by conscience to the good, perform evil. Their evil actions are a result of ignorance or a misapplication of the "applied conscience." Although Bonaventure's reasoning here leads to a number of questions, I will limit myself to two. The first concerns the authority of conscience, which Bonaventure discusses in detail. The second, which concerns the formation of practical principles, is only implied in Bonaventure's discussion, but it is very fruitful for a dynamic picture of the rules found in conscience.

Bonaventure discusses in some detail whether one should always follow one's conscience. He tells us that conscience may dictate any of three types of actions: those in conformity with God's law; those in addition to God's law; those contrary to God's law. In the first two types, one is obliged to follow one's conscience. It is the third type that is problematic. Because we can have an erroneous applied conscience, our conscience can command us to do what is against God's law. Needless to say, we must not do what is in conflict with God's law, so that it appears that we should not always follow our conscience. Yet, Bonaventure thinks that it is wrong to act against our conscience, in part because the conscience is, as it were, the representative within us of God.[15] So, we should never act against our conscience. There thus appears to be a dilemma: On the one hand, our conscience mistakenly requires us to act against God's law, and we seemingly should not follow conscience in this case; on the other hand, God's law requires us not to act against our conscience.

As part of his discussion of why we should not act against God's law, Bonaventure distinguishes what we do from the manner in which we do it (*Commentary*, 940b–941a). Acting against our conscience reveals that we are acting in an evil manner, for we are acting with the wrong intention, that is, to violate the internal representative of God. It appears, then, that Bonaventure can solve the dilemma of the authority of conscience presented above by pointing out that in a case of erroneous conscience we are in ignorance about what God's law requires, and so we are not responsible for acting against God's law in following our conscience. Interestingly, Bonaventure does not pursue this path of resolution because he seems to be more concerned with cases in which one has reason to suspect that one's conscience is in error. Specifically, he seems to have in mind cases in which a conscience arrives at dictates that are in conflict with established authority, particularly Church authority. In these cases, one should refrain from acting at all to avoid acting against conscience. One is then obligated to educate

---

15. Bonaventure, *Commentary*, 941a.

oneself properly so that the applied conscience can be brought into conformity with the authority. Self-education thus transforms an erroneous applied
conscience into a correct applied conscience and permits individuals to follow their own consciences in good faith. So Bonaventure encourages those
with an erroneous applied conscience to change their applied conscience to
the correct dictate so that they can avoid acting against the (erroneous)
applied conscience. Needless to say, Bonaventure's view has limited application. It applies exclusively to those situations in which a person recognizes a
superior, legitimate authority; knows what the legitimate authority says on a
certain matter; and is in a position to refrain (at least temporarily) from
performing any action concerning the matter in question. Although a significant number of cases fulfill these conditions, many do not. Perhaps in these
cases Bonaventure would agree that the best that can be done is to act in
accord with conscience because in such circumstances we would at least be
certain that it is wrong to act against our conscience.[16]

Although Bonaventure does not elaborate at length on the distinction
between what I have called the "potential conscience" and the "applied conscience" with its further division into the general and particular applied consciences, the distinctions are intriguing. Where do the principles that are
endorsed as true by the "potential conscience" come from? Surely, a good
number come from revelation, Church authorities, and natural law. But do
they all come from these sources? Can one generate very general practical
principles from experience? Or are these principles necessarily part of "general applied conscience" and thus not necessarily true? It certainly seems to
be the case that not all the principles of general applied conscience derive
from revelation, authority, or natural law. Principles such as "Exercising will
prolong one's life" or "Insomnia will shorten one's life" seem not to come
from these sources; rather, they come from experience. If this is the case, it
appears that Bonaventure views conscience as a dynamic faculty. There are
not a fixed number of true very general principles we are given at birth.

16. In Book IV, d. 38, a. 1, q. 2, ad 5, Bonaventure points out that there are two types of
erroneous conscience. The first type holds something that needs not be held even though it is not
required that the opposite of what it holds is to be held. In this case, a person is bound by
conscience. The second type holds as good what is evil. In this case, the person is required to
change his conscience. Reference to this question is found in *Lexicon Bonaventurianum Philosophico-
Theologicum*, comp. Antonii Mariae A. Vicetia and Joannis A. Rubino (Venice: Aemiliana, 1880).

In his *Summa Theologiae*, I–II, question 19, article 5, reply, Aquinas criticizes Bonaventure's view of
conscience and suggests that Bonaventure does not think that an erroneous conscience binds. It
appears that Aquinas's criticism is too general because Bonaventure discusses only those situations in
which one has a good suspicion that one is wrong.

Rather, we come to understand through experience more and more of the true very general principles as we grow older.[17] Moreover, the number of general applied principles we endorse constantly changes over time. We discover new general applied principles through experience and, perhaps, even reject previously held general applied principles. Conscience seems not to be a static faculty for Bonaventure; on the contrary, it is dynamic.

The dynamism seems apparent in another way. Bonaventure regards conscience as a dispositional potentiality.[18] The dispositional part seems to relate most closely to the "potential conscience." We have at birth the ability to see the truth of certain very general principles, and we can neither lose this ability nor improve it. Yet we can improve our ability to bring to our attention very general practical principles the truth of which we can endorse or reject. Clearly, the more experience we have, the more terms and concepts we possess, and, consequently, the more principles we can consider. Our ability to apply the very general practical principles also seems to be innate for Bonaventure. But we can certainly improve our ability to formulate the principles of the general applied conscience and our ability to apply the very general practical principles without error. In short, although conscience is innate to all people, it can be improved (or weakened) in its exercise. Once again, the fact that people perform evil actions comes into play; for one reason people do evil is that they fail to improve the exercise of conscience and so allow it to weaken. In fact, Bonaventure draws a useful connection with the virtues. Like conscience, the virtues are partly innate and partly acquired. Although we have no control over what is innate, we have a considerable amount of control over the development of what we can acquire.[19]

Bonaventure on Synderesis

Although conscience is obviously complex and important to Bonaventure, his remarks on synderesis are even more intriguing. One of the more astonishing claims he makes is that conscience is dependent on synderesis: "To the objection that synderesis is the 'spark of conscience,' it ought to be said that it is called spark insofar as conscience, in itself, cannot move or vex or

17. Compare Potts's discussion on 41ff. in his *Conscience*.
18. See Potts's discussion on 20ff. in his *Conscience*.
19. Bonaventure, *Commentary*, 437a.

stimulate without the mediation of synderesis, which is like the stimulus and flame [of conscience]. Thus, just as reason cannot move without the mediation of the will, so conscience [cannot move] without the mediation of synderesis."[20] This passage comes in response to an argument that, because synderesis is the "spark of conscience," it must reside in the same part (that is, the cognitive part) of a human being as the conscience. Bonaventure rejects the argument, for he places synderesis in the affective part. He consequently thinks of the phrase "spark of conscience" not as indicating that synderesis is a part of conscience, but rather as indicating that the synderesis provides a spark that conscience needs to operate. Given that, for Bonaventure, the conscience deals with practical principles, it appears that the spark synderesis provides conscience is the general drive to do good that is expressed in humankind's search for the good, in the drive to formulate true principles leading to the good, in the desire to follow these principles, and in the vexation at having failed to follow them. Each of these expressions of synderesis bears further comment.

When Bonaventure claims that synderesis is the desire to do good and avoid evil, he does not mean that we are directed by synderesis to pursue good objects in themselves; rather, we are directed to the good found in objects (*Commentary*, 951a). That is to say, we desire good objects insofar as they are good and avoid evil objects insofar as they are evil. Because synderesis is directed to the general good in objects, it can never be mistaken. Whatever it causes us to pursue contains good in general. Yet, because every being is good, synderesis as the general drive to the good appears to provide little practical advice about which objects to pursue and which to avoid. Providing this practical guidance, however, is the role of conscience.

As we have seen, according to Bonaventure, conscience provides human beings with the very general first practical principles as well as the application of these principles. It provides these principles and applications to give human beings the means to pursue the good. They are thus practical implementations of the drive of the synderesis toward good and away from evil.

---

20. Bonaventure, *Commentary*, 945b, my translation. It is interesting to note the variety of views in the thirteenth century about the placement of synderesis. Many thinkers seem to follow Philip the Chancellor's view that it is to be found in both the affective and cognitive orders: Odo of Rigaud (d. 1245), Bernard of Auvergne (c. 1300), William of Ware (c. 1274), Richard Middleton (d. 1287), Nicholas of Ockham (c. 1290). (See Lottin's summary of discussions of synderesis in *Psychologie et morale aux XIIe et XIIIe siècles*, vol. 1 [2d ed.], vol. 2 [Gembloux: J. Duculot, 1957, 1948], 2:338–44; hereafter Lottin, *Psychologie*.) Others, like Bonaventure, place it in the affective order. Still others, like Aquinas, place it in the cognitive.

As we have seen, Bonaventure expresses this connection between synderesis and conscience by claiming that conscience works with the mediation of synderesis.

It is, of course, one thing to formulate laws of behavior and quite another to follow these laws. Without the desire to put the dictates of conscience into play, conscience is little more than an extension of the imagination; that is, through conscience we would picture how to behave to reach the good, but not sense that we should do what we picture. Given that conscience is found in reason, it can by itself provide no basis for the desire to follow its dictates. This desire must be found in the affective part of human beings. It is Bonaventure's insight to place the desire to follow the dictates of conscience in the general context of the desire for the good, which is synderesis.

Although Bonaventure thinks that synderesis provides the positive drive toward the good that conscience directs, he believes that synderesis also indirectly guides us to the good by making us feel guilty when we follow evil. In fact, Bonaventure explicitly connects the regret one has in failing to follow correct principles with synderesis rather than conscience (Commentary, 935, ad 4). Again, his justification is that regret and guilt are emotions and fall within the affective part of human beings. Conscience, found in the rational part, lacks the emotional qualities required for regret and guilt. Bonaventure thinks that conscience provides the practical principles by which we move to the good. The failure to follow the principles of conscience effectively thwarts the desire for good, and the frustration of this desire leads to the emotions of guilt and remorse. Bonaventure's linking of synderesis with guilt plays a prominent role in his view that synderesis can never be extinguished even though its exercise can be prevented.

According to Bonaventure, synderesis can never be destroyed because it is natural and innate to human beings. It is thus unlike the impulse to sin, which for Bonaventure comes from a fault in the will that is contrary to nature (Commentary, 948a and b). Thus, the impulse to sin may be lacking in some human beings, for example, in Christ and the Virgin Mary, but synderesis is found in all human beings. In discussing how the exercise of synderesis can be prevented, he offers three possible impediments: "However, although its exercise cannot be taken away or extinguished altogether, it can be temporarily prevented, either by the darkness of blindness, or by the wantonness of pleasure, or by the hardness of obstinacy."[21] Bonaventure talks

---

21. Bonaventure, Commentary, 947a. Translated in Potts, Conscience, 117.

about these three impediments in detail, but it is important to see that the three impediments correspond to the three possible sources for evil doing. The first impediment, darkness of blindness, corresponds to Plato's explanation for human beings' performance of evil: They do it through ignorance.[22] The second impediment, the wantonness of pleasure, corresponds to Aristotle's explanation for human evil: It is done through weakness of will.[23] The third impediment, the hardness of obstinacy, is, in fact, moral perversity, in which one knows the good but chooses evil even when one knows that the choice leads to suffering. This third possibility for evil, perversity, is decidedly nonclassical, but it is a major point of discussion in the voluntarist tradition.[24]

In elaborating on the impediment of the darkness of blindness, Bonaventure says: "Synderesis is hampered by the darkness of blindness so that it does not murmur in reply to evil, because the evil is believed to be good, as e.g., in the case of heretics who, while dying for the impiety of their error, believe that they die for their piety of faith, so that they feel no guilt, but, instead a fictitious and vain joy."[25] The heretics, of course, are pursuing good in general under the influence of synderesis. Yet they are, in fact, holding to a mistaken belief in their pursuit of the good. This much seems to be in the background for Bonaventure's main point: The reason synderesis does not cause a negative emotional reaction to their embracing of what is evil is that what is evil (the heresy) is seen as good (the piety of faith). Thus, guilt, which comes from the activity of synderesis and should occur when evil is embraced, does not arise.

In describing the impediment of wantonness of pleasure, he says: "Similarly, it is hampered by the wantonness of pleasure, for sometimes in sins of flesh a man is so engrossed by the exercise of the flesh that a sense of guilt has no place, because men of the flesh are so far carried away by the impulse to pleasure that reason has then no place [in them]" (*Commentary*,

---

22. This doctrine is found in the *Protagoras* as well as in other dialogues.

23. Aristotle discusses weakness of will in *Nicomachean Ethics*, Book 7. See Chapter 1 above.

24. The grounds for the possible perversity of the will are especially emphasized by Scotus when he indicates that the human will has the power to turn away from good. See Allan B. Wolter's *Duns Scotus on the Will and Morality* (Washington, D.C.: Catholic University of America Press, 1986), 145–73 and 181–97. Ockham specifically mentions willing wickedness for the sake of wickedness (see Rega Wood's "Willing Wickedly" in *Vivarium* 37, 1 [1999]).

Bonaventure is not the first to discuss these three cases. They are traditionally discussed in this section of commentaries on the *Sentences*. See Lottin, *Psychologie*, 2:111, 134, 159, for examples of other discussions of these cases.

25. Bonaventure, *Commentary*, 947a. Potts, *Conscience*, 117.

947a). Again, we must assume that synderesis provides the impulse to the good in general. In this second case, a person embraces the evils of the flesh and has no guilt because the reason is so overcome by the pleasure that the evil cannot be seen as evil. Thus there is no regret.

In the cases of the darkness of blindness and the wantonness of pleasure, there is a clear drive to what is mistakenly seen as good. Of course, even the evil acts performed have some good in general so that synderesis is not mistaken in pursuing them. Yet their pursuit, because they are evil, should be prohibited by conscience: if not outright then by the guilt associated with doing what is evil. But there is no guilt or remorse in these two cases of impediments because what is done is not seen as evil and thus not seen as in violation of conscience. In the first case, ignorance prevents one from seeing the act as evil and deserving of regret; in the second case, being overcome by wantonness prevents one from seeing the evil and reacting with guilt.

The impediment of "hardness of obstinacy" is different from the other two impediments, for there is no pursuit of good: "Synderesis is also hampered by the hardness of obstinacy, so that it does not goad towards the good, as e.g. in the case of the damned, who are so strongly reinforced in evil that they can never turn towards what is good."[26] The damned are so hardened in their sins that they pursue evil in contrast to good. One cannot regard their case as one of ignorance (that is, the first impediment), for they know that what they pursue is evil. Nor can one explain their case as one of weakness of will, for they are punished for their pursuits and cannot regard them as leading to greater pleasure than the pursuits of good. The damned are simply perverse: They know what good is and turn away from it to pursue evil. It thus appears that synderesis as the desire for good is extinguished in them. Bonaventure's treatment of this case is intriguing:

> Thus synderesis [in the case of the damned] is perpetually hampered from goading to good and, consequently, can be said to be extinguished in respect of its exercise, but not extinguished without qualification, because it has another use, namely, to murmur in reply [to evil]. In this use, in which the function of synderesis is to sting and murmur in reply to evil, it flourishes most in the damned. I say this, in the sense in which murmuring in reply to evil is a punishment, not in the sense in which it is a matter of justice, because this murmuring in reply will be a commendation of divine justice but will not have

---

26. Bonaventure, *Commentary*, 947a. My emendation of Potts's translation, *Conscience*, 117–18.

> the purpose of bringing forth fruitful repentance. Hence, in the damned, synderesis murmurs in reply to their guilt, yet in relation to punishment.[27]

Synderesis murmurs in the damned; because it is the justified punishment of God, it is an indication of their guilt. Even though they have shut themselves off from repentance, the murmuring inside them is a sign of the guilt caused by their pursuit of evil; thus they must have, after all, the drive to good and the avoidance of evil, that is, synderesis. So, for Bonaventure, even the perverse must have synderesis, although its operation is reduced to punishment, not to any longer providing a real likelihood of repentance.

The case is intriguing for two reasons. In the first place, it is noteworthy how easily Bonaventure moves from the fact that there is an expression of synderesis, that is, murmuring or guilt, to the claim that synderesis must itself be present. Clearly, there is a very strong link in Bonaventure's mind between synderesis and its expressions. Synderesis must be found either as the drive for good, the working of conscience, or the guilt associated with the failure to follow conscience. Likewise, wherever one of these expressions is found, synderesis must be present. In the second place, it is important that this third case is presented in terms of the damned. In cases of perversity, it is tempting to see the perverse person as acting from ignorance or weakness of will. As I remarked, such a reduction is impossible in talking about the damned. Bonaventure thus presents the best case for the belief that there is such a thing as perversity, which cannot be reduced to ignorance or weakness of will. There are beings who know the good but turn from it without being overcome by passion.

It is also worth remarking that Bonaventure holds that synderesis cannot be corrupted by sin. It is directed to the good and cannot be changed in this respect. To be sure, the individual who possesses synderesis may be corrupted, and thus synderesis will be connected with corruption. But this is not to say that synderesis itself is corrupted. To make this point, Bonaventure draws an analogy with a soldier riding a horse.[28] The rider may sit correctly and direct the horse well, but if the horse falls, the rider may also be said to fall, even though he himself does not fall. Similarly, the synderesis

---

27. Bonaventure, *Commentary*, 947a. My emendation of Potts's translation, *Conscience*, 118. My reading of the third case is indebted to Robert Andrews, editor of *Franciscan Studies* (1993), where a slightly different version of the present chapter appears.

28. Bonaventure, *Commentary*, 950a. The example is also found in Odo of Rigaud's writings. See Lottin, *Psychologie*, 2:200–201.

can be found in what is corrupted without itself being corrupted. Bonaventure further explains that the synderesis may fall not from a fault in itself so much as from a fault in the virtues over which it has control (*Commentary*, 950a–b, ad 1)

This last remark is particularly interesting. Just as conscience and synderesis are different but closely related for Bonaventure, so, in Bonaventure's eyes, there are very close connections among synderesis, conscience, and the virtues. Although he does not elaborate on these connections, some of them seem clear. The virtues are first developed in line with the dictates of conscience. Continual development of them is kept in line by conscience and the murmurings of synderesis associated with the turning away from the good. Development of the virtues, which leads one toward the good, is a manifestation of the drive toward the good that is synderesis.

The Contribution of Bonaventure

As we have seen, Bonaventure regards conscience and synderesis as residing in different faculties: Conscience is part of the rational faculty, and synderesis is part of the affective. Yet, conscience and synderesis interpenetrate each other. Bonaventure sees the formation of ethical rules by conscience as an implementation of a human being's desire for the good (the synderesis). He also sees the following of these principles as another aspect of the desire for good. Because we naturally have a desire for the good, we also desire the means to that goal. The principles of conscience are such means, and so we are naturally disposed to carry out the principles of conscience. Similarly, the emotional reaction to doing evil (guilt or remorse) is a reaction to the frustration of the desire for good caused when one fails to adhere to what the conscience has determined leads to good. Bonaventure, although placing synderesis and conscience in different parts of a human being, does not isolate them. On the contrary, he views conscience as driven by synderesis and at the same time as directing synderesis.

The close interconnection between synderesis and conscience allows Bonaventure to answer an important question—why should conscience be followed—without moving outside a discussion of synderesis and conscience. Because synderesis is the desire for the good and conscience is an expression of synderesis, following one's conscience is the means for pursuing the good. The first principles of practical reason (found in the conscience) are ways to achieve the good and obviously require adherence. A purely intellectualistic

analysis of synderesis and conscience, which places them both in the intellectual faculty, must look beyond the rational order for explanation for why
first principles of practical reason should be followed.[29] It must move to the
appetitive order and posit a basic drive to the good in all human actions.[30]
But in moving to the appetitive order for such an explanation, synderesis
and conscience, found in only the intellectual order, must no longer be part
of the explanation. Bonaventure's placing of synderesis in the affective order
and conscience in the intellectual order while seeing conscience as an expression of the synderesis requires a profound interconnection of the various
parts of the moral agent. Although some might see in this interpenetration
of the rational and the affective orders untidiness, in fact it is a sign of
sophistication for it escapes the tendency to identify particular human functions with particular parts of the human being. Such identification paves the
way for regarding these parts as faculties, and any viable theory of conscience needs to avoid positing faculties. Indeed, a viable theory requires
conscience to operate among the various parts of human beings.

Of equal sophistication is Bonaventure's dynamic view of conscience. He
does not see conscience as a purely mechanical device for applying the
general principles of synderesis. Rather, he regards conscience as a faculty
that grows and changes with experience. To be sure, it directs behavior, but
it changes with the results of behavior as well. Not only does it increase
through experience in the world the number of very general practical principles it sees as true, but it also constantly changes the general applied principles as well as the specific applications of these principles based on experience.[31] The dynamism Bonaventure posits is crucial for a theory of

29. Potts, *Conscience*, 57. For example, D'Arcy in his *Conscience and the Right to Freedom* (52) argues
that Aquinas, who offers an intellectualistic analysis of conscience and synderesis, regards the principle "Good should be done and evil avoided" as a purely formal principle that governs all our moral
reasoning.

30. Odo of Rigaud also seems to make the point that there is a need for a motivating cause
outside the rational order for following practical principles. See Lottin, *Psychologie*, 2:208.

Bonaventure's emphasis on the need to bring in the affective order seems to anticipate more
recent analyses of conscience. For example, Gilbert Ryle reduces all activities of conscience to
affective activities in his "Conscience and Moral Convictions," as does Peter Fuss in his "Conscience." Similarly, Bernard Wand discusses the ways a purely intellectualistic view of conscience
fails to explain why we follow our conscience by distinguishing an intellectualistic "ought" from an
affective "ought" in his "The Content and Form of Conscience." All three essays are found in John
Donnelly and Leonard Lyons, eds., *Conscience* (Staten Island, N.Y.: Alba House, 1973) and are discussed in Chapters 6 and 7 below.

31. On 63ff. of his *Conscience*, Potts bemoans the fact that medieval thinkers did not carve out a
group of general ethical principles that could be known through experience. It is one of the inter-

conscience. The fact that the content of conscience changes in reaction to experience and teaching is essential to any proper understanding of conscience.

Bonaventure's view of conscience offers important considerations for any modern theory of conscience. Interestingly, his view has obvious connections to practical wisdom as it is found in Aristotle's writings. For practical wisdom is gained through experience and is closely tied to constantly changing rules of behavior. It is also key to the development and practice of the virtues, which for Aristotle are the chief means for achieving the good of human beings. Yet, Bonaventure did not explore the connections among conscience, synderesis, and the virtues, but others did.

---

esting aspects of Bonaventure's theory of conscience that he seems to incorporate such principles into his view of the twofold nature of conscience. Once again, his view has a decidedly modern ring.

. . . .

THREE

AQUINAS ON CONSCIENCE, THE VIRTUES, and WEAKNESS OF WILL

Bonaventure's voluntaristic view of synderesis and conscience presents synderesis as the drive to the good and places it in the appetitive faculty. In contrast, Aquinas (1225–74) claims that synderesis is in the rational part of human agents. It is a natural disposition of the human mind by which we apprehend without inquiry the basic principles of behavior; it is thus parallel to the disposition by which we directly apprehend the basic principles of the theoretical disciplines.[1] Once the basic principles are apprehended and become part of synderesis, conscience, also in the rational part, applies these first principles to particular situations. Aquinas holds that synderesis is never mistaken; he claims, in addition, that the first principles of synderesis are

1. Potts, "Conscience," 700.

necessarily true. A human agent does evil when conscience makes mistakes in its applications of synderesis through invalid reasoning or by joining a first principle with a false premise and deriving a false conclusion. Like Bonaventure, Aquinas holds that conscience is binding, but he treats the error of following a mistaken conscience in a slightly different way. If a conscience has made a factual mistake, for example, the agent does not know that a particular case falls under a general rule, the mistaken conscience is not culpable. If, however, the mistake comes from ignorance of a law the agent should know, the agent is culpable.[2]

Aquinas's ultimate justification of his view that conscience is binding centers on the precept that not to follow conscience violates a first principle of synderesis.[3] The relevant principle seems to be something like the claim that God ought to be obeyed. Because conscience is the voice of God, it follows that conscience ought to be obeyed. On the other hand, given that the contents of synderesis are first principles (unlike those of conscience, which derive from synderesis), it is difficult to understand how Aquinas can explain why the first principles of synderesis should be followed. Perhaps there is a first principle to the effect that the first principles should be followed. Of course, one can then ask why this principle should be followed, and we have entered into an infinite regress. As Potts suggests, it appears that the only way the regress can be stopped is to posit "a goal which calls for no further justification" (Potts, *Conscience*, 57). Eric D'Arcy claims that there is such a principle because, according to him, Aquinas views the principle "Good should be done and evil should be avoided" as a purely formal principle that governs all our moral reasoning.[4] In fact, it is crucial for correctly appreciating Aquinas's views about synderesis and conscience that we place them in the context of his ethical views as a whole. To do this, it is important to turn briefly to his *Summa Theologiae*.

There has been a tendency for people writing about Aquinas to discuss issues or problems in isolation from the whole of his thought.[5] This has been

---

2. Ibid., 703–4. As I remarked in the previous chapter, Aquinas criticizes Bonaventure's view of conscience because he believes that it commits Bonaventure to claiming that a mistaken conscience does not bind.

3. Potts, *Conscience*, 57. This principle is the main principle underlying D'Arcy's extension of Aquinas's comments on freedom of conscience to the question of freedom of religion in his *Conscience and Its Right to Freedom*.

4. D'Arcy, *Conscience and Its Right to Freedom*, 52. See pages 35–36 above.

5. Dan Nelson in *The Priority of Prudence* (University Park: The Pennsylvania State University Press, 1988) and Jean Osterle in *Treatise on the Virtues* (South Bend: University of Notre Dame Press, 1960) both stress this point.

particularly true of the *Summa Theologiae*. In part because it was the last work he composed, scholars frequently look on it as the best source for establishing Aquinas's final views on various matters.[6] So they frequently treat the sections of the *Summa Theologiae* that deal with a relevant issue without trying to put the issue in the overall context of the work.

The *Summa Theologiae* is divided into three parts. The first treats God and the procession of creatures from God.[7] The second is concerned with the movement of rational creatures back to God, who is their source. The third treats of Christ, who is the way back to God. The second part is itself divided into two parts. The first part of the second part (I–II) is concerned with human acts and virtues in general, whereas the second part of the second part (II–II) treats the acts and virtues in detail. The first part (I–II) has the following structure. The first twenty-one questions talk about the end of human action (happiness) and the acts needed to achieve it. The next twenty-seven questions (22–48) analyze the human will, passions, and emotions. The following eighteen questions (49–67) treat habits and virtues. The remaining questions (68–114) take up the topics of the gifts of the Holy Spirit (68–70), sin (71–89), and law (90–114).

The first part of the second part of the *Summa Theologiae* (I–II) is thus a systematic treatment of ethics. In general, it presents a teleological and eudaemonistic ethics that is, in the main, Aristotelian.[8] It is, however, also influenced by previous medieval thinkers, especially Augustine, who is in the background of Aquinas's comments about the relation between the moral virtues and the theological virtues.[9] In this section of the treatise (Question 52), charity appears as the principal virtue. In the other sections, prudence is presented as the most important virtue, for it perfects the practical activity of reason and directs the other virtues.[10]

Prudence is defined as right reason applied to human conduct.[11] This is, however, a misleading description of prudence, because it presents prudence

---

6. In fact, Aquinas never finished the *Summa Theologiae*. He stopped working on it two years before his death.

7. Compare Osterle, *Treatise on the Virtues*, xvi, and Nelson, *Priority of Prudence*, 31.

8. Nelson, *Priority of Prudence*, 32 and 36.

9. This is clear in *Summa Theologiae*, I–II, question 52, in which Aquinas talks about the relation between the natural and the supernatural virtues. He offers a moderate position compared with Augustine's by stressing that the natural virtues can be perfected by the supernatural virtues. He does not agree with Augustine that the natural virtues are vices without love of God determining their formation.

10. Nelson, *Priority of Prudence*, 77.

11. *Summa Theologiae*, II–II, questions 48 and 49 (36:57, 79).

as far narrower in scope than Aquinas believes it to be. A much better (although considerably longer) description of prudence is found in the response section of *Summa Theologiae*, I–II, question 58, article 5: "Can There Be Intellectual Virtue Without Moral Virtue." Here Aquinas tells us:

> All other intellectual virtues can exist without moral virtue, but there cannot be prudence without moral virtue. The reason for this is that prudence is right reasoning about what is to be done—and this not only in general, but also in particular, in respect to which man acts. Now right reasoning requires principles from which the reasoning proceeds. And reasoning about particulars must proceed not only from universal principles but from particular principles as well. As to universal principles about things to be done, man is rightly disposed by the natural understanding of principles, whereby he recognizes that no evil is to be done; or again by some practical science. But this is not enough for right reasoning about particular cases. For it sometimes happens that such a universal principle known by understanding or through some science, is perverted in a particular case by some passion; for example, to a person very desirous of something when the desire overcomes him, the object of it seems good to him, although it is contrary to the universal judgment of his reason.
>
> Consequently, just as man is disposed rightly with regard to universal principles by natural understanding or by the habit of science, so in order to be rightly disposed with regard to the particular principles concerning things to be done, which are ends or goals, he must be perfected by certain habits, so that it becomes connatural, as it were, to him to judge rightly about an end. This comes about through moral virtue, for the virtuous person judges about the end of virtue rightly, since "such as a man is, so does the end seem to him." Hence in order to reason rightly about what is to be done, which is prudence, man must have moral virtue.[12]

In this passage, Aquinas connects prudence with the correct perception of individual circumstances. In fact, he links prudence to the problem of weakness of will and to the development of particular principles of behavior. Although general moral principles, according to Aquinas, are given through synderesis, these principles are rather empty, consisting of general state-

---

12. Osterle, *Treatise on the Virtues*, 87–88.

ments like: "Do good and avoid evil" and "Obey God." For human activity, more content-full principles are required. Aquinas talks about these principles in various places.[13] He claims that they are not innate, but are derived from experience and instruction. In his discussion of the role of prudence in Aquinas's ethics, Daniel Nelson calls these secondary principles, and he claims that they are developed through prudence:

> Once again, these naturally known higher principles, the ends of human action, are so general as to be empty of material content. The content, which depends on prudence and the virtues, is learned. I am arguing that what Thomas sometimes calls first universal principles of practical reason or natural law play the explanatory role I have described, while the secondary principles, which are acquired over time, guide conduct. The primary principles are known through synderesis, while the secondary principles are the concern of prudence.[14]

With the mention of synderesis, we are, of course, brought back to issues concerning conscience. In fact, conscience is discussed in the first part of the second part of the *Summa Theologiae* (I–II, question 19, articles 5 and 6). Here Aquinas discusses the binding and excusing powers of a mistaken conscience. In the two articles, he defines 'conscience' as the "application of knowledge to activity."[15] There appear to be a number of links between conscience and prudence. Not only is prudence connected with carrying out the dictates of conscience, but prudence is also connected with the knowledge that is applied to activities.[16] The rules that apply to particular cases come from the secondary principles derived from prudence, and the apprehension of particular circumstances, which determines what secondary rules the circumstances fall under, is also a product of prudence. It seems clear, then, that for Aquinas, prudence works in tandem with conscience and synderesis. Although conscience may be understood by Aquinas to be simply an application of principles to individual cases, the richer activities of conscience found in Bonaventure's discussion of conscience are placed by him into issues surrounding prudence.

13. *Summa Theologiae*, II–II, question 47 (36:49). Also Nelson, *Priority of Prudence*, 101–2.

14. Nelson, *Priority of Prudence*, 101.

15. *Summa Theologiae*, 16:61.

16. See note f, 16:61, and Osterle, *Treatise on the Virtues*, 57, 78. Robert J. Smith in his *Conscience and Catholicism* (Lanham, Md.: University Press of America, 1998), 23–30, discusses some of the relations between conscience and prudence in Aquinas's thought.

Aquinas also sees a close connection among conscience, synderesis, the virtues, and weakness of will. As one of the best commentators on Aristotle's *Nicomachean Ethics*, Thomas Aquinas was deeply interested in the problem of weakness of will.[17] His interest was also informed by Christian views about sin and the will, developed in large part from Augustine's concern for these issues.[18] In line with renewed interest in Aristotle's views about weakness of will, there has recently been increased interest in Aquinas's views about incontinence.[19] Of particular note is the work of Bonnie Kent and Risto Saarinen.

In her article, "Transitory Vice: Thomas Aquinas on Incontinence," Kent discusses Aquinas's views about incontinence and their relation to the views of Aristotle on weakness of will. Although there are some key differences between Aquinas's and Aristotle's views about weakness of will, their analyses of the phenomenon share broad agreement. Both men contrast the incontinent man with the intemperate man as well as the continent man. The intemperate man (also called the self-indulgent man) has made his own pleasure his ultimate good. He lives by the rule that he should do whatever he thinks brings him pleasure. His life is, according to Aquinas, a habitual vice. He does not care that his pursuit of pleasure eventually ends in damnation. He has chosen his way of life and continually chooses in line with it. He has no sense that what he is doing is wrong, nor is it likely he will ever change. In contrast, the continent man understands what ought to be done. He is aware that some pleasures should not be pursued whereas others may be legitimately enjoyed. He has sensual desires (and thus is distinguished from the temperate man), but he chooses not to follow these desires when they involve what should not be done. Likewise, the incontinent man also knows what should be done, and, in the absence of contrary passions, he will choose to do what should be done. But the sensual desires he has often lead him to do what he knows he should not do. For sometimes his desires lead him to perform an action he knows should not be done. Unlike the intemperate man, the incontinent man does not make a life of following his desires. On the contrary, his departure from doing what he knows should be

17. Ralph McInerny offers this evaluation in his introduction to Aquinas's *Commentary on the Nicomachean Ethics* (South Bend: Dumb Ox Press, 1994).

18. Risto Saarinen claims that Augustine's influence was important on these issues throughout the Middle Ages in his *Weakness of Will in Medieval Thought*.

19. Aquinas used *incontinentia* for *akrasia*. Following many others, I translate *incontinentia* as 'incontinence.'

done is occasional and episodic. In fact, Aquinas compares the incontinent man to an epileptic who has seizures at random times.[20]

That the incontinent (*akratic*) man knows what he ought to do but does not do it is the problem of weakness of will that vexed Plato. According to him, there can be no such weakness. If one truly knows what one should do (effectively, what is best for the person), one cannot do anything else. If anything other is done, it must be done through some form of ignorance. Above (Chapter 1), we saw that Aristotle disagreed with Plato and claimed that there was, in fact, weakness of will. Yet, his analysis seems to emphasize Plato's point that such weakness must involve some form of ignorance.

In Aquinas's presentation of Aristotle's discussion of weakness of will, the fourth position offered in Book 7, Chapter 3 of the *Nicomachean Ethics* is emphasized. According to this position, the incontinent man knows the appropriate general principles of behavior concerning what should be done, for example, one should not fornicate. If the incontinent man sees a particular action as falling under this general principle, for instance, a man sees that having intercourse with an unmarried woman is a case of fornication, he will not perform the action. However, the incontinent man also holds the general rule that pleasures should be enjoyed. If the incontinent man, driven by his particular desire for a particular unmarried woman, sees the proposed sexual liaison as a case of pleasure, he subsumes it under the general rule about pursuing pleasure and pursues the relationship. The desire he has, as it were, blinds him to the general principle about fornication he still possesses, but only habitually. The actual knowledge he possesses is that the proposed liaison is a case of pleasure to be pursued. He thus has (habitually) the knowledge that he should avoid fornication, but he fornicates nonetheless because he actually sees the fornication as an act of pleasure to be pursued. As a general comment on Aristotle's analysis, Aquinas remarks: "It is not the knowledge of the universal but only the evaluation of the sensible, which is not so excellent, that is dragged about by passion."[21] The point Aquinas is making is that the incontinent man possesses the knowledge of what he should do, but he is driven by the passion he has for a particular; this passion leads him to act contrary to what he knows (habitually) should not be done.

According to Kent, Aquinas's analysis of incontinence differs from Aris-

20. *Commentary on the Nicomachean Ethics*, Book 8, lecture 8, paragraph 1424. Translation, p. 445.
21. Book 7, lecture 3, paragraph 1352.

totle's view of weakness of will in two critical ways.[22] In the first place, the incontinent for Aquinas judges his incontinent act to be good. In the second place, the incontinent, according to Aquinas, chooses the incontinent act he performs. In Kent's opinion, these two differences show up in both Aquinas's commentary on Aristotle's *Nicomachean Ethics* and in his own views about incontinence (210f.). Ultimately, the two differences are linked to the emphasis on the will found in Aquinas's medieval predecessors, which comes from Augustine's discussions of the roles of the will and sin in human activity.[23] Kent is convinced that Aquinas is wrong to interpret Aristotle as claiming that the incontinent sees his act as good.[24] If one distinguishes, however, between an "apparent good" and what is really good and bears in mind Aristotle's opening line of the *Nicomachean Ethics*—"All arts and all teaching, and similarly every act and every choice seem to have the attainment of some good as their object"—it seems plausible to attribute to Aristotle the view that the incontinent (*akratic*) man sees his incontinent act as a good.[25] Thus it is not at all obvious that Aquinas's interpretation of Aristotle is as flawed as Kent believes. But this issue is secondary in Kent's eyes to the second point of divergence.

In his commentary on the *Nicomachean Ethics*, Aquinas is very careful to indicate that Aristotle denies that the incontinent acts from choice.[26] He never asserts that Aristotle believes that the incontinent chooses his action. But, according to Kent, it is likely that Aquinas saw Aristotle's analysis here to be "correct but incomplete" (217). In his own theological works, Aquinas claims that the incontinent chooses to act as he does. But this claim seems in conflict with Aquinas's statement that the incontinent sins from passion or weakness while the intemperate sins from choice (207). Kent, however, resolves the conflict by pointing out that Aquinas distinguishes two different senses of choice: *peccare ex electione* (sinning from choice) and *peccare eligens* (sinning while choosing). According to Aquinas, the incontinent chooses his incontinent action (*peccare eligens*), but his act is not from choice (*peccare ex electione*). In elaboration of the distinction, Kent tells us:

22. "Transitory Vice," 206. Kent does not modify her views in her *Virtues of the Will: The Transformation of Ethics in the Late Thirteenth Century* (Washington, D.C.: Catholic University of America Press, 1995).

23. Both Kent and Saarinen make the point about Augustine's influence.

24. "Transitory Vice," 218.

25. Compare Aquinas's remarks on the passage in his *Commentary on the Nicomachean Ethics*, Book 1, lecture 1, paragraph 8.

26. "Transitory Vice," 217.

Incontinent action is chosen, but it is not done from choice. By an act done "from choice" Thomas means an act in accordance with the agent's moral disposition and hence reflecting his opinion of what is good in general. The basis for this might be *Ethics* VI, where Aristotle says that there is no choice without moral character (1139a32–35). Incontinent action, which is against choice, must thus be somehow "out of character." Aristotle's comparison between incontinence and epilepsy lends support to this idea. The incontinent is not consistently indulging his appetites any more than the epileptic is in a continuous seizure. Both function well for the most part, suffering only from intermittent flareups. ("Transitory Vice," 219–20)

Because the incontinent man wills to perform his incontinent act, he chooses the act in the sense of "peccare eligens." The intemperate man does the same. But because the incontinent's selection of the incontinent action is "out of character," he does not do the action from choice in the sense of "peccare ex electione." The intemperate man, on the other hand, has developed a lifestyle of choosing wrong actions, and his choice of a wrong action is from a habit he has freely developed. The intemperate's choice reflects his character and so is a choice in the sense of "peccare ex electione." The contrast here between the incontinent man and the intemperate man explains why Aquinas regards the intemperate man as subject to a habitual vice and the incontinent man as suffering from transitory vice.

In reviewing Kent's views, Risto Saarinen expresses considerable agreement with Kent, but he thinks he has a better explanation of how the incontinent chooses the incontinent action without acting out of choice. He offers a "two-step explanation of *akrasia*."[27] Like Kent, Saarinen proposes (following Aquinas) that we think of the incontinent man as possessing two general principles: one that forbids the action, the other that permits the action. (Using our earlier example, "One should not fornicate" is the forbidding general principle, and "Pleasures should be enjoyed" is the permitting rule.) When the incontinent person is faced with a particular opportunity ("This is a desirable, unmarried woman"), "concupiscence places this minor premise under the wrong major proposition" (125). According to Saarinen, the placing of the minor premise under the wrong major is the first step of a two-step process. This first step is "voluntary," but it is not deliberately chosen by the incontinent person. Saarinen, in fact, claims that this first

27. *Weakness of Will in Medieval Thought*, 125f.

step explains why Aquinas says that the incontinent person does not act wrongly in the sense of "peccare ex electione." Because the first step is not deliberately chosen (presumably because it is driven by concupiscence), it cannot be done "ex electione." Once the minor premise has been subsumed under the wrong major premise, the incontinent follows out the perverted syllogism and chooses the incontinent action. This choice after the perverted deliberation is the second step of the incontinent action, and the incontinent deliberately chooses this action. It is an action that is "eligens."

In many ways, Saarinen's proposal is best seen as an elaboration of Kent's basic analysis. He thinks that Kent has correctly analyzed the second step of an incontinent action, but he believes that there is a "first step" prior to this second step. This step occurs "contrary to the choice disposed toward the proper good" (129). This first step seems to be, essentially, perceptual; it is the point in the action where the opportunity is seen either as a desirable pleasure (contrary to the choice disposed toward the proper good) or as a forbidden object (in line with the choice disposed toward the proper good). The second step is a good deliberation, drawing the appropriate conclusion from given major and minor premises. Aquinas, in fact, emphasizes the difference between the perceptual and the deliberative in his commentary on Book VI of the *Nicomachean Ethics*. In Lecture IX, when discussing prudential action, Aquinas contrasts *eubulia* with *synesis*. *Eubulia* (the topic of Lecture VIII) is "good deliberation."[28] It is characteristic of prudential people. *Synesis* is good judgment about the things treated by prudence (391). It is also a critical part of prudence but is not to be identified with it. Aquinas's main point in the lecture is that a prudent person must judge particulars correctly and deliberate well about these particulars so that he may act correctly. Because an incontinent person lacks prudence, it is clear that the incontinent man must be lacking in either *eubulia* or *synesis*. In fact, Aquinas's third lecture on Book VII of the *Nicomachean Ethics* seems to emphasize that the incontinent is lacking in *synesis*.

In this text, Aquinas presents incontinence as a problem in practical reasoning. At paragraph 1339, he indicates that practical reasoning involves both universal and particular propositions. In the next paragraph (1340), he makes a critical point:

> We should note, however, that the universal can be taken in two ways. In one way as it is in itself, as in the example, "Dry things are

---

28. Translation, p. 389. Aquinas seems to connect *eubulia* with good deliberation to good ends.

good for every man"; in another way as it is in a particular object, for instance, "This is a man," or "That food is dry." Therefore it is possible that a man knows, both habitually and actually, the universal considered in itself but either he does not grasp the universal considered in this particular object, i.e., the universal is not known in an habitual way, or he does not bestir himself, i.e., the universal is not actually known. (422)

The issue of how a universal is seen in a particular is essential to Aquinas's explanation of the actions of the incontinent man as we can see in paragraph 1347:

On the first point the proper consideration is this—reason in the incontinent man is not so completely overcome that he is without genuine knowledge of the universal. Put it this way. The reason proposes a universal judgment forbidding an inordinate tasting of something sweet, e.g., it says that nothing sweet should be tasted outside a certain time. But the appetite proposes that every sweet thing is pleasant, something in itself desired by concupiscence. And, since in a particular case concupiscence may bind reason, the proposal is not accepted under universal reason so as to say also that this is outside the time; but it is taken under the universal aspect of concupiscence so as to say this is sweet. So the conclusion of the operation follows. In this syllogism of the incontinent man there are four propositions, as already indicated. (423–24)

Driven by concupiscence, the incontinent man sees the opportunity (a desirable unmarried woman in the case mentioned earlier) as an example of the permitting rule (Pleasures should be enjoyed). Under the influence of concupiscence, he is unable to see the opportunity as an example of the correct, forbidding principle (One should not fornicate). Given his perception of the opportunity, it is not surprising that the incontinent man performs the incontinent action. But why does he see the opportunity in the way that he does? As Aquinas says, he is driven by concupiscence. The continent man, who chooses correctly, also has concupiscence. Yet, he is not driven by it as the incontinent man is. Why, then, is the incontinent man driven by concupiscence and the continent man is not? Neither Kent nor Saarinen addresses this important issue in their discussions of weakness of will. But it is an extremely important one.

In Lecture 3 on Book III of the *Nicomachean Ethics*, Aquinas discusses Aristotle's views about what constitutes involuntary actions. For Aristotle, compulsion (where the active principle is outside the agent) and ignorance both render an action involuntary. In commenting on ignorance in paragraphs 505 and 506, Aquinas makes two important distinctions:

> Ignorance causes an involuntary [*sic*], as was explained before (406–424). If, however, we are the cause of this ignorance, the ignorance will be voluntary and we will be punished for it. A man can be the cause of his own ignorance in two ways. In one way directly, by doing something, as is evident in those who get drunk and for this reason are rendered ignorant. . . . In the other way a man is the cause of ignorance indirectly by reason of the fact that he does not do what he ought to do. On account of this, ignorance of the things a man can and is bound to know is considered voluntary and therefore he is punished for it. . . . The same is true of those things which men do not know apparently by reason of negligence, because they could have learned. They are masters of themselves and they can be diligent and not negligent. (164–65)

We are responsible for our ignorance of things we should know even when this ignorance is indirect, that is, from a failure to do what ought to be done. And this is precisely the situation of the incontinent man. When he performs his incontinent act, he is ignoring the forbidding principle he should follow because he sees the opportunity as an example of the permitting rule. He sees it in this way because he is driven by concupiscence. But he is so driven because he has neglected to develop the proper habits that would enable him to see the opportunity correctly as an example of the forbidden principle. The weakness of will the incontinent man suffers from comes from his failure to train himself adequately to see opportunities in the proper way.

Issues about habits and training, of course, connect directly to talk about the virtues. Given the context of the issue of weakness of will, that is, that it occurs in a work advocating an ethics of virtue, it is surprising that neither Kent nor Saarinen links weakness of will with the development of the virtues. Aquinas's *Commentary on the Nicomachean Ethics* clearly links the two issues. As I have mentioned, Aquinas links incontinence with a failure of practical reason, and he connects *eubulia* and *synesis* with the virtue of prudence. Of course, because weakness of will is essentially a problem of the failure of prudence (or the failure to develop prudence), it is not surprising that, for Aquinas, weakness of will also involves a failure of conscience. In his discussion of the binding and excusing powers of a mistaken conscience in the *Summa Theologiae* (I–II, question 19, articles 5 and 6), he discusses how someone will choose what is evil because it appears good as a result of some factor connected with its apprehension, and he discusses what types of ignorance excuse evil actions.[29]

Aquinas's linking of conscience with prudence and the virtues in general through his concern with weakness of will is extremely insightful. A viable view of conscience needs to see it in relation to success or failure in developing the virtues. Moreover, conscience needs to be seen not only as performing judging functions on the value of actions but also as connected to the assessment of moral situations. Clearly, Aquinas's own view of conscience departs from earlier discussions of conscience. In these discussions, the focus was on conscience and synderesis in isolation from other issues. It seems likely that Aquinas's shift is connected with his strong interest in the whole of the *Nicomachean Ethics*. Indeed, Aquinas's discussions of conscience as well as prudence are marked by constant reference to the *Nicomachean Ethics*. Whatever the explanation, Aquinas's shift from focusing on conscience in isolation from prudence and weakness of will is carried on by two prominent Franciscans: Duns Scotus and William Ockham.

---

29. Vol. 18, *responsio* section of article 5.

F O U R

· ·

SCOTUS AND OCKHAM ON SYNDERESIS *and* CONSCIENCE

Lottin's research (in *Psychologie et morale au XIIe et XIIIe siècles*) reveals that the topics of conscience and synderesis were extensively treated from the time of Philip the Chancellor (d. 1236) to that of Henry of Ghent (d. 1293). It is consequently surprising that these topics receive little direct attention from either Duns Scotus (1265–1308) or William of Ockham (1280–1349). Ockham devotes no explicit question to conscience (in fact, the closest he comes to a discussion of conscience is in the context of asking whether willfully following a mistaken intellect is ever meritorious), and Scotus's discussion of conscience in his *Ordinatio*, Book 2, distinction 39, is a rejection of Henry of Ghent's views without an articulation of his own. These two great thinkers' failure to treat conscience and synderesis explicitly in any detail is not so much a neglect of traditional issues of conscience and synderesis, however, as an indication that the focus of the discussion of these issues has changed to issues about the virtues. In the context of discussing the development of virtues like prudence, Scotus and Ockham present claims about the functioning of conscience that unite the views of Bonaventure and Aquinas and influence subsequent thinkers; many of their claims need to be incorporated in a viable view of conscience.

Given Bonaventure's view that synderesis is in the will, it is unexpected that his fellow Franciscan, Scotus, places synderesis in the intellect. Scotus's explanation is straightforward: "I reply to these questions: If synderesis is assumed to be something having an elicited act that necessarily and at all times inclines one to act justly and resist sin, then since nothing of this sort is in the will, we cannot assume it to be there. Consequently, it is in the intellect, and it cannot be assumed to be anything other than that habitual knowledge of principles which is always right."[1] As a Franciscan and voluntarist, Scotus would naturally be expected to follow Bonaventure's views about synderesis and conscience. Yet, this passage clearly indicates that Scotus follows Aquinas's views about synderesis: It is the habitual disposition for apprehending the truth of correct practical principles. Similarly, Scotus's views about conscience seem decidedly Thomistic: "Conscience is the habit of making proper practical conclusions, according to which a right choice of what is to be done is apt by nature to follow" (203). In this passage, conscience seems to be linked with the application of principles in a practical syllogism to obtain practical conclusions. Because it is synderesis that supplies the general practical principles from which conscience draws practical conclusions, Scotus has seemingly embraced Aquinas's views about synderesis and conscience: Synderesis, found in the intellect, supplies general and necessary practical principles that conscience applies in particular cases. Apparently, Bonaventure's emphasis on synderesis as residing in the will and consisting of the desire for the good that sparks conscience has been abandoned by Scotus. The situation, however, is more complicated than it appears.

Scotus's doctrine of the will is more developed and complicated than Bonaventure's. In contrast to Plato and Aristotle, who see the will as subservient to the intellect, Scotus regards the will as a self-determining agent that can choose to follow either the reasoning of the intellect or the demands of the passions and desires. He states a number of times that "the will with

---

1. Allan B. Wolter, *Duns Scotus on the Will and Morality* (Washington, D.C.: Catholic University Press, 1986), 201.

respect to the intellect is the superior agent" (175). One of his justifications for this view is that the will is a free power whereas the intellect is not: "But if 'rational' is understood to mean 'with reason,' then the will is properly rational, and it has to do with opposites, both as regards its own act and as regards the acts it controls. And it has to do with opposites not in the way that a nature, like the intellect, acts, which has no power to determine itself in any other way. But the will acts freely, for it has the power of self-determination" (157). The will is superior to the intellect because it is self-determined and makes choices whereas the intellect has no choice but to accept the true when presented to it. Scotus also regards the will as superior to the intellect because it can accept or reject the recommendations of the intellect: "And if some volition, such as choosing perhaps, first requires some judgmental knowledge about what the choices are, one of the contraries could be known through the other in this way, though at times the choice runs counter to that judgment" (165). Moreover, the will is superior to the intellect because it can control what the intellect considers:

> I say, therefore, that for one intellection that exists perfectly in the intellect, many confused and imperfect intellections can also be there. . . . Hence, by means of these confused and imperfect intellections present there, the will . . . can take complacency in any one of them, even though that intellection was not known actually as a [distinct] object, and . . . by taking pleasure in one, the will confirms and intends that intellection. Hence, that which was imperfect and disregarded becomes perfect and intense through this complacency, and thus the will can command thought and turn the intellect towards it. But by not willing some other intellection or taking no pleasure in it, that intellection diminishes in intensity and ceases to exist. Thus the will is said to avert the intellect from that intellection, just as the visual power, without moving and remaining within the same cone of vision, can focus on another point which it envisioned only imperfectly before. (175)

The will is surely an extraordinary power as Scotus describes it. It receives information from the intellect, but it can choose to focus on whatever information it wants according to the pleasure the particular information gives it.

The issue of the will taking pleasure is important for Scotus. Elsewhere, he talks about how the will "by taking pleasure in the intellection strengthens and intends it, whereas the intellection that is nilled or in which the intel-

lect takes no pleasure is weakened and dismissed."[2] The will as a self-determining agent determines itself by what gives it pleasure. This fact is important for understanding why the will chooses evil. Quite simply, the will that
chooses evil finds more pleasure in that choice than in the choice of what is
good and proper. This suggests, however, that moral training for Scotus is a
matter of training the will to take pleasure in what is proper and good. In
fact, this is the case, and the point relates to Scotus's views about the development of the virtues. Yet, there is another crucial aspect to Scotus's view of
the will.

Following Anselm, Scotus claims that there are two affections in the will:
an affection for benefit (*affectio commodi*) and an affection for justice (*affectio
justitiae*).[3] The first, the affection for benefit, is related to people's ability to
will what seems to benefit them, in the sense of bringing them happiness.
This disposition is in play, for example, whenever human beings will to eat,
will to protect themselves, will to gather possessions, and so on. The second, the affection for justice, is related to the ability to will what people
should do.

Scotus regards both affections as innate to the human will. Moreover, he
argues that only beings who possess both affections are free. If a being
possessed merely the affection for benefit, it would not be free to pursue
anything other than what is seen to benefit it. Only if the affection for
justice is also present is there the possibility of choice, which is required for
freedom.

Although the aims of the affection for benefit may be at odds with the
aims of the affection for justice, this is not always the case. As the highest
good, God is a principal object of the affection for benefit. And, in fact,
Scotus regards the affection for benefit as "a God-given drive implanted in
man's rational nature which leads him to seek his true happiness, the supreme degree of which is to be found in union with God."[4] Thus, the drive
toward good, which Bonaventure identifies with synderesis, is associated
with the affection for benefit in Scotus's thought. Given Scotus's assumption
that there are the two affections in the will, it is not at all surprising that he
gives a different role to synderesis than did Bonaventure.

2. Ibid., 173–75. Alan R. Perreiah in his "Scotus on Human Emotions" (*Franciscan Studies* 56
[1998]: 325–45) presents a clear overview of Scotus's doctrine about human emotions. In the second section of the article, he discusses emotions as inducements to actions.

3. Anselm offers these two dispositions in *The Fall of Satan*.

4. Marilyn Adams, ed., *The Philosophical Theology of John Duns Scotus* (Ithaca: Cornell University
Press, 1990), 153.

If we put aside the issue of terminology, there are parallels between Bonaventure's view of conscience and Scotus's. What Scotus labels the synderesis plays the role of the "potential conscience" in Bonaventure's view. This is the power found in the intellect to assent to the truths of very general practical principles. Similarly, what Scotus calls the "habit of conscience" corresponds to the "applied conscience" in Bonaventure's scheme. This is the intellectual power to apply general principles to particular circumstances. Of course, this correspondence can also be found between Bonaventure's and Aquinas's views. In fact, Scotus's view of conscience seems to draw from both Aquinas's and Bonaventure's views. From Aquinas, Scotus seems to have drawn the thought that both synderesis and conscience are to be placed in the intellectual order. From Bonaventure, Scotus seems to have given conscience much more of a dynamic role in the human personality than a mechanical application of general principles. It is Scotus's close linking of conscience and the development of the virtues that allows him to combine the two sources.

Scotus claims that moral virtues are most properly found in the will, even though there is something like virtue in the sense appetite.[5] The location of moral virtues in the will is obvious once one realizes that moral virtues are habits that incline the will to act rightly. As habits, moral virtues are acquired by repeated acts that are dependent on the will. Once a virtuous moral habit is established, the will is inclined to follow the right reason or dictate of the virtue and to act rightly. Thus moral virtues are formed in the will and serve to incline the will toward right actions. But how does one first act in accordance with the dictates of moral virtue to develop the habit that is the moral virtue?

For Scotus, a virtuous action is one that is performed in accordance with the dictate of right reason associated with the particular virtue. According to him, there is a right dictate associated with courage, another one associated with justice, and so on for all the moral virtues. Interestingly, he calls these dictates "proper prudences." The existence of the "proper prudences" is to be distinguished from the existence of a "general habit of prudence." This general habit, found exclusively in the intellect, seems to be a power to formulate the right dictates (the "proper prudences") associated with each moral virtue (411f.). According to Scotus, one can have this general habit of prudence without possessing the moral virtues. That is, one can have the ability to determine what is to be done so as to be virtuous in situations without

---

5. Wolter, *Duns Scotus on the Will and Morality*, 341.

actually doing what is virtuous. But it appears that one cannot possess "proper prudences" without also possessing the relevant moral virtues. That is to say, one cannot know the correct dictate associated with courage without performing courageous actions. But it is also the case that one cannot perform a courageous action without possessing the appropriate correct dictate, for an action done in ignorance is not meritorious. Thus there is a circularity between knowing the right dictates associated with the moral virtues to perform the moral virtues and the need that the relevant virtues be performed before the correct dictates can be known. How can one break into the circle? For Scotus, the answer is that conscience provides the way into the circle. His insight is in fact a critical part of any viable theory of conscience.

Although Scotus, in arguing against Henry of Ghent's view of conscience, says that "conscience is the habit of making proper practical conclusions" (203), he also states that "conscience is from one practical syllogism deducing evidently some conclusion from first practical principles."[6] That is to say, conscience is not simply a habit of deriving proper practical conclusions; it is at work wherever there is a deduction of a practical principle. Thus, whenever a person formulates what is to be done in some circumstance, there is an exercise of conscience. It appears, then, that one performs actions in accordance with the dictate of conscience, which has determined the proper action from the principles of the synderesis. These actions, performed voluntarily in accordance with the dictate of conscience, are meritorious, and they provide the basis for the development of the relevant virtues. For the performance of these acts from conscience leads to the type of habit that Scotus thinks of as a virtue.

Take, for example, the virtue of fortitude. Synderesis perhaps contains a very general principle like "Remain steadfast in one's devotion to God." When presented with a test of faith, for example, to renounce one's belief in God or suffer punishment, conscience deduces that one should not give up one's faith and one should thus act courageously. It is likely that the first act, or even the first several acts, of such courage is performed with unease and misgivings. But with repetition of such acts, their performance becomes easier. In fact, one may even develop an inclination to such acts and experience pleasure in their performance. It is at this point, according to Scotus, that one can talk about the formation of a virtue. Importantly, one cannot have the virtue without performing the relevant actions, but, likewise, the actions

6. Ibid., 198, my translation of the text.

leading to the formation of the virtue must be done in accordance with the appropriate correct dictate. Thus, following one's conscience allows one to develop the virtues.

Scotus regards prudence as different from practical reason. According to him, practical reason is concerned only with the means to pursue given ends. Prudence, on the other hand, is concerned with both the ends to be pursued by a person and the means for achieving these ends (409). This distinction suggests that there is also a difference between the correct dictate of conscience and the correct dictate of a proper prudence associated with a particular virtue. The correct dictate of conscience is essentially a practical conclusion to a practical syllogism, developed in the intellect and aimed at fitting a particular circumstance. The correct dictate of a proper prudence is a habit of making the appropriate choice in relevant circumstances. This habit is developed from appropriate acts and is directly related to the experience associated with the acts. Because it is a generalization from particular acts, it is undoubtedly more nuanced than is the correct dictate from conscience. Thus Scotus's view here parallels Bonaventure's view that practical principles both direct actions and are influenced by the results of the actions performed. The dynamism of Bonaventure's view of conscience is alive in Scotus's view of proper prudences. Moreover, although Scotus places the habit of prudence completely within the intellectual order, he regards proper prudences as falling within both the intellectual and moral orders. This placement is closely connected to the dynamic view of proper prudences that he endorses; it also parallels Bonaventure's sophisticated blending of the intellectual and affective orders.

It thus appears that there is an obvious explanation for Scotus's lack of explicit discussion about conscience and synderesis. What have been the traditional roles assigned to synderesis and conscience Scotus presents as part of his discussion of the moral virtues and their relation to the will. As we have seen, Bonaventure's view of synderesis as a drive to the good has become Scotus's notion of the affection for benefit. This innate and necessary drive of the will is tempered by the affection for justice, so that moral agents have a choice between following what they desire and what they should do. The moral agent's innate grasp of the truth of general practical principles (Scotus's and Aquinas's "synderesis" and Bonaventure's "potential conscience") is applied in particular circumstances by the conscience to form a correct dictate about what ought to be done (Scotus's and Aquinas's "conscience" and Bonaventure's "applied conscience"). The will can choose to follow the correct dictates or reject them. With the performance of acts following the correct dictates of conscience, the development of a habit (proper prudence) becomes possible, which can become the relevant moral virtue. An important part of the development of the virtue is a transformation of the affective order so that the person possessing the relevant virtue takes delight in performing the acts associated with the virtue. Scotus has thus closely linked the traditional discussions of conscience and synderesis with the virtue tradition, a direction Bonaventure hinted at in his texts but never fully developed and one Aquinas developed to a degree. Such linkage is an important part of any viable view of conscience.

Given Scotus's obvious interest in issues found in the virtue tradition, it is not at all surprising that he discusses the question of the unity of the virtues. He is quite clear that if there is any unity among the virtues, it can only be among the moral ones; there is no unity between the intellectual and moral virtues. Although this view is in line with classical treatments of the unity of the virtues, Scotus seems to be one of the first to make the point clearly.

It is, then, somewhat surprising that Scotus gives the very unclassical answer that there is no unity to the moral virtues. According to him, it is obvious that a person may possess the virtue of temperance but lack the virtue of bravery. But Scotus's view about the unity of the virtues is very subtle because it is complicated by his distinction between "the general habit of prudence" (found in the intellectual order) and the "proper prudences" (found in both the intellectual and moral orders) associated with each virtue. As we have seen, proper prudences, specific to each moral virtue, express the correct dictates, developed from experience, for each virtue. Thus, there is a proper prudence for courage, a different proper prudence for justice, and so on, because the correct dictates for the various virtues differ from one another. The general habit of prudence, as we have seen, is not related to specific dictates. On the contrary, the general habit of prudence is the ability to formulate the specific dictates. Thus, the general habit of prudence must obtain before any of the specific prudences obtain, and so it must be present when any virtue is present. Scotus talks about this situation as the general habit of prudence virtually containing all the moral virtues (413). To this extent, there is a unity to the moral virtues; they are all virtually contained in the general habit of prudence. Yet, there is a further unity to the virtues that Scotus acknowledges: "But one is not simply a moral person without all the virtues, just as one is not simply sentient without all one's senses" (389). Although certain virtues may be present without other virtues—for example, temperance may be found without courage—a moral man "is one who possesses all of the virtues." So there is a unity to the virtues in the sense that a moral person must have them all; one virtue cannot be present in a moral person without all the other virtues being present.[7] Elsewhere, Scotus calls the moral person a perfect, virtuous person:

> Hence, that dictum of the Philosopher should be understood in this way. Just as the virtuous person is inclined to choose rightly by reason of a correct habit, so too he has been conditioned by prudence to make at once a correct judgment as to what should be chosen, and to deliberate imperceptibly, as it were, because of the rapidity with which the practical inference is made. Another, imperfect individual, however, syllogizes practically only with difficulty and delay. And if at last he chooses correctly, he is said to act not suddenly but sullenly, whereas another, perfect person as it were acts quickly with respect to that thing, since the time it takes him to act is imperceptibly short.[8]

Scotus's perfect person seems very similar to Aristotle's person of practical wisdom. This is the person who has, through long experience, developed the moral virtues and is able to deliberate so well about all moral situations that in Aristotle's view "to be moral is to do what a man of practical wisdom would do."[9] Scotus's perfect, virtuous person, like the person of practical wisdom, is skilled at determining what should be done in given circumstances; takes delight in acting in accord with his virtues; possesses all the moral virtues, and has gained them through experience. Needless to say, Scotus's perfect, virtuous person will also be informed by God's law as to what is appropriate to choose and will be influenced by the theological virtues infused by God. So Scotus's notion of the perfect, virtuous person is not precisely Aristotle's notion of the person of practical wisdom. But the similarities that are present indicate how closely Scotus wishes to tie his moral theory to the virtue tradition.

When we turn to Ockham's discussion of similar issues—conscience, prudence, virtues—it is clear that he has followed Scotus's turn toward the virtue tradition. In fact, Ockham's discussion of the virtues and related matters is much more detailed than Scotus's. It contains very careful distinctions that Scotus did not make but should have made according to Ockham, who

7. There are obvious connections here with what Gregory Vlastos labeled "Pauline Predication" in his "The Unity of the Virtues in the *Protagoras.*"

8. Wolter, *Duns Scotus on the Will and Morality,* 345f.

9. Ibid., 385, for Scotus's citation of this phrase from Aristotle.

devotes a significant part of his writings to issues concerning the virtues. There are important discussions, for example, in his *Commentary on the Sentences*, Book III, Question 11 and Question 12; in his *Quaestiones Variae* (Questions 6, 7, and 8); and in his *Quodlibetal Questions* (question 20 of the Primum and questions 16 and 18 of the Tertium). His most extended treatment of issues related explicitly to conscience, found in Question 8 of the *Quaestiones Variae* ("Whether the will can have a virtuous act in respect to some object in regard to which there is an error in the intellect"), connects issues about mistaken reason and erroneous conscience to other discussions about the possibility that a person may simultaneously possess one virtue and the vice of some other virtue.[10]

Although in these works Ockham demonstrates considerable agreement with Scotus's views on the lack of a unity of virtues, on the various grades of the virtues, on the need of right reason for a virtuous act, and on the need to distinguish moral knowledge from prudence, he disagrees with Scotus on at least four points. The first is that Scotus is wrong to claim that the intellect and the will are formally distinct.[11] He has little patience with Scotus's "formal distinction" on this issue as well as others. He believes that the intellect and the will are really identical but their operations are distinct.[12] The second disagreement, found in many places in his writing, is that Scotus is wrong to believe that internal as well as external actions have moral worth. On the contrary, according to Ockham, only internal acts of the will are morally meritorious. External acts are morally significant only by extrinsic denomination; that is, their moral worth is a matter of the moral worth of the internal act of will to which they are related. This is a significant area of disagreement between Scotus and Ockham, but it has limited impact on the details of the relations between their views about the virtues and conscience.[13] Of more direct significance is Ockham's third objection that Scotus is wrong to think that the different degrees of virtue are of the same

10. William of Ockham, *Opera Theologica* (Saint Bonaventure, N.Y.: Franciscan Institute, 1984), 8:420. See Rega Wood's *Ockham on the Virtues* (West Lafayette: Purdue University Press, 1997) for a translation and discussion of "De connexione virtutum" (Question 8 of *Questiones variae*).

11. *Opera Theologica*, 5:434–35.

12. *Opera Theologica*, 5:435.

13. Some of the places where Ockham discusses this topic are *Reportatio*, III, Q. 11 (*Opera Theologica*, 6:351f.) and *Quaestiones Variae*, Question VII (*Opera Theologica*, 8:327, 385). Taina M. Holopainen discusses the relevant issues in her *William Ockham's Theory of the Foundations of Ethics* (Helsinki: Luther-Agricola-Society, 1991), 73ff. It is important to remark that Ockham's view here probably had great influence on Luther's view that external actions need not reflect the internal state of a person. See Randall C. Zachman's *The Assurance of Faith* (Minneapolis: Fortress Press, 1993), especially 74.

species and lead to one another.[14] According to Ockham, Henry of Ghent, who said there are four grades of virtues—perseverance, continence, temperance, and heroic virtue—completely misunderstands Aristotle's views and the nature of the degrees (342f.). On the contrary, there are five grades of the virtues (335f.). The first grade occurs when a person performs actions in conformity to right reason for the sake of the worth (*honestas*) of the virtue. The second grade occurs when someone performs an action in conformity to right reason with the intention of not ceasing to do so even in the face of death. The third grade is found when someone performs an action in accord with right reason for the sake of right reason itself. The fourth grade occurs when a person performs an action in accordance with right reason for the sake of love of God. (According to Ockham, this grade alone is the perfect and true moral virtue the saints discuss.) The fifth grade obtains when one chooses an action with a formally imperative act in accordance with right reason either for the sake of the end or for love of God. This grade of virtue is called heroic if it requires an action that exceeds the common state of men or is against the natural state of men. Scotus, in Ockham's view, believes that these grades represent various degrees of virtue. So one can, for example, move from the first grade to the second by increasing the degree of the virtue possessed (278). Ockham rejects this. According to him, these grades are different species of virtues. One can increase some grade infinitely, and it will remain the same species and not become a different grade. Moreover, as different species of virtues, the different grades do not incline one to develop the other grades (279).

Ockham's third criticism indicates a significant difference in the way Scotus and Ockham view the development of the virtues. His fourth criticism of Scotus seems even more serious for it indicates that he believes Scotus has failed to appreciate the influence of nonexperiential knowledge for moral action. Ockham distinguishes "practical knowledge" from "prudence."[15] Practical knowledge (*notitia practica*) concerns universal and necessary principles. Prudence, on the other hand, is more about particular actions we perform. It follows from this that, although all prudence is practical, not everything that is practical is a type of prudence.

In elaboration of the difference between moral knowledge and prudence, Ockham says there are two types of moral knowledge (*scientia moralis*).[16] The

14. *Opera Theologica*, 8:278.
15. *Opera Theologica*, 6:419.
16. *Opera Theologica*, 8:281.

first type is all scientific knowledge that can be derived from doctrine. This type involves deductions from *per se nota* (that is, self-evident) propositions. The second type is knowledge that can be derived only from experience and in no manner from doctrine. Likewise, there are two general types of prudence. The first type is evident knowledge of some singular proposition derived from experience. Ockham calls this "prudence properly speaking" (282). The second type is evident knowledge of universal practical principles learned through experience. Given these distinctions, it is clear, according to Ockham, that moral knowledge in the first sense is very different from prudence. However, moral knowledge in the second sense and prudence in the second sense are the same, for they both concern general moral principles derived from experience. Nonetheless, both types of moral knowledge, concerned with general principles, are to be distinguished from the first type of prudence (prudence properly speaking), which is concerned with particular cases.

Having made these general distinctions, Ockham proceeds to criticize Scotus for his way of distinguishing moral knowledge and prudence:

> From this it is clear that Johannes does not assign very well in his first book [of *Commentary on the Sentences*] the difference between moral knowledge and prudence [when he says] moral science is of universals and directs [actions] only remotely and mediately and prudence is of particulars and directs immediately and proximately. For this supposes that moral knowledge directs [actions] only mediately through prudence, which is false. Because someone can have evident knowledge of some universal proposition through doctrine (as for example "every benefactor should be benefitted") and evident knowledge of some contingent proposition falling under the universal proposition, as for example that this person is a benefactor because I saw him so act, the knowledge of which is not prudence because it is not directive. From these it can evidently be concluded that this person is to be benefitted. The knowledge of this particular proposition directs immediately practice whether interior or exterior. Nevertheless, knowledge of this conclusion is not prudence because it is acquired through doctrine and not through experience. (283)

Ockham is responding to a passage from the Prologue to Scotus's *Ordinatio:*

To the second I say that it concludes that moral science is prudence, for moral knowledge is an active habit with right reason. Therefore, I say that the definition of prudence ought to be understood as an active proximate habit, [for] such is a habit acquired from acts. As art is compared to the habit of an expert concerning things doable [*factibilia*], so is moral science to the habit of prudence concerning things doable, because the habit of art and moral science are as if remote in directing [acts] because they are universal; but the habit of prudence and of the expert, because they are generated from acts, are particular and proximate in directing.[17]

This passage from Scotus contrasts moral science, which consists of universal practical principles, with a "habit of prudence." This "habit of prudence" is what Scotus elsewhere describes as "proper prudence." It is the prudence of a particular type of virtue, for example, courage, derived from repeated acts of a certain type, that is, courageous acts. What is missing from this passage is any mention of the "general habit of prudence," that is, the ability of a person to formulate proper prudences. This lack is unfortunate, for it would be interesting to see what Scotus regards as the relation between "moral science" and the "general habit of prudence." In any event, Ockham's criticism of Scotus seems to be that, because a universal practical principle can direct a particular action through a nonprudential truth, Scotus is wrong to say that all moral actions must be proximately directed by a proper prudence that is derived through practice. What seems to be at issue in Ockham's objection is the moral value of acting from knowledge one is taught by another and not developed by oneself. Ockham understands Scotus as dismissing the possibility of acting morally from knowledge that is merely taught. Such a dismissal would seriously undermine the effectiveness of conscience in developing the virtues. For much of the direction that conscience provides such development comes from the education provided to agents before they act. To better understand Ockham's criticism of Scotus, it is important to examine Ockham's further comments about prudence.

In Question 8 of the *Quaestiones Variae*, Ockham draws a distinction between "aptitudinal or habitual prudence" (*prudentia aptitudinalis* or *habitualis*) and actual prudence (*prudentia actualis*). He defines aptitudinal prudence as

---

17. Duns Scotus, *Opera Omnia* (Rome: Vatican City Press, 1950), 1:227.

"the potency or aptitude before the act of having prudence."[18] Actual prudence seems to be the consciously formulated dictate that guides particular action. He claims that aptitudinal or habitual prudence is not sufficient for a virtuous action; actual prudence is required (409f.). Although he does not specifically say that aptitudinal prudence is required for actual prudence, there is no reason to think he does not grant this connection. But Ockham offers even finer distinctions concerning prudence.

He claims that prudence can be taken in four different ways (330f.). In the first way, it is understood as any knowledge that is mediately or immediately directive in respect to things to be done. This is the sense in which Augustine understood prudence in *De libero arbitrio*. In the second way, it is understood as evident knowledge immediately directive about some particular thing to be done, which evident knowledge comes from universal *per se nota* propositions. In the third way, it is understood as immediately directive knowledge gained through experience alone in respect to something that is to be done. This is the sense in which Aristotle talks about prudence properly speaking, and it is distinguished from moral knowledge. In the fourth way, it is understood as what is gathered from all immediately directive knowledge, whether this comes from doctrine or experience, that concerns human works necessary for living well. In this sense, prudence is not one simple knowledge; it includes as many distinct sets of knowledge as there are virtues required for living well, because each virtue has its own proper prudence and its own directive knowledge. These four senses of prudence are connected with the two general types of prudence discussed above (prudence properly speaking and evident knowledge of universal practical principles learned through experience), but they do not fit neatly with the earlier distinction. Having distinguished these ways of taking prudence, Ockham draws a number of conclusions about the relations among them and the five grades of virtue.

Like Scotus, Ockham rejects the view that there is a unity of the virtues. It is clear, for example, that the intellectual virtues can occur without the moral ones and that virtues in the first three grades can be found without the theological virtues (355). Moreover, virtues of the first two grades can be found with the vices of other virtues (350). Even the fifth grade of a virtue of philosophers (in contrast to a virtue of Christians) can be found with vice (354–55). Yet, there is a kind of unity to the virtues in at least three different ways. In the first place, all moral virtues are connected by

18. *Opera Theologica*, 8:411.

some universal principles that they fall under (347). Second, a virtue of the third or fourth grade inclines one to perform the first act of other virtues, which act can lead to the formation of the other virtues. Virtues of the first and second grade, however, do not so incline. Finally, one who has acquired the theological virtues (rather than having had them infused) is disposed toward the moral virtues if the right circumstances for developing them obtain (357).

Ockham makes several more observations about the relation of the theological virtues to the moral ones. Although one can have the moral virtues without the theological and the theological without the moral, one cannot possess the theological virtues and have actual moral vices (358). The reason for this seems to be that having the proper orientation toward the ultimate end (God) is incompatible with the culpable deformity necessary for a vice (358). Nevertheless, possession of the theological virtues, if they were infused, is compatible with the existence of the habit of moral vice even if it is not compatible with actual moral vice (359). A pagan, for example, who has a habit of performing some moral vice, after receiving the theological virtues through baptism, retains the habit but does not exercise it. If, however, one has acquired the theological virtues, possession of them is incompatible with either habitual moral vice or actual moral vice. This follows because to acquire the theological virtues one must have habits that eliminate the habits of moral vice (360). The distinction between virtuous habits and acts is important for grasping Ockham's claims about the relation between prudence and the other moral virtues.

Ockham, in line with Scotus, asserts that no moral virtue or any virtuous act can exist without prudence.[19] The reason is that no act can be virtuous unless it is in conformity with right reason (and each proper prudence represents the right reason associated with a particular virtue). On the other hand, prudence taken in the first way (described above) and prudence taken in the second way can both exist without any moral virtues (363, 371). It is also the case that prudence taken in the fourth way can exist without any moral virtues (374–75). However, some prudences taken in the third way can be found without moral virtue, and some other prudences taken in the third way require the existence of moral virtue (372–73). According to Ockham, some prudences can be derived from the activities of others, for example, knowing that a particular person can be mollified with pleasing words by seeing another person so mollify this particular person. Such

---

19. Ibid., 362. But a virtuous act can occur without the first or second mode of prudence.

knowledge can be gained by someone without that person's possessing the virtue in question. Other prudences taken in the third way, for example, knowing that acts of continence and prudence make one more disposed to knowing and loving God, can be known only through one's own possession of the relevant virtues. Having made the point that some moral virtues are required for some prudences, Ockham stresses that in these cases, the prudence cannot be the cause of the moral virtue (374). For if the moral virtue is critical for the development of the prudence, the prudence developed after the moral virtue cannot be the cause of the moral virtue. But if "right reason" is required for any moral virtue or moral act, where does the "right reason" come from that is critical for the first act of moral virtue that leads to the relevant prudence? Ockham does not provide an explicit answer to this question in this section of *Quaestiones Variae*. In the next section, however, entitled "Whether the will can have a virtuous act in respect to some object in regard to which there is an error in the intellect" (Question 8 of *Quaestiones Variae*), Ockham indicates that conscience provides a right reason that guides the performance of a moral act that may lead to a prudence (410–11). Like Scotus, Ockham sees conscience as providing the knowledge required to develop prudence. But, according to Ockham, Scotus treats this directing function of conscience as a form of proper prudence. This is a mistake on Scotus's part, however.[20] Proper prudences are connected with particular practices. Conscience, in contrast, can contain both rules derived from particular practices as well as rules given by others. Moral advice and instruction can lead to the habits necessary for the virtues. Unless this is recognized, a critical function of conscience can be lost, particularly if one sees conscience as a proper prudence as Ockham claims Scotus does. Conscience and proper prudence are linked, but they can be distinguished and should not be equated in a simple way.

It is clear that Ockham and Scotus have similar views about conscience and the virtues.[21] Where they differ, Ockham's criticisms are best seen as an indication that he believes that many of Scotus's general statements need clarification. Both men see conscience as providing a critical component of the development of the virtues: It provides the initial direction for action that can result in the development of proper prudences and eventually the

20. I leave aside consideration of whether Ockham has correctly interpreted Scotus on this point.

21. Oddly, Ockham does not mention synderesis at all. In his *Action and Person*, vol. 20 of *Studies in Medieval and Reformation Thought* (Leiden: E. J. Brill, 1977), Michael G. Baylor sees Ockham's apparent rejection of the synderesis as in line with his dismissal of all innate habits.

virtues—an insight important for any theory of conscience. Of course, the practice of the habits that virtues are based on can also influence conscience, as Bonaventure saw. In general, the view of conscience presented by Scotus and Ockham is a combination of the views of Bonaventure and Aquinas. In line with Bonaventure's position, conscience is closely connected to the drive to the good as well as to both the intellectual and emotional parts of human beings. It is a dynamic part of the human being consistently modified through experience. In line with Aquinas's view, conscience is closely related to practical reasoning and the development of the virtues, particularly prudence. These views advanced by Scotus and Ockham need to be part of any viable view of conscience. In many ways, the view of conscience offered by Scotus and Ockham presents a culmination of medieval views about conscience. Yet, despite its power, this sophisticated view was abandoned for a number of reasons.

F I V E

. . . .

LUTHER *and* THE RISE OF CONSCIENCE
AS A FACULTY

Luther on Conscience and Synderesis

Two recent, complementary studies have investigated Martin Luther's
(1483–1546) view of conscience. Michael G. Baylor's *Action and Person* traces
Luther's reaction to scholastic discussions of synderesis and conscience and
the development of his own innovative view that conscience has as object
not only actions but also the whole person.[1] Randall C. Zachman's *The Assurance of Faith* presents Luther's mature view of conscience, placing it within his
"theology of the cross" and linking Luther's views to Calvin's.[2]

---

1. Michael G. Baylor, *Action and Person: Conscience in Late Scholasticism and the Young Luther,* Studies in
Medieval and Reformation Thought, vol. 20 (Leiden: E. J. Brill, 1977).

2. Randall C. Zachman, *The Assurance of Faith: Conscience in the Theology of Martin Luther and John
Calvin* (Minneapolis: Fortress Press, 1993).

The studies reinforce each other; Zachman's, in fact, uses Baylor's as a significant source. Both studies emphasize that there is a tension in Luther's mature thought about conscience. On the one hand, a conscience that operates in isolation from God's grace and formulates ways of behaving that lead to salvation without the sanctification of God's grace is in conflict with faith. (A conscience informed, however, by God's sanctification can give testimony to the effectiveness of God's grace.) On the other hand, the sufferings of conscience, deriving from a sense of damnation, are necessary for the acceptance of God's mercy and justification through faith.

Zachman's contrast between the "theology of the cross" and the "theology of glory" is particularly useful for articulating the complex role of conscience in Luther's mature thought:

> In order to understand the role of the conscience in the theology of the cross, it is advisable first to understand the role of the conscience in the theology of glory. If the *theologia crucis* must be understood as the testimony of the Word to the conscience that contradicts what the conscience sees and feels, then the *theologia gloriae* must be understood as the testimony of the conscience to itself about God that is made on the basis of what is apparent and perceptible to the conscience, that is, works of the law. "That wisdom which sees the invisible things of God in works as perceived by man is completely puffed up, blinded, and hardened." (*D. Martin Luther's Werke: Kritische Gesamtausgabe*, 1.354.23–24; *Luther's Works*, 31:40–41)[3]

The "theology of glory" consists of falsely derived claims about the unknowable God. In fact, the only knowledge we have of God is what God reveals in Scripture. Other supposed sources of knowledge about God's nature, commands, or aims—whether reason or authorities other than Scripture—are spurious. They offer information about what, in principle, cannot be accessible to them. If conscience is seen as a device for articulating from human authority alone what is pleasing to God or what God requires human beings to do, it misleads and is a threat to faith. The only source of knowledge about God and his actions is Scripture. In particular, one must embrace the teachings of Christ and the message of his sacrifice: God has forgiven humankind, and acceptance of this forgiveness is crucial for salvation.

In some tension with the explicit affirmation of the ignorance of human

---

3. Zachman, *The Assurance of Faith*, 19.

beings about God is Luther's claim that the condemnations of conscience need to be accepted: People are powerless to do good, and their actions are intrinsically nonmeritorious; human beings are sinful and are damned. For, according to Luther, only if we recognize our true situation of sin can we recognize our helplessness and need for God's grace. With this recognition, we can cling to God in faith and accept his promise of mercy—even though we are unworthy—and be saved. The justification of faith is thus a recognition of our sinfulness and helplessness as well as an acceptance of the mercy of God.

Clearly, in the background of Luther's view of conscience, there is the assumption that conscience judges the state of a person. In fact, this seems to be the primary function of conscience. Before justification by faith, according to Luther, conscience must judge the person as damned. Although conscience may continue to judge particular actions as good or bad (consequent conscience) and help direct future behavior (antecedent conscience), it cannot see actions as in themselves justifying the individual before God. Works cannot justify; only faith can. After justification, the conscience can attest to God's merciful justification that is unearned by the individual. Ideally, good works follow justification by faith, but this need not be the case. The internal state of grace is what matters to an individual's salvation. External actions need not reflect the internal state, and, in fact, it is presumptuous to judge the inner person by external actions—another case of reason exceeding its proper boundaries.[4]

Baylor argues that Luther's mature view of conscience reflects Luther's scholastic training and his increasing discontentment with it. At Erfurt, under the tutelage of Trutfetter and Arnold von Usingen in the faculty of arts and of Paltz and Nathin in the faculty of theology, Luther was trained in a scholasticism heavily influenced by Ockham's thought as interpreted by Gabriel Biel.[5] Most of his earliest views on conscience fell within the usual range of medieval views. He saw conscience as working in tandem with synderesis in human beings (129). Moreover, he located synderesis and conscience within the intellectual or rational side of human nature (130). He held that vexation and tribulation are connected with synderesis and may benefit "speculative reason by refreshing it through experience" (132–33). In general, the young Luther seems to have viewed conscience as operating within the framework of practical reason (134). That is, conscience was seen

4. In fact, this issue is a point of major disagreement between Luther and Calvin.
5. Baylor, *Action and Person*, 119–20.

as the activity of the practical intellect that applies general practical principles to particular situations. Despite the general agreement with scholastic analyses, the young Luther also held some views that were not part of standard medieval positions.

Most later scholastics accepted the twofold claim that to act against conscience is always sinful and that to act according to conscience is not always good. The first part of the claim was often connected with the view that conscience is the voice of God within us and it is wrong to disobey God's commands. The second part of the claim was connected with the general problem of an erroneous conscience, one that holds as correct something that is wrong. Many scholastics, following Aquinas, held that there were two types of erroneous conscience. The first type is a culpably ignorant conscience. This conscience holds as correct (or incorrect) what it should know is incorrect (or correct). Because it should know the truth of the matter, this conscience is held morally responsible for its error. The second type is an inculpably ignorant conscience. This conscience suffers from "invincible ignorance" about a particular matter and cannot be held morally responsible for its error.

Luther also embraced the twofold claim. Interestingly, his understanding of the second part of the claim was not the usual interpretation that the scholastics offered. According to the young Luther, one can follow conscience because one has faith in the authority of conscience, or one can follow conscience because of faith in Christ (147f.). For Luther, only the latter reason is a good reason for following conscience. Those who follow conscience, even a correct conscience, because of a faith in conscience are wrong to follow it. So following one's conscience, according to Luther, is not always good. Interestingly, the young Luther's views here led him to reject the entire medieval notion of invincible ignorance (152f.). They are also closely related to the mature Luther's doctrine of justification by faith.

Another area of tension between the young Luther's views on conscience and the general scholastic position concerns synderesis. Although the young Luther sharply distinguished the will from the intellect, he held that synderesis should be seen as operating in both faculties. To be sure, a number of medieval thinkers, Bonaventure above all, thought that synderesis had connections with both the intellect and the will. But the young Luther thought that there were two syndereses: one in the intellect and one in the will (157f.). Although some have argued that the influence of Jean Gerson explains the young Luther's postulation of two syndereses, Baylor argues against this view because Luther's account does not appeal to a mystical, suprarational faculty as does Gerson's. Baylor's own explanation is that "the double *synteresis* which the young Luther developed may well have been the result of a deeper appreciation of Ockham's thought than that shown by Biel" (165). What is of more interest, however, is that after 1516, Luther's views about synderesis underwent a change that resulted in altogether eliminating synderesis from Luther's thought by 1519 (173f.).

Baylor recounts various explanations for the disappearance of synderesis in the mature Luther's views and explains their failings. Luther did not reject synderesis because it committed one to Pelagianism or semi-Pelagianism (177f.). Nor did he reject it because synderesis was seen as having soteriological as opposed to ethical significance (188–89). Nor did he reject it because it was an unbiblical notion (190). On the contrary, he rejected it because it no longer played a useful role in his view of conscience:

> In short, Luther has established a new object for the working of the conscience: its judgments are not just about actions—"What is to be done or is not to be done, or what has been done or done badly," as he put it in his more traditional definition—it also judges about the agent who performs these actions, the individual or person as a whole.
>
> Here is the important reason that Luther discarded the synteresis from his conception of the conscience. The synteresis notion, as described by late scholasticism, fixed the conscience firmly within the framework of the Aristotelian practical reason. The synteresis was the anthropological foundation for the action of conscience. The content of the synteresis was self-evident and inextinguishable truths of a practical and universal nature. This analysis of the synteresis implied that the conscience must judge about the application of these truths, or principals [*sic*] derived from them, to particular cases. The object of the action of conscience is restricted to particular moral actions within the power of the will. In order to develop a view of the conscience which depicted the conscience as concerning itself, on the highest level, with the person as a whole rather than just his particular actions, Luther was forced to discard the synteresis as the ontological base and, in this sense, determinant of the conscience. (201–2)

After rejecting synderesis, the mature Luther incorporated much of what he had attributed to synderesis to conscience (207). Luther placed conscience at the center of human beings and often seemed to equate it with the "heart" or the whole conscious life of the individual.

For Baylor, then, Luther's important contribution to views about conscience is to move conscience from the framework of practical reason concerned with the value of particular actions (as found in late scholastic thought) to understanding it as judging the whole person, particularly the state of damnation. Baylor is careful not to say that Luther claims that conscience no longer judges about individual actions. Rather, he sees the judgment of the whole person as added to the judgment about individual actions. According to Baylor, this judgment of the person is not to be found in late scholastic thought. At best, the scholastics recognized an indirect or inferential judgment about the person: "If, for example, the conscience judges that some particular action is a mortal sin, then the inference would follow that the person himself is no longer in a state of grace or friendship with God. This is implied in St. Thomas's notion of the 'stain of sin' (macula peccati). It is noteworthy, however, that the scholastics did not explicitly connect the power of drawing this inference with the conscience" (212). Although Baylor's analysis of Luther's changing views of conscience is impressive, it fails to take into account the movement in scholastic thought toward blending discussions of conscience with discussions of the virtues. To be sure, Baylor acknowledges the close association between talk about conscience and the virtue of prudence, but this acknowledgment is connected to Baylor's linking of prudence with practical reasoning. There can be little doubt that prudence is connected with practical reasoning, but, as we have seen, the emphasis in Ockham's writings (as well as Scotus's before him) is on how prudence relates to the other virtues—whether theological or moral.

Baylor's discussion of scholastic theories about conscience and synderesis focuses on the *via antiqua* (represented by Aquinas) and the *via moderna* (represented by Ockham and Biel). He does not directly address Scotus's views other than to acknowledge that they were important and that in Luther's early career the Scotistic school was one of three real options open to him.[6] Baylor emphasizes the differences between Scotus and Ockham and fails to appreciate the similarity in their thought. Throughout his discussion of Ockham, Baylor treats right conscience as equivalent to right reason.[7] But

6. Ibid., 119. Baylor does not remark on the fact that Luther's rejection of the view that synderesis is a necessary drive toward the good reflects Scotus's criticism of the same view (see *Duns Scotus on the Will and Morality*, 201, for Scotus's dismissal of the view).

7. See, for instance, *Action and Person*, 82, where Baylor states: "Right reason or right conscience is reason which is in agreement with divine precepts."

because right reason may be principles, revelations, or truths based on experience, it should not be confused with conscience. Because of these difficulties, Baylor fails to see that the connection between conscience and the virtues found in Scotus's and Ockham's writings paved the way for Luther's "new object of conscience": the person. For the development of the virtues in the virtue tradition is fundamentally geared toward the development of the person. Developing the virtues through actions and experiences is seen as a transformation of the individual. The person is made to enjoy the practice of the virtues and to delight in their fruits. In fact, when one becomes a virtuous (moral) person, actions are seen as moral because they flow from the individual rather than because they meet some objective criterion of worth.

To be sure, the focus on the person one finds in Scotus's and Ockham's writings is not a focus specifically through conscience as it is for Luther. But Luther's new view of conscience is prepared for by the linking of conscience with the virtues found in Scotus's and Ockham's writings. What may be called the "Protestant turn" in relation to views about conscience, that is, the focus on the state of the person, was prepared for by the "turn to the virtues" in Scotus's and Ockham's views about conscience.

One of Luther's most lasting contributions to the history of views about conscience has, however, been mostly overlooked by Baylor and Zachman. Luther did not completely divorce conscience from the function it traditionally held in practical reason, but he clearly downplayed this function in emphasizing its role in judging the whole person. Once conscience is no longer thought of as part of a process (of practical reason) and is viewed as something like a judge of the whole person, the way is prepared for conceiving of conscience as an independent entity, a most unfortunate turn in the history of the concept of conscience. Although Luther does not depict conscience as a faculty separate from the faculties of the will and the intellect, his views on conscience lead that way. The story of this development, however, is tied up with the phenomenon of "casuistry."

Conscience as a Faculty

As Johann P. Sommerville remarks in his "The 'New Art of Lying': Equivocation, Mental Reservation, and Casuistry," there are two general meanings to 'casuistry.'[8] In the first, casuistry is part of practical reasoning in that it is "the

8. In Edmund Leites, ed., *Conscience and Casuistry in Early Modern Europe* (Cambridge: Cambridge University Press, 1988), 159.

art or science of bringing general moral principles to bear upon particular cases." In the second, casuistry is "sophistical, equivocal, or specious reasoning." The first meaning links casuistry with the discussions of Aristotle, Augustine, Aquinas, Scotus, and Ockham about the role of conscience and the mechanisms of practical reason. The second denigrates the importance of casuistry. Given Luther's emphasis on the lack of continuity between the internal grace state of an individual and his or her external actions, one would expect the Protestant reformers to embrace the critical view of casuistry. Although this negative view of casuistry finds its strongest exponents in the Protestant tradition, a number of Protestants in fact embraced casuistry.[9] To a certain extent, the existence of Protestant casuists can be explained by a major disagreement between Luther and Calvin (1509–64) on the importance of the relation between the inward state of grace and external actions. The two men agreed that justification comes through faith alone, but, unlike Luther, Calvin thought that there was a strong connection between how a man acted and the state of grace he was in or to which he could lead others.[10] The Calvinistic attention to external actions and their relation to inward grace gave a decided support to those Protestants who wished to link casuistic reasoning to practical judgments. But there is, perhaps, another explanation for the existence of Protestant (as well as Catholic) casuists.

Reacting to the success of Pascal's *Lettres provinciales* of 1656–57 in diminishing the reputation of casuistry as well as the Jesuits, Gabriel Daniel argues that casuistry was not intended for direct use by the laity but rather was intended for clergy who were to advise laity about morality.[11] Typically clergy gave advice that was juridical in nature: It was intended to determine whether an already completed action was a serious (mortal) or minor (venial) sin. Such advice, given after the performance of actions, would undoubtedly have the effect of making the layperson more contemplative about the nature of his or her actions. It would undoubtedly affect future behavior (128–29). Casuistry practiced in this way seems on a line with issues of the development of the virtues, and this connection helps to explain casuistry's continued importance for Catholic and Protestant thought. On the traditional analysis coming from Aristotle and preserved by the great

9. See Edmund Leites, "Casuistry and Character," in *Conscience and Casuistry*, 119.

10. Zachman, *The Assurance of Faith*, 242.

11. *Conscience and Casuistry*, 74f. Compare Joseph V. Dolan's "Conscience in the Catholic Theological Tradition," in William C. Bier, ed., *Conscience: Its Freedom and Limitations* (New York: Fordham University Press, 1971), 14. Dolan views many of the historical trends and persons in a light different from my own.

thinkers of the Middle Ages, there are two components to the development of the virtues: a material and a formal. The material component is directly linked with the habit of virtuous acts. Performance of the appropriate (to the virtues) actions leads to the habit of performing such actions. The formal aspect involves the states internal to the agent: whether the actions in themselves are pleasurable to the agent; whether they are done with the right intentions and consciousness. The casuistic advice of the clergy was intended to foster the habits of performing acts that were virtuous. It was not intended to speak to the formation of the formal aspects of the virtues. But this is in line with the virtue tradition, for that tradition, following Plato, held that these formal aspects of virtue cannot be taught but can only be cultivated through the performance of appropriate actions. So the casuists' emphasis on actions fit well with the virtue tradition's emphasis on development of appropriate habits.

Nonetheless, the casuists' downplaying of the direct cultivation of the formal aspects of the virtues ran afoul of an increasing interest in individual autonomy, especially in England. Edmund Leites explains this conflict with particular emphasis on the role of moral autonomy:

> This change was at least in part a function of the rise to cultural power of the belief that from the point of view of spirituality and morality, nothing was more important for the individual than his possession of a truly moral will. To encourage the formation and maintenance of such a will, of "character" in a laudatory sense, was therefore seen to be a chief task of both moral and religious instruction. The methods of casuistry, however, had never been meant to create or transform character. Moreover, they generally dealt with questions about what was forbidden or permitted, rather than about what it would be morally and spiritually best for the individual to do. (120)

This conflict between the need for development of character and casuists' emphasis on acts eventually led to the waning of the importance of casuistic reasoning for Protestant religious leaders. Interestingly, many aspects of casuistic reasoning found their way into secular law where the emphasis was on modification of behavior rather than on transformation of will and character.[12]

---

12. Ibid., 128–30. See also Lowell Gallagher's *Medusa'a Gaze: Casuistry and Conscience in the Renaissance* (Stanford: Stanford University Press, 1991), 5f.

Some casuists attempted to cultivate character as well as influence actions: Jeremy Taylor (1613–67), William Perkins (1558–1662), Thomas Barlow (1607–91), and Richard Baxter (1615–91) among others.[13] These thinkers influenced later Protestant thinkers who rejected casuistry out of a concern for the development of character. One of the most important of these later thinkers was Joseph Butler (1692–1752), an extremely influential Anglican clergyman and perhaps the person most responsible for the modern view that conscience is a faculty.

Although Butler regarded his *An Analogy of Religion* as his major work, his most influential writings were his *Fifteen Sermons Preached at the Rolls Chapel* (including "A Dissertation on the Nature of Virtue").[14] Written as a response to Thomas Hobbes's view in *Leviathan* that human beings always act in accordance with their strongest desires, these sermons influenced David Hume, Henry Sidgwick, G. E. Moore, and countless other ethicists. In fact, *Fifteen Sermons* was reprinted several times during the nineteenth century and was used extensively by utilitarians and deontologists (3). In these sermons, Butler presents several claims. He states, for example, that there is a divinely given harmony to people as well as to the universe such that acts of human self-interest invariably lead to the common good. Moreover, he asserts that people have not only a drive for self-interest but also naturally possess an instinct of benevolence toward others. But his views about conscience are of even more interest.

Butler sees human beings as divided into parts that constitute a system by virtue of the domination of conscience:

> Thus it is with regard to the inward frame of man. Appetites, passions, affections, and the principle of reflection, considered merely as the several parts of our inward nature, do not at all give us an idea of the system or constitution of this nature, because the constitution is formed by somewhat not yet taken into consideration, namely, by the relations which these several parts have to each other; the chief of which is the authority of reflection or conscience. It is from considering the relations which the several appetites and passions in the inward frame have to each other, and, above all, the supremacy of

13. See Edward Leroy Long Jr.'s *Conscience and Compromise* (Philadelphia: Westminster Press, 1954), 37.

14. From the introduction by Stephen L. Darwall to *Joseph Butler: Five Sermons Preached at the Rolls Chapel and a Dissertation upon the Nature of Virtue* (Indianapolis: Hackett, 1983), 1.

reflection or conscience, that we get the idea of the system or constitution of human nature. (14–15)

Butler goes on to argue that the system of human nature dominated by conscience is directed toward virtue. In fact, he defines virtue as following human nature and sees vice as what is contrary to it (13). Conscience's role in the movement toward nature is, of course, crucial:

> But that is not a complete account of man's nature. Somewhat further must be brought in to give us an adequate notion of it, namely, that one of those principles of action, conscience, or reflection, compared with the rest as they all stand together in the nature of man, plainly bears upon it marks of authority over all the rest, and claims the absolute direction of them all, to allow or forbid their gratification—a disapprobation of reflection being in itself a principle manifestly superior to a mere propension. And the conclusion is that to allow no more to this superior principle or part of our nature than to other parts; to let it govern and guide only occasionally in common with the rest, as its turn happens to come, from the temper and circumstances one happens to be in; this is not to act conformably to the constitution of man; neither can any human creature be said to act conformably to his constitution of nature unless he allows to that superior principle the absolute authority which is due to it. (16–17)

The authority of conscience over the parts of a human being should be absolute. Any failure to follow the directions of conscience is, in fact, a failure to follow one's own nature.

Butler is not shy in attributing qualities to conscience. He regards it as an unerring faculty that judges actions as well as the agent; it is essentially a law unto itself, and it always leads us to the good (37, 43, 45, 69). Its one defect seems to be that it cannot enforce its decisions for, although possessing authority, it lacks power (39). But there is no doubt in Butler's mind that the world would be better off if conscience had such power: "Had it strength, as it has right; had it power, as it has manifest authority, it would absolutely govern the world" (40).

The strong view of conscience one finds in Butler's writing is a departure from the more limited conception found in scholastic writers. It is, however, reminiscent of Luther's views about conscience. Butler, of course, goes beyond even Luther's views, seeing conscience as an unerring faculty. He was apparently influenced by William Perkins on this issue. Perkins considered conscience as the vice-gerent of God, so that the voice of conscience was the infallible voice of God.[15] Similarly, Butler sees conscience as implanted by God to represent God's own commands.[16] Interestingly, Butler does not link conscience to issues about the cultivation of virtues, for his stress is not on the need that conscience has for development. On the contrary, given his view that it is infallible, Butler stresses that conscience needs only to be freed from its lack of power. If we but listen to our conscience, we will do what is virtuous.

There is a similar view of conscience in the writings of Kant (1724–1804):

Consciousness of an *internal court* in man ("before which his thoughts accuse or excuse one another") is conscience. Every man has a conscience and finds himself observed, threatened, and, in general, kept in awe (respect coupled with fear) by an internal judge; and this authority watching over the law in him is not something that he himself (voluntarily) makes, but something incorporated in his being. It follows him like his shadow when he plans to escape. He can indeed stun himself or put himself to sleep by pleasures and distractions, but he cannot help coming to himself or waking up from time to time; and when he does, he hears at once its fearful voice. He can at most, in extreme depravity, bring himself to *heed* it no longer, but he still cannot help *hearing* it.

Now this original intellectual and (since it is the thought of duty) moral predisposition called *conscience* is peculiar in that, although its business is a business of man with himself, a man constrained by his reason sees himself constrained to carry it on as at the bidding of another person. For the affair here is that of trying a case (causa) before a court. But to think of a man who is accused by his conscience as one and the same person as the judge is an absurd way of representing a court, since then the prosecutor would always lose. For all duties a man's conscience will, accordingly, have to think of *someone other* than himself (i.e., other than man as such) as the judge of his actions, if conscience is not to be in contradiction with itself.

15. *Works of William Perkins* (Abingdon, England: Sutton Courtenay Press, 1970), 64.
16. See Terence Penelhum's *Butler* (London: Routledge and Kegan Paul, 1985), 77.

This other may be an actual person or a merely ideal person that reason creates for itself.[17]

As does Butler, Kant conceives of conscience as a judging entity that should control the agent's actions. In line with his ethical system, Kant explains this by viewing conscience as possessing the duties moral agents should follow to be morally good. In this way, Kant turns conscience into something like a universal moral judge. Its judgments, connected to duties, are true not just for the particular moral agent, but for all moral agents.

Kant's fullest remarks about conscience are found in the second part of *The Metaphysics of Morals*, which is entitled "The Doctrine of Virtue." In fact, Kant is very interested in the virtues, but this interest results in a view of the virtues that is very different from the view we find in the virtue tradition. Kant, for example, separates cultivation of the virtues from the teleological aim of achieving happiness:

> When a thoughtful man has overcome incentives to vice and is aware of having done his often bitter duty, he finds himself in a state that could well be called happiness, a state of contentment and peace of soul in which virtue is its own reward. Now a eudaemonist says: This delight, this happiness is really his motive for acting virtuously. The concept of duty does not determine his will *directly*; he is moved to do his duty only *by means of* the happiness he anticipates. But since he can expect this reward of virtue only from consciousness of having done his duty, it is clear that the latter must have come first, that is, he must find himself under obligation to do his duty before he thinks that happiness will result from his observance of duty and without thinking of this. (183)

This passage reflects common themes in Kant's ethical system. According to Kant, one is moral when one performs an action for the sake of duty without attention to the consequences or benefits of such an action. He often calls doing one's duty for the sake of duty the moral point of view. In

17. *The Metaphysics of Morals* (Cambridge: Cambridge University Press, 1991), 233–34. David Little also treats Kant's view of conscience (especially in comparison to Calvin's views) in his "A View of Conscience Within the Protestant Theological Tradition," in Bier, ed., *Conscience: Its Freedom and Limitations*. Thomas E. Hill Jr. presents a Kantian theory of conscience in his "Four Conceptions of Conscience," in Ian Shapiro and Robert Adams, eds., *Integrity and Conscience* (New York: New York University Press, 1998), 31f. (Hereafter Shapiro and Adams, eds., *Integrity and Conscience*.)

the present passage, Kant links the moral point of view with being virtuous, and so, according to Kant, one is virtuous (acting in accordance with the virtues) when one does one's duties for the sake of the duties themselves. Interestingly, as for Joseph Butler, there is no indication in Kant's thought that practice of the virtues leads to being virtuous (acting in accord with the moral point of view). On the contrary, doing one's duty for the sake of duty seems to be accomplished through rational analysis or instruction. Formation of habits and attention to the actions agents perform and what can be gleaned from these actions in terms of goals and further practices have little place in Kant's views about the virtues.

Kant has in effect focused on the formal component of virtues: What should be the state of a person when he or she performs a virtuous action? And he has linked the formal aspect of the virtues with his concept of universal duties and the need for indifference to the pleasure (or pain) of acting virtuously. Moreover, he has positioned conscience as the faculty that acts as a judge to ensure that moral beings do their duties and do them in the proper way. His position is clearly linked to earlier scholastic discussions about virtues and the conscience, but it marks a significant departure from the assumptions of those discussions. It is not surprising that Kant dismisses casuistic reasoning as misguided, for, according to Kant, attention to the practical details of the moral value of actions misses the critical importance of the proper moral point of view.

With Butler and Kant, we have a significant and unfortunate change in the understanding of conscience. Although scholastic discussions emphasized that conscience plays a role in practical reason and is closely connected to the development of the virtues, under the influence of Butler and Kant, conscience is conceived of as an independent entity (a faculty) that is infallible, directive, and punitive, and the guarantor of morality. This newer view of conscience became the standard view of the nineteenth and early twentieth centuries much to the detriment of the contemporary importance of conscience. Freud, of course, modified this view somewhat, but even his modifications preserved the basic picture articulated by Butler and Kant. It is this view of conscience that has fallen into disfavor in more recent times.

PART TWO

THE CONTEMPORARY
DISMISSAL
OF CONSCIENCE

FREUD *and* RYLE ON CONSCIENCE

Freud's View of Conscience

One of the major developments of the twentieth century is the theory of psychoanalysis. Although many have criticized the theory, it has become a fixed feature of the present intellectual landscape. The theory itself is the creation of Sigmund Freud (1856–1939), but it has undergone continual revision. Psychoanalytic theory as it is practiced today is more of a synthetic product than simply an application of Freud's views. Yet it is still important to look at Freud's own thoughts, if only to understand a major source for present theory.

The historical background for Freud's views is often neglected. This seems particularly true of his views about conscience. Once one examines his statements about it, it is clear that his view of conscience bears some striking similarities to views presented in Part I. Because Freud's understanding of

conscience has molded the way it is viewed by twentieth-century philosophers and theologians, it is necessary to look at some basic components of
Freud's psychoanalytical theory as it is presented in his *Outline of Psycho-
analysis.*

According to Freud, there are three parts to the psychic apparatus of
human beings: the id, the ego, and the superego. He claims that the postulation of these is based on extensive studies of many human beings.

The id is present at birth and contains the instincts.[1] The ego develops
from the id in a physiological manner: "Under the influence of the real
external world around us, one portion of the id has undergone a special
development. From what was originally a cortical layer, equipped with the
organs for receiving stimuli and with arrangements for acting as a protective
shield against stimuli, a special organization has arisen which henceforth
acts as an intermediary between the id and the external world. To this re-
gion of our mind we have given the name of ego" (145). This description of
the ego makes it clear that it develops from the id. This development is
closely linked to the presence of the organs of sense. It is as if the physiological impact of stimuli on the brain causes the physical development of a
part of the brain that becomes the ego. Once the ego is formed, the superego can develop: "The long period of childhood, during which the growing
human being lives in dependence on his parents, leaves behind it as a pre-
cipitate the formation in his ego of a special agency in which this parental
influence is prolonged. It has received the name of superego. In so far as this
superego is differentiated from the ego or is opposed to it, it constitutes a
third power which the ego must take into account" (146). Freud's notion of
parental influence is much wider than the term implies. It includes "the
family, racial and national traditions handed on through them, as well as the
demands of the social milieu" and also "teachers and models in public life of
admired social ideas" (146). The superego thus is not a static replication of
one's parents' demands and behaviors. Rather it is something like a repository of authority that has been internalized. To be sure, the authority of
one's actual parents provides the core of the superego, but this content
changes over time through the influence of other authorities or even psy-

---

1. *An Outline of Psycho-Analysis*, Standard Edition of the Complete Psychological Works of Sigmund Freud, 23 (London: Hogarth Press and the Institute of Psycho-Analysis, 1964), 145: "To the
oldest of these psychical provinces or agencies we give the name of id. It contains everything that is
inherited, that is present at birth, that is laid down in the constitution—above all, therefore, the
instincts, which originate from the somatic organization and which finds a first psychical expression
here [in the id] in forms unknown to us."

chotherapy.[2] The agent modifies the content of the superego and modifies
or rejects the injunctions of past parental influences. It is, of course, unclear
how much change in the superego is possible in Freud's eyes. But it is at
least clear that change does occur.

Freud clearly links, but does not identify, the conscience with the superego: "We call this agency the superego and are aware of it in its judicial
function as our conscience" (205). In explaining this relationship in the last
(unfinished) chapter of *An Outline of Psychoanalysis*, Freud once again summarizes the development of the superego:

> The picture of an ego which mediates between the id and the exter-
> nal world, which takes over the instinctual demands of the former in
> order to lead them to satisfaction, which derives perceptions from
> the latter and uses them as memories, which, intent on its self-preser-
> vation, puts itself in defence against excessively strong claims from
> both sides, and which, at the same time, is guided in all its decisions
> by the injunctions of a modified pleasure principle—this picture in
> fact applies to the ego only up to the end of the first period of
> childhood, till about the age of five. At about that time an important
> change has taken place. A portion of the external world has, at least
> partially, been abandoned as an object and has instead, by identifica-
> tion, been taken into the ego and thus become an integral part of the
> internal world. (62)

In this passage, Freud once again stresses that the superego is the internalization of external parental authority. Once internalized, "This new psychical agency continues to carry on the functions which have hitherto been
performed by the people [the abandoned objects] in the external world: it
observes the ego, gives it orders, judges it, and threatens it with punishments, exactly like the parents whose place it has taken" (205). Thus, according to Freud, the superego functions in various ways. Only in its judging and threatening actions is the superego identified as conscience. So
conscience appears to be a functional part of the superego: the part that
judges and threatens with punishment. The rest of the superego continues

2. Ibid., 75. "Moreover, the relation of transference brings with it two further advantages. If the
patient puts the analyst in the place of his father (or mother), he is also giving him the power which
his superego exercises over his ego, since his parents were, as we know, the origin of his superego.
The new superego now has an opportunity for a sort of *after-education* of the neurotic; it can correct
mistakes for which his parents were responsible in educating him."

to observe the individual and to dictate what the individual should do. The individual who fails to live up to the demands of the superego is judged negatively and threatened with punishment.

Freud indicates that the "torments caused by the reproaches of conscience correspond precisely to a child's fear of loss of love" (206) and are clearly connected to a feeling of anxiety (146). Essentially, the superego creates tensions in the ego when it fails to measure up to the superego's demands, and this failure increases the feeling of unease. This emotional discomfort leads the agent to want to abandon behavior in conflict with the demands of the superego.

Because Freud sees conscience as the judging function of the superego, he allows conscience to have both a conscious and an unconscious function. We are most aware of the conscious function when we weigh alternative actions in the light of articulated beliefs, as, for example, when a person who believes in the sanctity of life contemplates registering for the military draft. Our conscience bothers us if we go against our conscious beliefs. The unconscious function of conscience is more tied to the unconscious or pre-conscious dictates of the superego. We often react to certain situations with unpleasant "security feelings" like anxiety, fear, or dread. These feelings are generated by threatening situations or by situations in which behavior or potential behavior is at odds with the content of the superego. As a result of these feelings, for example, a strictly raised young adult might well uncon-sciously avoid situations in which he or she is tempted to violate inculcated beliefs.

Although some content of the superego is conscious ("I know that being a thief is wrong"), much of it is preconscious. That is to say, it is not conscious but could become conscious (160f.). For example, we might be completely unaware that we avoid eating ice cream until in an introspective moment we discover this fact and can attribute the cause for it to early childhood train-ing. The preconscious dictates of the superego, however, clearly affect one's behavior. In fact, until one becomes introspective and examines one's beliefs, the preconscious dictates are probably more determinative of behavior than one's conscious dictates. Moreover, even when we are able to articulate our beliefs and assumptions, we are not always actively conscious of them. Many return to the preconscious where they exert an important, although unconscious, influence.[3] Freud's postulation of conscience as the judging

3. See G. Zilboorg's comments in his "Superego and Conscience," in C. Ellis Nelson, ed., Con-science, Theological and Psychological Perspectives (New York: Newman Press, 1973), 220.

function of the superego treats the unconscious prohibiting activity of the superego as a part of conscience. In fact, this unconscious prohibition is one of the dominant activities of conscience for Freud. He is unwilling to limit the activities of conscience to the conscious consideration of beliefs and attitudes that take place in conscious moral reasoning or in conscious reflection on moral feelings like shame, guilt, and remorse. We perhaps are most aware of conscience and its power when we consciously think about how our actions violate our beliefs, but this fact does not undercut Freud's belief in the power of our preconscious beliefs to guide behavior.[4]

Surprising as it might initially seem, Freud's notion of conscience bears striking resemblance to theories about conscience we have already examined. Freud's views are similar to Butler's and Kant's insofar as he regards the conscience as a judging entity. He carefully calls it a function of the superego (the judging function), but his dynamic view of the superego leads to the view that conscience is something like an entity that enforces the dictates of the superego. In similarity to Luther's views, the conscience as judge finds the agent unworthy and in need of punishment and change. And, perhaps most surprising, the relationship between the superego and the conscience parallels the traditional relationship between the synderesis and the conscience. Just as the synderesis stands as the repository of the universal moral rules one should obey, so the superego is the repository of the agent's beliefs and dictates that guide behavior. Conscience in the medieval view applies the general laws to specific cases, and failure to follow appropriate behavior results in suffering and vexation. Although Freud does not talk about conscience as applying the dictates of the superego to specific situations (except in cases of conscious moral reasoning), he obviously sees conscience as punishing the agent when the agent's actions violate the dictates of the superego.

Ryle: Conscience as Personal Monitor

Subsequent discussions of conscience in the twentieth century, although relatively few, have been deeply influenced by Freud's views—whether this is acknowledged or not. A case in point is Gilbert Ryle's advocacy of the view that "conscience is a private monitor," presented in his well-known article,

---

4. For a challenge to Freud's views, see David H. Jones's "Freud's Theory of Moral Conscience," in Donnelly and Lyons, eds., *Conscience*, 90f.

"Conscience and Moral Convictions."[5] In elaboration of his view, he tells us: "We limit the verdicts of conscience to judgments about the rightness or wrongness of the acts only of the owner of that conscience."[6] Ryle clearly thinks that the operations of conscience are person specific. As he puts it, "It is absurd to say, 'My conscience says that *you* ought to do this or ought not to have done that'" (*Collected Papers,* 2:185). Ryle's view that the dictates of conscience pertain only to the owner of the conscience is, of course, a widely held one. It is, in fact, a part of most analyses of conscience one finds in the twentieth century. As I indicated in the first chapter, this aspect of the modern sense of 'conscience' is at odds with the etymological history of the word deriving from 'syneidesis' and 'conscientia.' An examination of how Ryle arrives at his view is therefore important not only for understanding Ryle's view but for clarifying general issues about the nature of conscience and how we presently understand the notion. His essay has been definitive in modern philosophical discussions about conscience.

As the title suggests, in the essay Ryle is interested in the relation between the contents of conscience and moral convictions. In fact, Ryle regards the contents of conscience as a type of moral conviction: "My particular verdicts of conscience are applications of general rules, imperatives, or codes. My conscience says, 'You aren't being honest,' and this involves understanding both what being honest is, and that it is a general desideratum" (186). Assuming that "general rules, imperatives, or codes" are part of what Ryle means by "moral conviction," Ryle here claims that conscience is the self-application by a particular person of moral convictions he or she holds. But this is not a sufficient reason to hold that conscience is only a personal monitor, for one may easily think that the moral convictions one holds should apply to other people. In fact, for Ryle, the *way* in which moral convictions are applied is crucial for seeing that conscience is a personal monitor. To understand the different ways moral convictions can be applied, we must first look at Ryle's further analysis of moral convictions.

Obviously anticipating claims he later made in *The Concept of the Mind,*[7] Ryle claims that a moral conviction is really a disposition to a certain type of behavior: "So there seems to be a sense in which real acceptance of a principle (does not lead to, but) *is* being disposed to behave in accordance with

---

5. Originally published in *Analysis* 7 (1940). Reprinted in *Collected Papers,* vol. 2 (London: Hutchinson and Company, 1971). Also in Donnelly and Lyons, eds., *Conscience,* 25f.

6. *Collected Papers,* 2:185.

7. *The Concept of Mind* (New York: Barnes and Noble, 1949), esp. chapters 1, 2, and 5.

it."[8] As it turns out, according to Ryle, we can hold moral convictions in either an academic sense or in an operative sense (*Collected Papers*, 2:186–88). If a person holds a moral conviction in an academic sense, he or she is inclined to utter "it regularly, relevantly, and without hesitation," and "other things which he says regularly, relevantly, and unhesitatingly, presuppose it" (187). When we apply moral convictions to others, we can do it only in this academic sense. We can say that others should follow these convictions and even exhort them to do so (187–88). But we cannot control the behavior of others through applying to them the moral convictions we hold.

A person holds a moral conviction in an operative sense, when he or she "regularly and readily behaves in accordance with it, on occasions when it is relevant" and "when he does not behave in accordance with it, he feels guilty, resolves to reform, etc." (187). To hold a moral conviction operatively is, in effect, to allow it to work on one's own volitions, emotions, and behavior. Clearly, only moral convictions one applies to oneself can be operative. Not surprisingly, Ryle identifies conscience as connected with operative moral convictions. As a result, he distinguishes conscience from moral convictions by viewing 'moral convictions' as a general notion that is divided into two more specific notions—'academic moral convictions' and 'operative moral convictions'—and stipulating that conscience and only conscience deals with operative moral convictions. Of course, given the nature of operative moral convictions, it is easy to understand why conscience is a personal monitor. A person can have operative moral convictions only about himself and his own behavior.

However, why should we think that conscience has to do with operative moral convictions alone? Why should we not also maintain that academic moral convictions are also in the power of conscience? Ryle, in fact, gives an explicit answer to these questions, but it is not at all clear that his explicit answer is the real justification for his view: "Conscience, then, is one species, among others, of scrupulousness; and scrupulousness is the operative acceptance of a rule or principle which consists in the disposition to behave, in all modes of behavior, including saying to oneself and others, teaching, chiding, etc., in accordance with the rule" (191). Scrupulousness is connected with operative rules or principles, not necessarily morals, according to Ryle. His justification for this claim is rather thin; he merely cites examples of rules of prudence, etiquette, and arithmetic and draws his conclusion

---

8. *Collected Papers*, 2:187.

(189–91). To Ryle's credit, however, it seems to be the case that we use the notion of 'scrupulousness' so that we can be scrupulous only about our own behavior. But why does Ryle think conscience is to be considered a form of scrupulousness? His answer is disappointing:

> Scruples, whether of conscience or of any other species of scrupulousness, occur only when the normal actualization of the disposition is impeded or balked. And they, too, are only a special way in which the disposition is actualized, viz. when it cannot be *normally* actualized. The reason why my conscience is not spoken of as either judging or commanding other people is the same as the reason why, in general, a man can be described as scrupulous only about his own acts, namely, that full operative acceptance of the rule can (logically) take the form only of conducting oneself in accordance with the rule. Your actions can't (logically) be exercises of or exhibit *my* skill, readiness, capacity, enthusiasm, etc. (191–92)

The answer is disappointing because Ryle uses the person-specific nature of conscience to explain why conscience is a form of scrupulousness. But this is circular because the appeal to scrupulousness was an attempt to justify why conscience is person specific.

Ryle's professed argument that conscience is a form of scrupulousness is unsuccessful because it is circular. Implicit in his just-quoted remarks, however, is another argument. Ryle points out that a person's scruples occur when his or her scrupulousness is challenged in some way. Using his own example, if one is an Oxford don and is scrupulous about obeying the social custom at Christ Church of dressing for dinner and if one is prevented from dressing before dinner and dines "in mufti," one feels uncomfortable (190). One's sense of decorum nags. One experiences scruples. Similarly the scrupulous mathematician experiences scruples if he arrives (correctly) at an answer without having carefully gone through the necessary reasoning (191). Ryle, in fact, labels the mathematician's scruples "a sense of guilt." Scruples, whether a sense of warning or actual discomfort, arise when scrupulousness is challenged or violated. Moreover, they occur only to the person who is scrupulous in the relevant way. One cannot have scruples about the behavior of others. These facts provide the basis for Ryle's real reason for viewing conscience as a form of scrupulousness. To see this, we must turn to Ryle's remarks about the activity of conscience.

Conscience is not something other than, prior to, or posterior to moral convictions; it is having those convictions in an operative degree, i.e., being disposed to behave accordingly. And it is active or calls for attention when this disposition is balked by some contrary inclination. Conscience has nothing to say when the really honest man is asked a question and when he has no temptation to deceive. He then tells the truth as he signs his name, without considering what to do or why he should do it or how to get himself to do it. Conscience is awake only when there is such a conflict. The test for the existence of such a conflict is the occurrence of attention to the problem of what is to be done. Pangs or qualms of conscience can occur only when I am both disposed to act in one way and disposed to act in another and when one of these dispositions is an operative moral principle. (184)

Like scrupulousness, conscience is experienced most when there is a violation of convictions. In the case of conscience, the agent experiences guilt or remorse. Moreover, when there is a conflict about behavior, the convictions associated with scrupulousness and the moral convictions associated with conscience become conscious. Where scrupulousness is followed and the moral convictions of conscience are followed, the agent is unaware of his or her scrupulousness and conscience. Given such parallels, Ryle concludes that conscience is a form of scrupulousness.

It is clear that this is not convincing. Simply put, one cannot generally conclude that one phenomenon is a type of a second phenomenon by citing a number of attributes they have in common. Much more needs to be done. Moreover, there are some striking dissimilarities between scrupulousness and conscience as Ryle defines them. In the first place, scrupulousness, even when it is not the subject of awareness, strongly guides an agent's behavior. The Oxford don dresses in his robes for dinner because he is scrupulous. The mathematician goes through various deductions because he is scrupulous. They do not do so from fear of scruples. They are scrupulous people and behave unthinkingly in accord with their scrupulousness. Does conscience guide in a similar way for Ryle? Apparently not. Conscience passes judgment on a person's actions (185). It "has nothing to say when the really honest man is asked a question and when he has no temptation to deceive" (189). When Ryle describes conscience as a personal monitor, he pictures conscience as something internal to an agent, which, like Socrates' voice in the *Apology* and the *Phaedrus*, warns (or punishes) when an agent is about to do (does) wrong. This is a striking difference between scrupulousness and conscience, and it makes it difficult to see conscience (as Ryle sees it) as a type of scrupulousness. What is perhaps even more interesting is that Ryle's view of conscience as a private monitor is similar to Freud's view that conscience is the judging function of the superego, which affects behavior by means of producing anxiety in the agent. Of course, this similarity does explain why Ryle views conscience as a personal monitor. One experiences anxiety over one's own actions, not over the actions of others.

Surprisingly, Ryle is not consistent in following this Freudian tack. He often identifies conscience with operative moral convictions: "[W]e use the word 'conscience' for those moral convictions which issue not in verdicts but in behaving or trying to behave" (188). Of course, if there really is an identification here, one could strengthen the comparison with scrupulousness. Operative moral convictions, even when unconscious, do shape an agent's behavior much as scrupulousness does. Honest persons have as an operative moral conviction that they should not steal, and this conviction guides them unconsciously as they habitually and honestly fulfill their obligations and agreements. As I indicate above, Freud views this unconscious direction as a function of conscience. We might, of course, wonder how a moral conviction can cause discomfort in the way conscience does, but we can put this problem aside and concentrate on a much more severe problem: If conscience is just one's operative moral convictions as Ryle claims, how can anyone ever act against conscience?

Take, for example, the general situation in which we are faced with options: "Wondering what to do is a manifestation of a balked disposition to act; if it was not balked, I would act as I am disposed to act for that is what 'disposed' means. Consulting my conscience entails attending introspectively to my conflicting dispositions to act" (189). If my conscience is my operative moral convictions, and if convictions are dispositions to act, and if, in cases where I appeal to my conscience, I judge between my dispositions to act, whatever disposition I choose to follow is in accord with my conscience. I can never violate my conscience, and I can therefore never experience the guilt or discomfort Ryle discusses. One might object that this argument is misguided because it fails to distinguish the general moral convictions I endorse (and think others should follow) from the momentary conviction I endorse, which is at odds with the general moral convictions. Unfortunately, given Ryle's identification between convictions and dispositions to behave, it is hard to see how Ryle can distinguish the general convictions from the momentary ones. I believe I should not steal (a general conviction). I steal from the poor box at my church by actualizing a disposition to so behave. The disposition behind my stealing is not newly created. It has been as much a part of me as the disposition that is the general moral conviction "I should not steal." Perhaps the disposition behind my stealing is even a general disposition such as "I should act in ways that benefit me." In any event, given Ryle's equating of convictions with dispositions to behavior, it is difficult to see how we can act against conscience.

There is another difficulty with Ryle's position. Given his view that a conviction is really an inclination or disposition to a certain behavior, it is not surprising that Ryle finds little interest in classical problems about following one's conscience: "This answer to the original puzzle will, of course, provoke the objection that it denies the hallowed distinctions between cognition, emotion, and volition. For I am saying that in one sense, and a very important sense, of the word my being 'convinced' of something or my 'knowing' it do not *cause* but *consist in* my tending to feel certain feelings and to enact certain actions" (192). Because a belief of conscience is just an inclination to behave in a certain way, there can be no question of following a dictate of conscience. One might be confused about what dictate is appropriate because there may be conflicting dictates, but once one has the proper dictate there can be no question but that it will be followed, for the dictate is an inclination to behave in the proper way unless impeded. So Ryle dismisses the whole issue of weakness of will where an agent knows what ought to be done, has (in Ryle's terms) a disposition to behave appropriately, but does not behave properly. Yet, weakness of will is an undeniable phenomenon. A theory of conscience that rejects it flies in the face of experience, as Aristotle points out,[9] and should not be endorsed.

Ryle's views about conscience are intriguing, but they suffer on close analysis. The argumentation one finds Ryle consciously offering consists more of assertion than reasoning. The position he advocates, dependent on his equating convictions with inclinations to behavior, contains many serious problems. It results in thinking that no one acts against conscience and in denying the phenomenon of weakness of will. Finally, his view of conscience as a personal monitor is best supported by seeing his view as essentially Freudian: Conscience judges and warns when convictions are violated. But Ryle's view is at odds with Freud's notion that conscience as a function of the superego unconsciously controls actions.

Ryle's failure to show that conscience is a personal monitor is surprising.

9. *Nicomachean Ethics*, Book 7, chapter 2.

As I remarked before, most twentieth-century discussions of conscience take it for granted that conscience can have only a personal authority: What persons hold on the basis of conscience binds them but does not apply to others. But these discussions base this assumption on Ryle's arguments. Given the failure of Ryle's arguments, one can only conclude that there has been no demonstration that conscience has only personal authority.

To be sure, there is a unique and crucial link between a person and a person's conscience, and a viable theory of conscience needs to incorporate this link. A person's conscience controls his or her own behavior in a way that cannot be extended to the behavior of others. For example, the guilt I feel over missing a doctor's appointment is not something that inflicts my child. Nor does my need to fulfill my promises cause workmen I hire to fulfill their promises to me. But we certainly can think that others should feel guilt over missing appointments and should fulfill their promises. That is, we can and do think that the contents of our consciences should be followed by others. And we think that the content of our consciences should be authoritative for others even though we acknowledge that our consciences cannot control the behavior of others. Indeed, in many moral debates—for example, the abortion debate—both sides of the dispute think the other (false) side should follow the content of their (true) side's consciences. Thus, if we distinguish the content of conscience from the influence of the conscience, it is easy to see in what sense conscience has merely personal authority and in what sense it has authority over others. Although one's own conscience has a unique personal authority over one's own actions, the content of one's conscience has authority beyond the personal and extends to the behavior of others. Yet, the claim that conscience has content has also been challenged in the twentieth century.

SEVEN

CONSCIENCE AS SOMETHING
OTHER THAN A FACULTY

Although discussions of conscience in the philosophical literature of the last half of the twentieth century are rare, in general there are three different views about the nature of conscience in the literature.[1] Some writers advocate a cognitive view of conscience. According to this view, conscience is the device by which one contemplates and evaluates one's own actions or moral standing. By and large, those who view conscience as a faculty advocate this understanding of conscience.[2] Clearly this view regards conscience as closely connected to moral reasoning. A second view of conscience, as an affective faculty, regards conscience as the unpleasant emotional reactions to

---

1. Broad discusses the three theories of conscience in his "Conscience and Conscientious Action," in Donnelly and Lyons, eds., *Conscience*, 8.
2. Butler, Kant, Freud, and Ryle can all be seen as taking this approach to conscience.

moral actions or moral standing that control or modify one's behavior. This second view is distinguished from the first in that it sees conscience as having little to do with the formulation of moral imperatives; this formulation is more likely an aspect of moral reasoning. On the second view, conscience is concerned with the enforcement of imperatives through feelings like guilt and remorse. The third view regards conscience as a conative disposition to follow out what is thought to be right. (In many ways, this view of conscience seems similar to Bonaventure's notion of synderesis as the drive to the good in human beings.)

Each of these three views has its advocates, but a number of writers argue against them. Moreover, there has emerged during this century the view that there is no such thing as conscience. To a large extent, this view is tied up with the rejection of the notion of faculties, but it is also linked to the reductionistic view that conscience can be reduced to moral reasoning or emotional conditioning.

Joseph Butler's views of conscience are frequently taken as the starting point for twentieth-century discussions of conscience. This is fitting, of course, because Butler is one of the most influential proponents in the history of the notion of conscience of a number of claims about conscience. He regarded conscience as a faculty that is a supreme moral authority. Conscience is the formulator of universal moral principles that have authority for all human beings, not simply the individual possessor of a particular conscience. Modern critics point out that the notion that conscience is a supreme moral authority in Butler's sense is highly suspect. One need only point to two obvious facts to show this. In the first place, the conscience of an individual comes up with different verdicts on the same issue at different times. This occurs whenever an individual acts in good conscience and later comes to think the action was wrong. If conscience were a supreme moral authority, its verdicts would be essentially infallible and not subject to later revision by the same individual. In the second place, it is clear that the consciences of different individuals vary: What one individual finds permissible another finds forbidden. If conscience were a supreme moral authority, such variation should not occur. Moreover, this last point cuts against the view that conscience legislates universal moral principles. If individual consciences in various societies establish different general moral rules, it is difficult to see conscience as establishing universal moral rules. In fact, variations in conscience among individuals and groups strongly suggest that, as Ryle urged, conscience has only personal authority. But such a view of conscience does not fit well with Butler's view that the universal dictates of conscience are authoritative for all human beings.

Although such criticisms of Butler's view seem well founded, it is not at all clear that they undermine all cognitive views of conscience. A more moderate view of the cognitive aspect of conscience holds that there may be some universal principles common to everyone, but many of the dictates found in conscience vary from culture to culture and even in the same person over time. Other cognitive views, directly influenced by Freud, hold that conscience contains dictates gained from external authorities and internal reasoning and is not the sole originator of dictates as Butler indicates. To link the issue of the limited personal authority of conscience to the problem of the cognitive status of conscience is misguided. It is not at all clear that conscience has only personal authority, as I have suggested in the previous chapter, and it is not convincing to use the claim that conscience has only personal authority to establish that it has no cognitive content. Moreover, even if conscience had only personal authority in the way Ryle and others advocate, it is unclear that this fact shows that there is no cognitive content to conscience. The personal authority of conscience might well be tied to personal principles that are cognitive. To be sure, these cognitive contents might be applied through noncognitive mechanisms like emotions and feelings, but this fact does not count against the fact that there is cognitive content to conscience.

It is clear that one may well question Butler's statement of the cognitive power of conscience. However, it is also clear that a rejection of Butler's particular formulations of the cognitive view should not cause one to reject completely the view that there is cognitive content to conscience. There are cognitive theories of conscience that can avoid many of the problems associated with Butler's theory. I present in Chapter 9 a theory of conscience that understands conscience to have cognitive content.

Those who equate conscience with emotional responses like guilt and anxiety have been seen as following in the steps of John Stuart Mill (1806–73) who claimed:

> The internal sanction of duty, whatever our standard of duty may be, is one and the same—a feeling in our own mind; a pain, more or less intense, attendant on violation of duty, which in properly cultivated moral nature rises, in the more serious cases, into shrinking from it as an impossibility. This feeling, when disinterested and connecting it-

self with the pure idea of duty, and not with some particular form of it, or with and of the merely accessory circumstances, is the essence of conscience.[3]

In this quotation, Mill seems to equate conscience with the affective responses themselves. This seems to be a mistake, however, for one should separate what occasions feelings of guilt and remorse, for example, from the feelings themselves. Not doing so relegates such chemical disorders as generalized anxiety disorder to overactive conscience. Those who endorse an emotive theory of conscience see the principal function of conscience as controlling behavior through emotions like guilt and remorse and do so without equating the emotions with conscience. They relegate the issue of cognitive content to moral reasoning and see conscience as enforcing such reasoning through guilt and remorse.

Two of the best articulations of the conative theory of conscience are found in Peter Fuss's "Conscience" and Bernard Wand's "The Content and Function of Conscience." For his part, Fuss is dissatisfied with the cognitive and emotive views of conscience, and he proposes a notion of conscience as a "conative disposition to seek what one believes good and to shun what one believes bad, and to do what one believes right and avoid wrong."[4] Fuss is particularly emphatic that conscience should not be seen as either an entity or a faculty: "Finally, conscience is not a conative faculty or disposition in any substantive sense—that is, it does not as such move the agent to pursue this or that object of value or to perform this or that morally worthy act. However, it does constitute the disposition to integrate or harmonize moral knowledge or belief with the appropriate moral action" (44). In his rejection of the notion that conscience is a faculty, Fuss is following trends in twentieth-century philosophy and psychology away from faculty psychology. In reaction to Freud's postulation of unobservable entities, psychologists embraced empirical and behavioral methods and rejected the postulation of entities like psychological faculties as superfluous to explanation. Explanations in terms of systems, processes, or behavior were deemed to be more accurate and complete, and belief in the existence of faculties was lost.

3. Quoted in Donnelly and Lyons, eds., *Conscience*, 38. Rashdall Hastings offers some considerations about this view of conscience in his *Is Conscience an Emotion? Three Lectures on Recent Ethical Theories* (Boston: Houghton Mifflin, 1914). Thomas E. Hill Jr., in his "Four Conceptions of Conscience," in Shapiro and Adams, eds., *Integrity and Conscience*, 21–22, discusses feeling theories of conscience.
    4. Donnelly and Lyons, eds., *Conscience*, 42.

Many philosophers also rejected belief in faculties, and with this rejection they did away with the entire notion of conscience.

Some philosophers, and Fuss is among them, do not want to follow this route completely, however. According to them, although one might want to deny that conscience is a faculty, this is not equivalent to claiming that there is no conscience. On the contrary, one needs to be very careful in articulating exactly what conscience is to avoid denying its existence. Ordinary discourse about conscience, in fact, is a danger to maintaining a viable notion of conscience. Because it is imprecise and unsophisticated, ordinary discourse dangerously attributes to conscience qualities and powers it does not possess. When it is discovered that such qualities or powers are aspects of something other than conscience, the very existence of conscience is questioned. Fuss warns us of the dangers of ordinary discourse used by the typical layperson:

> Lacking the philosophical sophistication needed to make careful distinctions, he is given to calling the entire process of moral investigation, deliberation, decision, and their affective consequences by the name of conscience. But after all there is little harm in it: his everyday moral concerns do not require careful theoretical distinctions. The moral philosopher, on the other hand, is concerned with the precise nature of conscience; he fails to make the necessary distinctions at his peril. (45)

For Fuss, it is a mistake to blur together the processes of moral investigation, deliberation, decision, and their affective consequences and call the whole conscience. One needs to separate the process of moral reasoning and deliberation and talk about it as what moral agents do when they think about moral issues. As a different consideration, one must think about the emotional consequences of not following what is decided on through moral reasoning. In fact, these emotional reactions must be seen in the light of a general orientation toward seeking what one deems to be good and avoiding what is seen as evil. It is the failure to pursue what is thought good that results in negative emotional reactions. Once these distinctions are made, it becomes clear that the real nature of conscience is connected to the commitment to pursue what is thought good. To enlarge conscience to include moral reasoning and emotional reaction is simply unsophisticated.

Bernard Wand also embraces a conative view of conscience rather than rejecting the whole notion. He is skeptical of cognitive views of conscience

like the one proposed by Broad. He is even critical of pragmatic accounts of
conscience like Ryle's that focus on the function of conscience: the doing of
that action that ought to be done. Like Fuss, he sees conscience more as a
drive to follow what one deems ought to be done. To make his points,
Wand focuses on the hypothetical proposition "If anyone thinks he ought to
do x, then he ought to do it" (134). The antecedent is concerned with the
content of conscience. The sense of 'ought' in that clause is an indication of
the result of moral reasoning. Through our moral considerations, we determine what it is that we should do. Those offering a cognitive analysis of
conscience stress that this determination of what we should do is a function
of conscience. For other theorists, the 'ought' of the consequent is an indication that we need to put into effect what it is that we have (intellectually)
determined we should do. It is pragmatic in the sense that this 'ought' expresses the fact that we need to put into practice what it is that we have
determined we should do. For Ryle, this need to put into practice the content of moral deliberation is the sole operation of conscience.

The hypothetical "If anyone thinks he ought to do x, then he ought to do
it" is also useful to Wand for emphasizing that most people make the "assumption that there must be a gap between our moral beliefs (or reason) and
our moral practice (or volitions), which conscience, sharing the characteristics of each, bridges" (142). He, in fact, ties this assumed gap to viewing
conscience as a faculty. But Wand states that there is no such gap. If one
understands the logic of moral discourse and the role conscience plays in it,
one has a very different view of conscience:

> The two opposing types of difficulty are avoided once it is recog-
> nized that, in appealing to conscience, a person *by that very appeal,*
> is committing himself to act morally. Had he not already decided
> that he ought to do something, the appeal would never have been
> made. The attribution of moral responsibility to a conscientious
> person is warranted only on such grounds. The connection between
> the content and function of conscience, between moral belief and
> moral practice, is not causal, because, although distinct, these fac-
> tors are not separable. They would be separable only if what a man
> ought to do were externally dictated to him. But on the above in-
> terpretation an appeal to conscience is pre-eminently the attempt
> to determine for oneself what one ought to do in a given situation.
> (142–43)

What Wand seems to say is that the role of conscience in moral discourse is something like a logical one. It is an explicit acknowledgment that what one determines (intellectually) one should do ought to be (functionally) done. To announce internally or externally that one is going to look at one's conscience about what one should do is to do nothing more than to commit oneself to willing to do what one determines (intellectually) one should do. There is not something over and above moral reasoning that is the conscience. It is merely the acknowledgment of the need to will the results of moral reasoning.

It is noteworthy, however, that Wand blurs the distinction between willing what we should do and doing what we should do.[5] Willing to do something and putting it into practice are two distinct activities—as anyone who has willed to lose weight but failed to refrain from eating forbidden foods can attest. Wand apparently does not link conscience with actually carrying out one's volitions. The reason for this is not hard to find, for Wand's article is, in fact, a subtle attempt to place conscience in the context of moral reasoning. If moral reasoning is that by which we determine what we should do, and conscience is merely the indication that the logic of moral reasoning involves the belief that we should will what we determine we should do, there is really nothing intrinsic to conscience that is not already contained in moral reasoning. Wand agrees with Fuss that the function of conscience is to move us to pursuing what we think of as good and avoiding what is seen as evil. According to Wand, moral reasoning is the process by which we identify good and evil, and so conscience is the commitment to doing what we deem we ought to do. Conscience is not the moral reasoning; it is the commitment to following the moral reasoning in our attempt to follow good and avoid evil.

There seem to be a number of implications to the conative view espoused by Fuss and Wand. In the first place, according to the theory, "[T]here is no such thing as a 'strong' or 'weak' conscience" (46). On the conative theory, conscience has no content. It is merely the requirement to seek what is thought to be good through moral reasoning and avoid perceived evil. This requirement is equal for all human beings, and so conscience is equally strong for all people. This claim fits poorly with the phenomenology of conscience, of course, for we assume that some people are more conscien-

5. See p. 142, where Wand blurs the two with the comment: "The assumption that there must be a gap between our moral beliefs (or reason) and our moral practice (or volition)."

tious than others. Fuss is sensitive to the problem. He suggests that although the disposition that is conscience may be uniform among people, the voice of conscience may be only one among several competing voices, and so conscientious behavior may differ from individual to individual. In the second place, on Fuss and Wand's view, there is no such thing as a "more or less enlightened or developed conscience" (46). Instead,

> Intellect is what is more or less enlightened, and moral character as a whole is what is more or less developed. The development of moral character, in turn, has to do with the informed tendency (a function of knowing and willing) to give our various impulses, dispositions, etc., their proper due and to act accordingly. Our varying degree of success and failure in so doing does not militate against the notion that the "voice" of conscience may be the only constant in the economy of the human makeup. (47)

Conscience apparently has nothing to do with the development of moral character. We develop it or not in isolation from our disposition to follow our moral knowledge. Moreover, conscience has nothing to do with the increase in our moral knowledge over time. These seem implausible claims in the light of the phenomenology of conscience, and they suggest that Fuss and Wand's view is problematic. But there is an even more serious problem. If the disposition that is conscience is the same for all people, why do people in the same circumstances develop very different moral characters? This is merely a variation of Plato's question about virtue asked in the *Protagoras*. Why should the children of a virtuous man themselves lack virtues? Although it is difficult to answer this question on the basis of any theory of conscience, Fuss and Wand's view seems particularly ill equipped to answer it.

Why is the conative theory subject to such serious objections? In a sense, the answer is that it fails to account for what the phenomenology of conscience reveals: Conscience does have cognitive, affective, and conative components. One can say as does Fuss that such evidence comes from the philosophically unsophisticated, but such evidence, as Aristotle remarked, is what sophisticated philosophers need to pay attention to.[6] In fact, to limit conscience to its conative elements is to impoverish the notion of conscience.

---

6. *Nicomachean Ethics*, Book 1, chapter 1.

Although Wand, Fuss, and others want to retain the notion of conscience and limit it to a unique function, other thinkers want to do away completely with the notion. To a large extent, the motivation for doing away with conscience is directly related to a dismissal of faculties. If conscience is a faculty and the notion of faculties plays no explanatory role, it is a small step to eliminating conscience. There is another motivation. The term *conscience* has undoubted usage in ordinary discourse. But careful examination of ordinary usage reveals that 'conscience' in ordinary discourse is only convenient shorthand for more cumbersome expressions. Take for example the sentence, "My conscience has been bothering me." This sentence can be rephrased in the following way: "I have been bothered in a moral way about my personal behavior."[7] And the sentence, "I couldn't with a good conscience do that" can be rephrased as "There would be a moral objection to doing that which would weigh heavily with me" (77). The rephrasings communicate the same information, but they do so without committing us to conscience. We are left with endorsing such uncontroversial things as persons and morality and ordinary events such as vexation, behavior, and moral objection. There is no need to postulate some nonempirical entity like conscience.

We need not, however, eliminate 'conscience' from our ordinary vocabulary. It is a very useful word, and its eliminative paraphrases are often colorless, slightly cumbersome, and fail to express adequately important aspects of an issue. J. F. M. Hunter suggests that we think about uses of 'conscience' as on a par with the adult use of 'Santa Claus' (75). We find sentences like "Santa Claus was very good to me this year" as accepted ways of saying things like "I received a lot of presents this year" or "I was very good this year." These expressions presuppose public notions of Santa Claus without assuming that there really is a Santa Claus. Similarly, we can use the term *conscience* with a background of public agreement about its definitions and applications without assuming that there is such an entity. Of course, philosophers are more aware of the fact that there are effectively two languages being used here. Philosophers, in their analytic moments, use language devoid of the term *conscience*. Most people, on the other hand, use the less exact ordinary language in which the term is used; under the guidance of philosophers, they do so without making an ontological commitment to the actual existence of conscience.

The reductionism of Hunter's essay seems to be the culmination of certain

---

7. Donnelly and Lyons, eds., *Conscience*, 75.

twentieth-century philosophical views of conscience. Because much of the literature on conscience after Joseph Butler took conscience to be a faculty, once the notion of faculties is abandoned in psychology and philosophy it is easy to abandon belief in the existence of conscience. Activities traditionally attributed to it—moral knowledge, direction of behavior, vexation—are attributed to other sources in the moral agent. But must conscience be considered a faculty, and must it be considered an entity? Before addressing these questions, it is important to explore a twentieth-century view of conscience that is very different from the strictly philosophical material examined in this chapter.

MORE TRADITIONAL VIEWS
OF CONSCIENCE

Conscience in the Catholic Church

As Bernard Wand points out, the topic of conscience has been relegated to casual mention in the twentieth century. The important discussions in the Anglo-American tradition, which I have treated in the last two chapters, have tended toward reductionism or elimination. Yet, there are still champions of the existence of conscience in the twentieth century. The Roman Catholic Church, not surprisingly, has been one of the principal exponents in the twentieth century of the view of conscience one finds expounded in the Middle Ages. In the *Catechism of the Catholic Church*, conscience is defined in a very Thomistic fashion: "[C]onscience is a judgment of reason whereby the human person recognizes the moral quality of a concrete act that he is going to perform, is in the process of performing, or has already completed."[1] The emphasis is on judging actions, as it was in the writings of Thomas Aquinas. Similarly, according to the *Catechism*, "A human being must always obey the certain judgment of his conscience" (paragraph 1790). Moreover, "Man has the right to act in conscience and in freedom so as personally to make moral decisions. He must not be forced to act contrary to his conscience" (paragraph 1782). A conscience may be in error, however. If the ignorance can be imputed to personal responsibility, that is, "when a man 'takes little trouble to find out what is true and good, or when conscience is by degrees almost blinded through the habit of committing sin,'" the person is culpable for the evil he commits (paragraph 1791). "If—on the contrary—the ignorance is invincible, or the moral subject is not responsible for his erroneous judgment, the evil committed by the person cannot be imputed to him" (paragraph 1793). These comments reflect much of Aquinas's view about the binding nature of an erroneous conscience.

In addition to the similarity to Aquinas's claims about conscience, the description of conscience in the *Catechism* also contains some of the views championed by Bonaventure. "Conscience includes the perception of the principles of morality (synderesis); their application in the given circumstances by practical discernment of reasons and goods; and finally judgment about concrete acts yet to be performed or already performed" (paragraph 1781). Whereas Aquinas separated synderesis from conscience and assigned to synderesis the role of perceiving the general principles of morality, the *Catechism* absorbs synderesis into conscience. Conscience thus takes on the dual role of determining moral principles and applying them to specific acts. This dual role is much closer to Bonaventure's view of conscience than to Aquinas's. Moreover, there are elements of Bonaventure's view of the binding power of an erroneous conscience in the *Catechism*'s discussion of this issue. When describing the invincible ignorance associated with some erring consciences, the *Catechism* affirms that "one must therefore work to correct the errors of moral conscience" (paragraph 1793). Earlier the *Catechism* lists the sources of errors of judgment and includes "rejection of the Church's authority and her teaching" (paragraph 1792). It seems clear that the *Catechism* here embraces Bonaventure's claim that, in cases where one has a good reason to think one's conscience is in error because there is tension with the teachings of the Church, one must re-educate one's conscience or be at fault.[2]

---

1. *Catechism of the Catholic Church* (New York: Image Books, 1995), paragraph 1778.
2. This principle seems to have been at work in the Catholic Church's censures of Hans Küng and Charles Curran.

In line with the views of both Aquinas and Bonaventure, conscience is seen as the voice of God: "Deep within his conscience man discovers a law which he has not laid upon himself but which he must obey. Its voice, ever calling him to love and to do what is good and to avoid evil, sounds in his heart at the right moment. . . . For man has in his heart a law inscribed by God. . . . His conscience is man's most secret core and his sanctuary. There he is alone with God whose voice echoes in his depths."[3] The laws discovered within conscience are regarded as unerring, universal principles written by God. True for all human beings at all times, they are very different from the temporary and contingent laws set up by human beings. The unerring, universal laws found in man are also expressed and defended by the Church.

The placement of the *Catechism*'s discussion of conscience is also worth noting. It is positioned immediately before the discussion of the virtues. And the *Catechism* notes that there are close ties between conscience and the virtues. In describing the uprightness of moral conscience, the *Catechism* affirms that "[t]he truth about moral good, stated in the law of reason, is recognized practically and concretely by the *prudent judgment* of conscience. We call that man prudent who chooses in conformity with this judgment" (paragraph 1780). The connection between prudence and conscience is further emphasized in the description of the virtue of prudence: "It is prudence that immediately guides the judgment of conscience. The prudent man determines and directs his conduct in accordance with this judgment. With the help of this virtue we apply moral principles to particular cases without error and overcome doubts about the good to achieve and the evil to avoid" (paragraph 1906). The connection to Aquinas's views is obvious, and the *Catechism* acknowledges its debt to "St. Thomas Aquinas, following Aristotle," in its discussion of prudence's relation to conscience.[4]

The *Catechism*'s discussion of conscience never asserts that conscience is to be regarded as a faculty. Following medieval paradigms, the description offered does not even treat conscience as an entity. It appears to be a part of practical reasoning and is tied closely to the virtues. In fact, the *Catechism* follows *Dignitatis Humanae* (one of the documents of Vatican II) in focusing its interest in conscience on the issue of freedom of con-

3. *Catechism,* paragraph 1776.
4. Ibid. Josef Pieper in *Prudence* (trans. R. Winton and C. Winston [New York: Pantheon, 1959], 27) equates conscience with prudence.

science, particularly as it affects religious liberty.[5] Religious liberty is based on the dignity of the person.[6] As part of their dignity as human beings, people are morally responsible beings, obligated to seek the truth (801). But they cannot be externally compelled to seek the truth; rather, they must seek it freely and without coercion. In particular, they must be free to follow their conscience and not be forced to act against the dictates of conscience. So it appears that freedom of religion is connected to freedom of conscience.[7] Of course, the Church recognizes limits to the freedom of conscience. In forming one's conscience, "the faithful must pay careful attention to the sacred and certain teaching of the Church."[8]

In the *Pastoral Constitution of the Church in the Modern World* (another document of Vatican II), the relation of conscience to other moral issues is discussed.[9] Issues concerning the morality of war and the possibility of conscientious objection within the Catholic tradition are addressed.

In general, then, the view of conscience one finds in the *Catechism* and in the documents of Vatican II is derived from medieval sources. The views of both Aquinas and Bonaventure are prominent. Importantly, conscience itself is not focused on so much as its connection to the virtues and its relation to freedoms like religious liberty.

The view of conscience in the *Catechism* and proposed in Vatican II is treated in great detail by Philippe Delhaye in his *The Christian Conscience*.[10] He distinguishes the "psychological conscience" from the moral conscience (255). The psychological conscience is people's awareness of themselves and their impulses, tendencies, perceptions, and reflections.

5. Richard J. Regan, "Conscience in the Documents of Vatican II," in William C. Bier, ed., *Conscience: Its Freedom and Limitations* (New York: Fordham University Press, 1971), 29, states: "In one sense, the whole work of the Second Vatican Council can be said to deal with problems of 'conscience,' at least the conscience of Catholics." Robert J. Smith in his *Conscience and Catholicism* (New York: University Press of America, 1998) offers a general discussion of Roman Catholic views about conscience. He takes Aquinas's theories as the base for comparison and articulates a "revisionist" school of thought (which is, ironically, more faithful to Aquinas's views on conscience) and a "traditionalist" school of thought (less faithful to Aquinas's views on conscience).

6. Austin P. Flannery, ed., *Documents of Vatican II* (7th printing; Grand Rapids: Wm. B. Eerdmans, 1984), 1:806.

7. Richard Regan cites John Courtney Murray who says that the Church does not base the right to free exercise of religion on freedom of conscience (in Bier, ed., *Conscience: Its Freedom and Limitations*, 31). The logic of the document, however, suggests that the Church should do so.

8. Flannery, ed., *Documents*, 1:811.

9. Ibid., 199–308. See Bier, ed., *Conscience: Its Freedom and Limitations*, 34.

10. Translated from the French by Charles Underhill Quinn (New York: Desclee, 1964).

The moral conscience is the aspect of the human person involved with moral reasoning and actions. It is what most people mean when they talk about a person's conscience.

The moral conscience can be divided up into the habitual and the actual (256). The habitual conscience, also called synderesis, is not a faculty but a *habitus* of the first principles of the practical order. The actual conscience is the actual judgments of the conscience about particular acts.

Delhaye is favorably disposed to the Thomistic revival in Catholic thought of the twentieth century, and he advocates closely tying conscience to prudence, as understood by Aquinas (260, 262). But he wishes to keep them separate because the action of prudence is more extensive than that of conscience.

Similarly, Delhaye favors an objectivist view of conscience (259). According to him, there needs to be a collaboration between the internal forces of an individual and objectivity in the moral judgment of the conscience (259). This is to be achieved through an education of the habitual conscience that emphasizes the teachings of the Church (261).

Delhaye presents his view of conscience in the context of a historical treatment of issues in the writings of figures like Saint Paul, Bonaventure, and Aquinas as well as moral treatments in various handbooks. His work has influenced a number of Catholic and non-Catholic thinkers.[11]

Charles Curran's analysis of conscience offered in works like *Christian Morality Today* bears some similarity to Delhaye's views. Like Delhaye, he sees Saint Paul as bringing a Stoic notion of conscience into the Christian tradition,[12] and he has praise for scholastic analyses. He is critical of the manuals of moral theology written in the seventeenth and eighteenth centuries for their legalism, extrinsicism, and impersonalism (134).

Curran says that there are three parts to conscience: synteresis (synderesis), moral science, and conscience.[13] Synteresis is the rational part of conscience that tends to the truth. Conscience is the concrete judg-

---

11. For example, the authors of the essays in Bier's anthology.

12. "The Christian Conscience Today," in C. Ellis Nelson, ed., *Conscience: Theological and Psychological Perspectives* (New York: Newman Press, 1973), 133.

13. Ibid., 135. In his most recent book, *The Catholic Moral Tradition Today* (Washington, D.C.: Georgetown University Press, 1999), Curran views conscience as the intersection of the personal and objective. He does not use the threefold division of synteresis, moral reasoning, and conscience. There is no reason, however, to think that he rejects the views he offers in "The Christian Conscience Today."

ments of the practical reason. Moral science is "the knowledge of the less general principles of the moral law which man deduces from the primary principles. The category of moral knowledge also includes whatever man knows from revelation or authority. It pertains to the objective, the conceptual, the essential order" (135). What Curran calls "moral science" seems to be similar to Bonaventure's notion that conscience articulates general principles of behavior. It is also similar to Aquinas's secondary principles of behavior that fall under the activity of prudence (see Chapter 3). This aspect of conscience is not emphasized by Delhaye or the *Catechism*. It is, obviously, a crucial aspect of conscience, and Curran claims that Catholic theologians generally embrace all three parts of conscience (135).

Given the distinction between synteresis and moral science, it is easy to distinguish, as the *Catechism* does, between necessary and contingent principles of behavior. Norris Clarke, for example, expresses the distinction in this way:

> It seems to me, reflecting on the nature of human consciousness and morality, with its intrinsically evolutionary character, as well as upon the history of moral thinking, that there are really very, very few particular moral principles which are absolute, transcending all possible diversity of contexts and circumstances. The great, general moral values, such as love and respect for one's fellow man because of his eminent dignity as a person, hence not treating another person as a mere means—these indeed are absolute. But they are very general and formal, and do not tell us directly how to apply these values here and now in real life. I am talking rather about moral principles with a specific content, such as killing, or stealing, justice, the morality of sex, and the like. It seems to me that *almost* all these hold only for the most part.[14]

The general, universal principles are found in synderesis. The content-rich principles by which we regulate our actions are part of moral science.

Curran also (as does Delhaye) distinguishes between the antecedent and consequent consciences.[15] The consequent conscience offers verdicts on acts

14. "The Mature Conscience in Philosophical Perspective," in Bier, ed., *Conscience: Its Freedom and Limitations*, 356–66.

15. C. Ellis Nelson, ed., *Conscience: Theological and Psychological Perspectives*, 132.

that have been performed. In contrast, the antecedent conscience considers the quality of actions to be performed. There is not, of course, a complete separation between the two types of conscience. Presumably, one can exercise antecedent conscience better after being informed by consequent conscience. That is to say, one's evaluation of actions to be performed can be better informed by consideration of actions that have already been performed. Yet, the notion of an antecedent conscience opens up a number of possibilities.

If we briefly return to Freud's view of conscience, it is clear that his notion of conscience falls for the most part under the consequent conscience. Conscience judges one's actions and punishes. To be sure, part of the aim of punishment is to modify future behavior. But there is another way to motivate behavior: Strive to attain an ideal.

Freud, of course, talked about an "ego-ideal" that we strive toward. According to Robert J. Campbell, in 1923 Freud subsumed both conscience and the ego-ideal under the superego.[16] Moreover, in contrast to the superego:

> The ego-ideal, as it is called, is the love side, rather than the hate side, of early relationships with the parents, and probably begins as a kind of magical union with the omnipotent and loving mother. The imagined participation in her omnipotence sets a standard—unrealistic and unattainable—that the superego uses as a measure of what the ego achieves. The ego-ideal may well be a source of comfort and security to the ego, offering it guidance, protection, and empathetic concern, and keeping its faith in the ego when all else has failed. But it also has its negative aspects, for persisting failure to draw near to a goal impossible to reach may produce chronic disenchantments and depression, and no achievement seems worthy when compared with the perfection of infantile phantasies. (Cameron 1963, 85)

Thus, even the ego-ideal serves a punitive function for Freud.

Conscience as a Positive Force

In general, Freud failed to present any sense of a positive function for the conscience, and many have criticized Freud for his essentially punitive no-

16. "Superego and Conscience," in Bier, ed., *Conscience: Its Freedom and Limitations*, 83.

tion of the conscience and the ego-ideal. John Macquarrie, for example, in his *Three Issues in Ethics*, talks about two distinct types of conscience: a conventional conscience and an authentic conscience.[17] He identifies the conventional conscience with the Freudian superego and says that "it reflects the standards of a particular society or even a segment of a society, and conformity to these standards is required if one is to be acceptable in that society" (157). In contrast, he identifies the authentic conscience with "a positive image toward which man transcends himself" and claims that recent psychoanalytical theory has understood this positive image as the ego-ideal. Macquarrie also thinks that this authentic conscience is very close to the Latin notion of 'conscientia' and the Greek notion of 'syneidesis.' The Latin and Greek notions express the idea that conscience is our knowledge or disclosure of ourselves to ourselves.

According to Macquarrie, our authentic conscience is not only the repository of our ideal image, but it "discloses the gap between our actual selves and that image of ourselves that we already have in virtue of the 'natural inclination' toward the fulfillment of man's end" (158). But the awareness of this gap is not punitive; rather, it is stimulating. The image of what we should ideally be in the context of our perceived final goals encourages us in a positive fashion to live up to the ideal. It forms the basis for choosing the activities and qualities that lead us to our final goals.

It is easy to undervalue Macquarrie's correction of Freud, but it is a mistake to do so. While acknowledging the negative role of conscience in penalizing agents when accepted beliefs are violated or challenged, Macquarrie attributes to conscience a more positive, formative role in the development of character (158). The notion that the ideal image of ourselves can be a part of conscience and serve as an encouragement to the development of the character associated with that image is a critical aspect of conscience that is overlooked in Freud's own views as well as in many of the views of conscience in the twentieth century we have examined. Any well-balanced theory about conscience must take into account this positive function of conscience, and, in fact, a number of recent writers have emphasized the positive aspect of conscience while discussing what is frequently called "the mature conscience."

John R. Cavanagh defines a mature conscience in this way: "The person with a mature conscience is one who, when confronted by difficult decisions

17. Reprinted as "The Struggle of Conscience for Mature Selfhood," in Bier, ed., *Conscience: Its Freedom and Limitations*, 158.

in the ethical order, carefully evaluates, insofar as he can, all aspects of the matter. On this basis he comes to a practical judgment about what is right and what is wrong. Then he acts on the matter with a functional certitude— that is, without unreasonable fears and doubts."[18] The mature conscience is a product of training and experience. There is an autonomy to it that requires moving beyond simplistic adherence to laws and authorities. Cavanagh goes on to say: "Maturity of conscience gives great freedom of thought and activity because the mature person is not restricted by taboos, fears, obsessions, or ambivalence, or other restrictive forces. Such maturity gives an incentive to seek greater freedom, which gives even greater maturity and hence greater peace of mind" (384). The mature conscience has overcome the primitive restrictions of the superego and strives to fulfill the ego-ideal. It strives toward this ideal without undergoing anxiety or suffering pain inflicted from a failure to reach an ideal. On the contrary, the ideal functions as a desired goal that the person strives for. The closer the individual comes to the goal, the greater the self-esteem.[19]

Ewert Cousins ties the mature conscience to imitation of Christ: "For the Christian, the mature conscience is one that is illuminated by the Spirit and conformed to Christ, and through Christ is united to the Father."[20] The imitation of Christ seems to involve two important qualities. In the first place, "[T]he mature person does not look upon the moral law as something merely outside himself: as a command of his parents, a decree of his Church or government, a taboo of his culture, an impersonal law of nature, or an edict of God." On the contrary, "the mature person realizes that the moral order, while extrinsic to himself, is also intimate to his subjectivity" (145). The autonomy a mature person displays is one that embraces the moral order rather than opposes it. It is as if the mature person regards him- or herself as a moral everyman, subject to universal laws.

The second quality is that the moral stance of the mature individual is not blind; it is marked by an awareness of ambiguity and limitation, a tragic sense, and responsibility. Living "east of Eden and after Cain," the mature person realizes that there is evil in the world and that morality is not as clear-cut as one might think as an adolescent (150). Evil must be opposed, but the route of this opposition is not obvious. Moreover, maturity involves

18. "The Mature Conscience as Seen by a Psychiatrist," in *Conscience: Its Freedom and Limitations*, 384.

19. Campbell, "Superego and Conscience," in Bier, ed., *Conscience: Its Freedom and Limitations*, 89.

20. "The Mature Christian Conscience," in E. Ellis Nelson, ed., *Conscience: Theological and Psychological Perspectives*, 144.

suffering and failure. In part this is a function of the moral ambiguity of the world. But it also seems to be a part of the fabric of life. In addition, the mature person's sense of responsibility moves far beyond him- or herself to embrace family and community.

Cousins finds Christ to be the teacher of the mature conscience, and he urges imitation of Christ to achieve this conscience. Although the Church is the principal source of Christ's teaching and thus a means toward the imitation of Christ, the mature person no longer sees "the Church as providing moral security in each age by giving definitive solutions to all problems of conscience" (152). Mature people must form their own consciences. This point is also emphasized by Norris Clarke:

> The most basic characteristic of the mature moral conscience and the necessary condition for all else is the habit of making its moral judgments truly personal ones. By this I mean that they proceed truly from within, from one's own moral convictions, according to one's own sincere judgment, in the light of one's own moral ideals and values freely and responsibly accepted as one's own; in a word, when the voice of my conscience is really the voice of my own deepest and most authentic self speaking out to guide my actions.[21]

Clarke thinks of this as the "personalized" aspect of the mature conscience. People with a mature conscience follow their own autonomy without blindly following the dictates of an external authority. In addition, Clarke expresses wonder at an unexpected aspect of personalization: "This is the spontaneous, intuitive, non-analytical character of its judgment in so many cases, even quite complex ones, in which it comes out with clear-cut judgments—'This is right; do it; that's no good; avoid it'—even though we find it very difficult to justify or organize these in any explicit analyzable reasoning" (361). This intuitive sense of what is appropriate is surely linked to what Clarke considers the main characteristic of the mature conscience: practical insight. This insight is gained from teaching and experience. It involves the ability to "relativize all or almost all moral principle dealing with specific types of actions, in the name of the few great general moral values which are ultimate and absolute" (366). It also involves the willingness of the mature conscience to follow its own decisions even "at the risk of condemnation by other good people or even by legitimate authority" (366).

21. Bier, ed., *Conscience: Its Freedom and Limitations*, 359.

Within the Catholic tradition, the notion that one can be duty bound by conscience to oppose Church doctrine is, of course, a deeply contested one. It was part of Luther's defense of his position at Worms. Avery Dulles in "Conscience and Church Authority" sees the freedom of choice of a mature conscience to be an essential ingredient of the Church, which is a voluntary society.[22] Realizing full well the authority of the Church but understanding that the magisterium is not omniscient, people of mature conscience must follow their consciences even at the risk of leaving the Church:

> If anyone feels in conscience that he cannot accept the Church's basic stance, he should not be made to feel guilty about leaving. Catholic pastors and educators should not so inhibit the psychological freedom of the faithful that they can no longer take any responsible attitude, either for or against the Church. At such a price, it would not be worth while trying to keep people within the fold. We must have enough faith to believe that in the long run it is better for mature people to follow their conscience in full freedom than to be kept in servile dependence, even though we may regret the immediate consequences of a particular conscientious decision. (121)

Although many in the hierarchy of the Catholic Church might dispute Dulles's views here, it is difficult to fault Dulles for following the logic of the authority of a mature conscience.

The importance of viewing conscience as a positive source cannot be overemphasized. In a century that tends not to discuss the nature of conscience in depth, the portrayal of conscience as a positive, formative force is a major innovation. It differs markedly from the notion of conscience as a reactive punisher of misdeeds offered by Freud and taken for granted by many thinkers in the twentieth century. The positive view of conscience is tied to cultivation of the virtues, especially prudence (in the sense of practical wisdom). It also has no commitment to thinking of conscience as a faculty.

22. In C. Ellis Nelson, ed., *Conscience: Theological and Psychological Perspectives*, 121. Robert J. Smith, following Bernard Haring, advocates a similar position in his *Conscience and Catholicism*.

NINE

THE EXISTENCE OF CONSCIENCE

At the root of many of the reductionistic criticisms of conscience examined in Chapter 7 was the assumption that conscience is a faculty. For example, Hunter's suggestion that the notion of conscience be taken as a convenient fiction is guided by the assumption that conscience is a moral knowledge-giving faculty. In fact, his pointing to its status as a faculty gives strength to the analogy with the entity Santa Claus. Why should we assume, however, that if there is a knowledge part to conscience that conscience is an entity (faculty)? Of course, if we regard conscience as the exclusive source of moral knowledge (as Hunter seems to suppose in his article), it is difficult not to see conscience as an entity (faculty). But do we need to think of it as an entity (faculty) if it involves moral knowledge?

The term *entity* has many uses. Perhaps its most common use is to refer to "a substantial being." We thus call tables, chairs, cabbages, and kings "entities." Perhaps derived from this use, 'entity' is also used in the context of fictitious beings like "the Great Pumpkin" or "the pot of gold at the end of the rainbow." If these fictitious entities were to exist, they would be substances. Yet, we also use 'entity' to talk about nonsubstances. Oxford University (as distinct from the colleges of Oxford University) is an organization but not a substance. Yet, we think of it as an entity. Certain scientific notions like gravity and energy are looked on as entities even though they are not substances. Moreover, we often regard nonsubstantial parts of substantial entities as entities. For example, take the electrical system of an automobile. The automobile itself, of course, is a complex, substantial entity. It is composed of smaller entities like fenders, hoods, and seats. But it is also composed of various systems: the electrical system, the braking system, the fuel system, and so on. Each of these systems is complex. The electrical system, for example, typically involves a number of substances: a battery, an alternator, fuses, distributor, condenser, light bulbs, wires, switches, and so on. It is governed by certain chemical and physical laws. It is closely related to other systems like the fuel system. Certainly, any major modification of a substantial part of the electrical system affects the system. If, for example, the battery goes dead, the system will not operate. If a critical fuse blows, a certain part of the system (such as the horn) will not work. But it would be misleading to think of the electrical system itself as a substance. It is more correct to think of it as an aspect of the automobile that relates to various substances and processes but is not itself a substance or process. In fact, the construction, functioning, and maintenance of an electrical system depend on understanding the system in this way. For lack of a better term, I call entities like the electrical system of an automobile "relational entities." The term is chosen to distinguish such entities from "substantial entities" as well as to indicate that they exist as a relation among various entities, processes, and systems. I also want to claim that the conscience is a relational entity. But it must be seen as a particularly complex relational entity—in large part because of the historical discussions concerning it.

As Bernard Mayo suggests in his *Ethics and the Moral Life*, discussions of the nature of the soul have followed either a political model (as did Greek discussions) or a mechanical model (as did Cartesian discussions) or a combination of the two.[1] Behind both models was an assumption that there were "parts to the soul" and that these substantial parts (for example, intellect, will, memory) interacted in various ways (129). Discussions of conscience

1. *Ethics and the Moral Life* (New York: St. Martin's Press, 1958), esp. chapters 7, 8, and 9.

since Butler's contribution have tended to regard conscience as a substantial part of the human psyche and to view it as a faculty. In fact, Mayo suggests, the dominant metaphor used about conscience seems to be a politicolegal metaphor in which conscience is seen as a judge of the other parts of a human being (127). Kant and, to a certain extent, Freud can be considered as advocating this metaphor. As we have seen, more recent writers who have critiqued the notion of conscience have regarded it as some type of faculty.[2] It thus appears that our ordinary use of 'conscience' presupposes that conscience is a substantial entity that is sometimes labeled a faculty. But this view of conscience results in either discovering the substantial entity and its attributes we call "conscience" or failing to discover such an entity and concluding that there is no conscience. Because 'conscience' is so connected to the notion that a conscience is a substantial entity, denying that it is a substantial entity seems to be equivalent to denying its existence. Moreover, viewing conscience as a substantial entity results in seeing its characteristics as unique to it. If conscience, for example, is a faculty different from intellect, the notion that it involves moral reasoning, which seems to be a characteristic of the intellect, seems paradoxical. If conscience is a substantial entity, it must be distinct from the other substantial entities (faculties) of the human psyche.

Needless to say, our historical discussions have shown that conscience has not always been regarded as a faculty. Many medieval schoolmen, for example, saw it as an aspect of practical reasoning closely related to the intellect and emotions. But our modern conception of conscience seems wedded to its existence as a substantial entity. Is it possible for us to see conscience as something other than a substantial entity? As it turns out, we might be able to retain our ordinary notion of conscience while understanding that it is not in fact such an entity. The case of the electron presents a possible model for doing this.

Until the early twentieth century, the planetary model of the atom was in vogue. This model, inspired by readily observable phenomena like the revolution of the moon around the earth, was easily grasped. An entity with negative electrical charge, the electron, orbited a larger entity, the nucleus. The nucleus itself was composed of protons and neutrons, and it possessed a positive charge that balanced the number of negative electrical charges in its electrons. Yet, there were widely recognized intrinsic difficulties with this

2. In his book, Mayo rejects thinking of the conscience as a faculty. He advocates thinking of it as an organization.

model.[3] Because charged particles moving along curved paths emit electro-magnetic energy, it should be the case that electrons are continually gener-ating such energy. But if this were true, electrons would lose their energy while orbiting the nucleus and would spiral into it. Clearly, this does not happen. Moreover, when electrons emit energy, they do so only in certain and discrete wave lengths, not over the whole spectrum as one would ex-pect if the planetary model were correct.

To cope with the difficulties of the planetary model, physicists like Max Planck, Albert Einstein, Neils Bohr, Clinton Davisson, Louis de Broglie, Er-win Schrödinger, and Werner Heisenberg developed quantum mechanics. According to this theory, electrons do not orbit nuclei; they are found in discrete energy levels around the nucleus. This explains the distinct wave lengths they emit. Moreover, according to quantum mechanics, an electron is not really a thing. It is something like an abstract entity that functions as if it were both a wave and a particle and has either momentum or location but not both. As Heisenberg and Von Neumann suggest, it cannot be mea-sured correctly because the act of measuring affects it and distorts the mea-surement (26–28).[4]

Despite the paradoxical status of the electron in quantum mechanics, which makes it appear that the electron is not an entity, treating it as if it were an entity still gives correct results in many experiments. In fact, regard-ing electricity as "the flow of electrons" as do most physicists and describing the paths of electrons in cloud chamber experiments readily result in think-ing of the electron as an entity. It then appears that, despite the overthrow of classical mechanics at the subatomic level, retaining the notion of an electron as an entity has distinct advantages. This suggests that the current use of the term *electron* is a type of shorthand. Although current use gives it an entitative existence, the electron as we now conceive of it seems to be an abbreviation for a set of mathematical relations connecting different obser-vations. These relations do not require that there be an entity, but using an entity in explanations of the relations is a useful tool (25).

So the electron offers a case where what was assumed to be a simple, independent entity by classical mechanics was shown not to exist. Yet, a complete reduction of the entity to mathematical relations was found to be

3. *The Ghost in the Atom*, ed. P. C. W. Davies and J. R. Brown (Cambridge: Cambridge University Press, 1986), 2.

4. For a somewhat different account of the uncertainty principle, see Roger Penrose, *The Em-peror's New Mind* (Oxford: Oxford University Press, 1989), 248ff.

undesirable. The result has been the retention of prominent features of the electron of classical mechanics and the reinterpretation of this entity as representing certain mathematical relations.

We can also turn to our notion of the will to give another example of an entity once regarded as a substance that is no longer so regarded. Although our modern conception of the will has its roots in Greek thought as well as in the letters of Saint Paul in the New Testament, the most important figure in the early formulations of the notion of will was Saint Augustine.[5] In *De Trintate*, Augustine divided the soul into three parts—understanding (intellect), will, and memory—which paralleled the divine trinity.[6] Although 'will' seemed to be a term that referred to the whole soul in action, Augustine often wrote as if it were a distinct part of the soul. In any event, the notion that there were three faculties of the soul became part of the standard view in the Middle Ages, and the relations among the faculties became an important topic. Intellectualists like Thomas Aquinas regarded the intellect as superior to the will. In contrast, voluntarists like Duns Scotus and other Franciscans regarded the will as the dominant faculty. In fact, the voluntarists presented the will as a free power that can act in accord with reason or against it. It is able to control what the intellect considers, and it is the source for choice within the human being.

The strong picture of the will offered by the voluntarists presents it as an independent entity within the human makeup. Issues about free choice and the morality of actions were seen as issues involving the will as the initiator of actions in human beings. The soul's status as a noncausally determined mover came down to the causal independence of the will. The view that the will is an independent faculty and the explanation for human activity was accepted by many. John Locke, however, in discussing freedom, indicates that it is a mistake to talk about a will as free. On the contrary, the human being is free or unfree.[7] Moreover, the person, not the will, is morally responsible for actions performed. Although Locke did not clearly reject the notion that the will is a faculty, he suggested that many of the powers attributed to it are better attributed to the whole person.

---

5. See Martha Nussbaum's *The Fragility of Goodness* (Cambridge: Cambridge University Press, 1986), for comments on Greek views. See also John M. Bowers's *The Crisis of Will in Piers Plowman* (Washington, D.C.: Catholic University of America Press, 1986), chapter two, for a readable history of medieval views about the will.

6. Bowers, *The Crisis of Will in Piers Plowman*, 44

7. *Essay Concerning Human Understanding*, Book 2, chapter 21, paragraph 14.

With the general rejection of faculty psychology, most modern theorists dismiss the idea of the will as a substantial entity in the human psychic makeup. In line with Locke, modern discussions of freedom analyze the freedom of the individual and see the person as the originator of actions and the center of moral responsibility. Yet, 'will' still retains its usefulness. In modern discussions, it is used to mark out an area of discourse that concerns human actions like volition, deliberation, choice, and decision. The term is used not to mark out some substantial entity in the human psyche, but to talk about action-related notions in contrast to notions having to do with remembering or reasoning. In expressions like "One must train one's will so that one will not fall prey to idleness," the term *will* is used as a type of shorthand to say that one should practice not being lazy. In expressions like "The child is willful," it is suggested that the child displays an independence of spirit that is (probably) undesirable. The uses of 'will' are so different, in fact, that it is difficult to see any common thread other than that all the uses have some relation to action.

Although one may urge that the term *will* can be replaced in many expressions by some paraphrase that talks about a specific type of action, it is awkward to do it. Moreover, such replacement tends to lose the sense that there are various ways to consider a human being and his or her actions. The term *will* carries with it often-unspecified connotations of effort and emotional content, not to mention desire, which are left out in paraphrases. The term seems to pick out an important and distinct network of concepts, the loss of which impoverishes descriptions of the human psychic makeup. Perhaps recognition of the harm of this impoverishment explains the continued use of 'will' despite its early identification with a specific substantial entity.

The cases of the electron and the will suggest that words originally used to refer to a substantial entity can retain features of this original reference in ordinary discourse even though it is denied that there is a relevant substantial entity. 'Conscience' is another such word, although with a striking difference: Conceiving of conscience as other than a substantial entity is in fact recapturing its original sense. Earlier, I suggested that we think of conscience as a "relational entity." If we are, on a parallel with 'electron' and 'will,' to use 'conscience' in ordinary discourse as if it picked out a substantial entity but in fact see it as referring to a relational entity, it is important to understand what it means to think of conscience as a relational entity.

Perhaps the best presentation of the multiple facets of conscience is Broad's definition of conscience in its widest sense:

To say that a person "has a conscience," when this phrase is used in its widest sense, is equivalent to asserting the following three closely connected propositions about him. (1) That he has and exercises the cognitive power of reflecting on his own past and future actions, and considering whether they are right or wrong; of reflecting on his own motives, intentions, emotions, dispositions, and character, and considering whether they are morally good or bad; and of reflecting on the relative moral value of various alternative ideals of character and conduct. (2) That he has and exercises the emotional disposition to feel certain peculiar emotions, such as remorse, feeling of guilt, moral approval, etc., in respect of the moral characteristics which he believes these to have. (3) That he has and exercises the conative disposition to seek what he believes to be good and to shun what he believes to be bad, as such, and to do what he believes to be right and avoid what he believes to be wrong, as such.[8]

In this passage, Broad does not claim that conscience is a faculty. He chooses, instead, to work with the expression "A person has a conscience." Moreover, he claims that the phenomenon of having a conscience involves cognitive, emotional, and conative elements. As we have seen, although some theorists wish to reduce conscience to one of these three elements, it is important to understand that conscience as a relational entity involves all three elements. Elaborating on Broad's comments, we may say that, on the cognitive side, conscience is related to the moral principles individuals initially inherit from their upbringing (the conventional conscience of Macquarrie) and the moral principles individuals develop through reasoning and experience (what many call the mature conscience). These principles are not necessarily true, nor do they need to be universal to all people (even if some of them, in fact, are common to all). Moreover, they are a dynamic set, constantly changing throughout people's lives. They are not exclusively prohibitions; positive ideals one tries to attain constitute a large part of the principles. The agent is not always consciously aware of these principles. In fact, most principles are so deeply embedded in the character of an agent that they rarely become present to consciousness; but they determine behavior as much as Ryle's scruples do. On the emotional side, conscience is as much related to the pangs of guilt and shame when one consciously violates

---

8. C. D. Broad, "Conscience and Conscientious Action," in Donnelly and Lyons, eds., *Conscience*, 8.

one's moral principles as it is to the feelings of satisfaction when principles are followed or progress is made toward attaining ideals. Importantly, conscience is connected to the pleasure an agent experiences in acting in accordance with his or her character traits, especially when impediments to so acting are overcome, as Macquarrie suggests in his notion of an authentic conscience. Finally, on the conative side, as Bonaventure emphasized, conscience is related to the desire to pursue one's ultimate goals through following the moral principles one has formulated as a means toward these goals. It is also connected to the desire to follow its own dictates.

This last desire is particularly relevant for issues surrounding weakness of will. It is not sufficient that one's conscience be developed to the point of cleverly formulating moral principles that lead one to ultimate goals. Unless one develops the habit of following one's principles (as Aquinas maintained), there is a danger that one will not follow one's conscience. Bonaventure placed the desire to follow the principles leading to the good in the synderesis. Subsequent thinkers either ignored the issue of this desire (and assumed that weakness of will was merely a type of ignorance) or placed the desire in the conscience itself. Wherever this desire is placed, it is important to realize that it must be developed. Although each person may claim to do what is perceived as good in any circumstances, the desire to pursue what has been discovered to lead best to the ultimate good can easily be lost. Unless there is constant reinforcement for pursuing what may be a long-term goal, there is a danger that one will pursue only immediate goods that, in fact, may lead away from long-term goods.

It would also be a mistake to see the three elements—cognitive, emotional, and conative—as the exclusive property of conscience. The development of moral principles, for example, is an aspect of moral reasoning that is similar to other forms of reasoning—scientific, logical, intuitive—that are considered functions of the intellect. Moral sentiments like guilt, shame, and pleasure are not exclusively tied to the functioning of conscience. One takes pleasure, after all, in seeing a movie and feels guilt over dressing inappropriately for certain occasions (as does Ryle when dining in mufti at Oxford). Similarly, desire for ultimate goals may be rooted in human nature, and following principles may be a conditioned response found in one's vocation or avocations. It is much better, then, to view conscience as overlapping with other parts of the human psychic makeup, as did Bonaventure. It shares characteristics with these other parts but does not have exclusive right to them.

We can easily refrain from viewing the parts of the psychic makeup of human beings as faculties. The intellect, for example, can be seen as a system based in the neurological network of a human being. Likewise, we do not need to see the conscience as a faculty or even connect it with a particular organ. It can be seen as a system that relates to the intellect, will, and memory and involves emotions as well as desires. It seems to be particularly connected to behavior of a certain sort: acting in ways that moves one toward one's ultimate goals. Like the will, it seems to be a unique and irreducible aspect of human beings.

Even if conscience is conceived of as a system that overlaps with and is connected to various parts and systems of the human psychic makeup, there is little harm in treating it as if it were a substantial entity, and much good in doing so. Although one can discuss improving the system that conscience is, it is much easier to talk about improving the conscience by, for example, training it or educating it. Instead of saying "My conscience is bothering me," one could talk about the relation of the conscience system to the emotions; but this is very awkward. In fact, treating the conscience as if it were an entity might allow one to focus on the most relevant aspect of a particular problem.[9]

Viewing conscience as a relational entity that is particularly tied to the practice of principles related to the pursuit of ultimate goals closely connects conscience to the practice of the virtues, and these connections are treated in the third part of this work. This view of conscience also has implications for issues about the authority of conscience. If part of the development of conscience involves the development of the desire to follow the dictates of conscience, conscience must be authoritative for the individual. This is to say that an individual ought to follow the dictates of conscience or be immoral. Because there are different types of principles in one's conscience, following the authority of one's conscience is not a simple matter. Certainly, up to a certain age, one acts in accord with the conventional conscience. For the most part, the principles of this part of conscience consist of the rules of behavior formulated by one's parents or society. These rules may be guides for attaining ultimate goals, but it is doubtful that they have been formulated with this in mind.[10] But these principles must be the

9. I have in mind situations in which people try to adjust their emotional reactions to rules or norms they think they must obey instead of challenging the rules or norms themselves.

10. Needless to say, a lot depends on who one's parents are and what society one lives in. If we were to agree with Alasdair MacIntyre's *After Virtue, Whose Justice? Which Rationality?* and other writings, we would even say that earlier Western societies were better groups for giving such guides to ultimate ends than our modern, liberal (and fragmented) society.

moral starting point. At a certain point, however, one must begin to develop one's own set of moral principles and develop a mature conscience. Depending on one's personal circumstances, the principles of one's mature conscience may be very similar to the principles of one's traditional conscience. Yet, there is a profound difference. The principles of a mature conscience are there because one has determined by reasoning and experience that these are the best principles to follow to attain one's ultimate aims. It is antithetical to a mature conscience to accept a principle on the unjustified authority of an external agent. Yet, it is consistent with this conscience to accept the authority of an external agent even when the claims of this authority conflict with one's own views—so long as the authority of the external agent has been justified. Take, for example, the advice a seasoned faculty member might offer to a junior faculty member about a vote on a change in faculty requirements for tenure. The junior colleague might have studied the issue and read the relevant documents. He might have, in fact, come to the conclusion that a change in procedures would be good. Yet, the trusted senior colleague argues for the opposite view. Although the junior colleague has not been swayed by the arguments of the senior colleague, the junior colleague knows from experience that the position of the senior colleague is usually correct. This senior colleague has an uncanny ability to sense the undesirable results of procedures even if she is unable to articulate them fully or convincingly. The junior colleague is also aware that his own reasoning is colored by his own desires to be tenured and understands that what he sees as beneficial may be beneficial in his case but not for the institution as a whole. The junior colleague has effectively justified accepting the authority of the senior colleague over his own views. And he is morally correct in following the opinion of the senior colleague, but only because he has effectively justified the authority of the senior colleague in this issue. If he had not made this justification, he would be abrogating his own authority for the authority of an external agent. In fact, given the process of justification, the junior colleague has effectively followed the authority of his conscience by following its justification of the senior colleague's authority in this particular matter. So, instead of seeing this as a situation of the imposition of an external authority, it is better to see the case as an example of internal and critical justification. Seen in this way, the junior colleague is really recognizing his own authority, for until he has justified the authority of the senior colleague, his acceptance of the position of the colleague cannot be allowed.

There are other examples of this aspect of the authority of conscience, of course. Issues of obedience to Church authority discussed by those who are concerned with the relation of the "mature conscience" to Church authority immediately come to mind. In agreement with Cousins and Clarke, it appears that the central question of authority is whether the statements of an external authority are autonomously accepted (by some process of justification) by the agent. If the statements are so accepted, the personal authority of the individual's conscience is not compromised. If the statements are not so accepted, compromise is apparent.

Because the view of conscience as a relational entity connects conscience to moral reasoning (although it does not identify the two), the results of conscience have more than personal authority. What individuals propose for themselves as appropriate in certain circumstances can be endorsed as appropriate for others in similar circumstances. For example, deciding that lying about the whereabouts of an innocent victim to a persecutor intent on harm is the correct thing to do can be advocated as the appropriate response for others in similar circumstances. To be sure, one's own moral reasoning has special connection to one's own actions, but this special connection does not require one to think that the dictates of one's conscience are appropriate only for oneself. In fact, the whole enterprise of instilling the conventional conscience in children and the very idea that people learn morally through imitation suggest that dictates of conscience can have more than exclusively personal application.

Finally, there is an intuitive aspect to conscience that also needs to be emphasized. We are often faced with situations in which we have time to deliberate about the situation and we are able to weigh the ways different solutions may move us to our ultimate goals, but often we do not have the luxury to so deliberate. Faced with the need for an immediate response— Should I give money to this person on the street or should I ignore her—we often need to rely on conscious principles we have adopted that generally lead us to our ultimate goals. If our experience has shown that acts of mercy sometimes benefit others and always reinforce positive character traits in ourselves, we act accordingly in situations. Ideally, we have formulated these rules from experience and practiced them so well that they are practically unconscious assumptions in our behaviors. In this case, we immediately act in accordance with our rules, for we have developed the habit of so acting. We have trained ourselves to act immediately in accord with what we have deemed in times of more reflection to lead us to our ultimate goals. At this point, we are not acting so much on the rules of conscience as acting according to the habits we have developed from conscience. As Aquinas suggests, immediate action may involve how the situation is perceived. With proper habits, we develop the ability to evaluate a situation correctly and act in the way that best leads us to our ultimate goals. This is, however, one of the areas where conscience and the virtues are closely connected. So the view of conscience as a relational entity, tied to the cognitive, emotional, and conative aspects of a moral agent and connected to our pursuit of our ultimate goals, has brought us to the relation between conscience and the virtues.

PART THREE

CONSCIENCE AS A KEY
TO VIRTUE ETHICS

T E N

· ·

CONSCIENCE AMONG THE VIRTUE ETHICISTS

It is by now a commonplace to remark that, among philosophers, there has been during the last twenty years a resurgence of interest in the virtues.[1] To be sure, many more articles and books espousing either a deontological or a consequentialist ethics are still being written than ones espousing a virtue ethics, yet the marked renewal of interest is undeniable. Many trace the renewal to Prichard's essay "Does Moral Philosophy Rest on a Mistake?"[2] but the scarcity of work on the virtues between 1912 and the 1960s suggests

1. Among those who claim this are John McDowell in "Virtue and Reason" (*The Monist* 62 [July 1979]: 331–50); Gregory E. Pence in "Recent Work on Virtues" (*American Philosophical Quarterly* 21 [1984]: 281–96); Gregory Trianosky in "What Is Virtue Ethics All About?" (*American Philosophical Quarterly* 27 [1990]: 335–44); and Robert B. Kruschwity and Robert C. Roberts in *The Virtues: Contemporary Essays on Moral Character* (Belmont, Calif.: Wordsworth, 1987).
2. Published in *Mind* (1912): 21–37.

more recent sources. Anscombe's "Modern Moral Philosophy" and Von
Wright's *The Varieties of Goodness* seem more likely sources of recent interest.[3]
But most people would regard Alasdair MacIntyre's work as playing a key
role in the revival of virtue ethics. Odd as it may seem, however, MacIntyre's influence, while immense, occurs in spite of the intellectual project he
is engaged in.

MacIntyre and the Virtues

In 1981, Alasdair MacIntyre published his remarkable book *After Virtue*.[4] Offering an analysis and critique of the reigning contemporary moral theory—
liberalism—the book generated a number of reactions. Some people questioned just what kind of book it was, because it blurs the distinction between philosophy and history.[5] Others wondered about the correctness of
MacIntyre's account of the virtues.[6] Still others wondered at MacIntyre's
account of how easily the Aristotelian tradition of the virtues entered into
the developing Christian tradition of the Latin West.[7] The second edition of
After Virtue, published in 1984, responded to these reactions and offered a
promissory note that a forthcoming volume would further MacIntyre's intellectual project. The promissory note was paid off in 1988 with the publication of *Whose Justice? Which Rationality?*[8] An added bonus was the publication
of *Three Rival Theories of Enquiry: Geneology, Encyclopedia, Tradition* in 1990.[9]

Although *After Virtue* struck a resonating chord among ethicists interested
in the role of the virtues in ethics, MacIntyre wrote in his preface to *Whose
Justice? Which Rationality?* that "this enabled me to respond to another lacuna
in *After Virtue*, one emphasized by more than one critic who misrepresented
that book as a defense of 'a morality of the virtues' as an alternative to a

---

3. G. E. M. Anscombe, "Modern Moral Philosophy," originally published in *Philosophy* 33 (January 1958): 1–19. Reprinted in *The Collected Papers of G. E. M. Anscombe, Vol. I: Ethics, Religion, and Politics*
(Minneapolis: University of Minnesota Press, 1981), 26–42; George Henrik Von Wright, *The Varieties of Goodness* (London: Routledge and Kegan Paul, 1963).

4. *After Virtue* (Notre Dame: University of Notre Dame Press, 1st ed. 1981, 2d ed. 1984). All
subsequent references to the work are to the second edition.

5. See MacIntyre's presentation of William K. Frankena's remarks in *After Virtue*, 265.

6. See MacIntyre's presentation of Samuel Scheffler's remarks in *After Virtue*, 272.

7. See MacIntyre's presentation of Jeffrey Stout's remarks in *After Virtue*, 278.

8. *Whose Justice? Which Rationality?* (Notre Dame: University of Notre Dame Press, 1988).

9. *Three Rival Theories of Enquiry: Encyclopedia, Geneology, Tradition* (Notre Dame: University of Notre Dame Press, 1990).

'morality of rules.'"[10] This comment reveals a remarkable aspect of MacIntyre's tripartite intellectual project: It is not chiefly concerned with the virtues in the same sense that classical and medieval proponents of the virtue tradition were concerned with them. In fact, the main focus of MacIntyre's project is on the rationality and commensurability of traditions. This emphasis comes to the fore in *Whose Justice? Which Rationality?* as well as in *Three Rival Theories.* The virtues—and the virtue tradition in ethics—have never been MacIntyre's principal interest. Even *After Virtue* was intended more to show the poverty of modern-day liberalism (and Marxism; see page x of *After Virtue,* 2d ed.) than to resuscitate the tradition of the virtues. Yet MacIntyre did stimulate interest in the virtues and the virtue tradition in ethics, and he offered many illuminating comments about the nature of the virtues. Perhaps not surprisingly, he has little to say about conscience and its relation to the virtues.

MacIntyre's most detailed discussion of the virtues is to be found in chapters 10 through 15 of *After Virtue.* There, he traces the development of the virtues in the "heroic societies" of Greece through the role of the virtues in Athens, Aristotle's thought, and the medieval period. He concludes with an analysis of the nature of the virtues and their necessary embedding in a moral tradition.

His discussion of the virtues begins with the critical observation: "In all those cultures, Greek, medieval, or Renaissance, where moral thinking and action is structured according to some version of the scheme that I have called classical, the chief means of moral education is the telling of stories" (121). The emphasis on story (or narrative) forms a critical part of MacIntyre's view of the virtues. The stories of a culture are the chief means for moral instruction in societies. Through them, roles and statuses are defined, and the framework holding the society together is communicated. Whereas people in a heroic society are defined as the roles they play in society, even in a more individualistic society a person is seen in terms of his or her role (122, 129).

A culture's stories also portray the values of the culture and point toward the goals of the society. MacIntyre sees these goals as important. Without them, individual actions lack intelligibility (210). Unless we know the context of an individual's action and its place in an individual's overall life, we cannot really understand the action (204f.). The simple act of gardening, for example, needs to be placed within the story of an individual's life before it

10. *Whose Justice? Which Rationality?* ix.

is seen as a form of exercise, as an expression of aesthetic activity, as a way of pleasing one's spouse, and so on.[11] Moreover, the intelligibility of the story of one's life, which is formed in part through interactions with the lives of others, needs to be understood in the context of the aims and assumptions of one's own society. Giving up a satisfying career in a metropolitan area to resettle near one's parents as they become less able to care for themselves can be seen as part of filial duty or as an exercise in self-sacrifice; it all depends on the society one inhabits.

For MacIntyre, then, an individual at any one time is a moment in a complex story that is a small part of the ever more complex story of a society. This view informs his account of the virtues. According to MacIntyre: "A virtue is an acquired human quality the possession and exercise of which tends to enable us to achieve those goods which are internal to practices and the lack of which effectively prevents us from achieving any such goods" (191). Although the idea that virtues are qualities or states of an agent acquired through the practice of certain actions is widely emphasized in the literature on the virtues, MacIntyre's comments on practices need to be highlighted. MacIntyre defines a practice as "any coherent and complex form of socially established cooperative human activity through which goods internal to that form of activity are realized in the course of trying to achieve those standards of excellence which are appropriate to, and partially definitive of, that form of activity, with the result that human powers to achieve excellence, and human conceptions of the ends and goods involved, are systematically extended" (187). Clearly, given this notion of a practice, not every repeated activity constitutes one. MacIntyre, in fact, tells us that tick tack toe, throwing a football with skill, bricklaying, and planting turnips are not practices. Chess, the game of football, architecture, and farming, however, are. One might disagree with MacIntyre about his lists, but his contrast is clear. Bricklaying, throwing a football, and planting turnips are parts of practices (home construction, football, farming), but they are not themselves practices. The action of bricklaying finds intelligibility in a larger context—the practice of home construction—but is not intelligible on its own. Tick tack toe is, on the one hand, a game, but, on the other hand, it is a very limited one with little ingenuity and skill required; it lacks complexity. One quickly exhausts its possibilities, whereas the possibilities of football are much greater in number. Perhaps more important, with its need for coordination among players, development of physical stamina, and

---

11. Ibid., 207, for this example.

elaborate, if often flawed, offensive and defensive strategies, the practice of football requires players, coaches, and spectators to develop skills that can apply to other practices and the general pursuit of the goods of the society. To understand this point, we need to understand MacIntyre's contrast between goods internal to a practice and goods external to a practice. To illustrate the difference, MacIntyre tells the story of teaching a child to play chess (188). He offers the child fifty cents worth of candy to play chess once a week. Moreover, he promises the child another fifty cents worth of candy if the child can win the game. The child is motivated to get as much candy as possible and does what is necessary to get it. Getting candy, however, is not part of chess; at best, it is an external reward for playing chess. Certain highly particular "analytical skill[s], strategic imagination, and competitive intensity" are intrinsic to chess and are necessary for winning (188). These are the internal goods for chess whereas getting candy is an external good. Although the internal goods of chess can be got only by engaging in chess, the skills developed are useful beyond playing chess. Employing strategies, focusing attention, and mastering rules are all skills that help players function successfully in their society. If an activity is to be understood as a practice, the skills of the activity (its internal goods) must help agents to achieve the goals of their own society.

The importance of a society's goals for MacIntyre's analysis of the virtues thus emerges. Only if a society has such goals—perhaps best expressed as its notion of what the good is for human beings—can the society be seen as morally coherent. Moreover, the intelligibility of the actions of agents in a society depends on the existence of societal goals, and only with such goals can there be a sense of a society's virtues. MacIntyre usually talks about the goals of a society in terms of what he calls a "moral tradition." In fact, much of MacIntyre's tripartite intellectual project is an investigation of different moral traditions: heroic, Aristotelian, medieval, Scottish Enlightenment—to name a few. In *After Virtue*, MacIntyre examines certain moral traditions and offers a core account of the concept of a virtue in an attempt to argue that modern liberalism is not a moral tradition at all:

> What is it in the account which I am about to give which provides in a similar way the necessary background against which the concept of a virtue has to be made intelligible? It is in answering this question that the complex, historical, multi-layered character of the core concept of virtue becomes clear. For there are no less than three stages in the logical development of the concept which have to be identi-

fied in order, if the core conception of a virtue is to be understood, and each of these stages has its own conceptual background. The first stage requires a background account of what I shall call a practice, the second an account of what I have already characterized as the narrative order of a single human life, and the third an account a good deal fuller than I have given up to now of what constitutes a moral tradition. Each later stage presupposes the earlier, but not vice versa. Each earlier stage is both modified by and reinterpreted in the light of, but also provides an essential constituent of each later stage. The progress in the development of the concept is closely related to, although it does not recapitulate in any straightforward way, the history of the tradition of which it forms the core. (186–87)

Based on what MacIntyre says about practices, narrative, and moral tradition, this summary of the core account of the virtues is somewhat misleading. Given how he defines 'practice,' the notion is more than "modified by and reinterpreted in the light of" a personal narrative and a moral tradition; it requires these notions to distinguish a practice from some merely repeated activity. But this is of minor concern, for the implicit mutual dependence of the three notions—practice, narrative, moral tradition—seems no more viciously circular than the view that one needs to possess all the virtues to have any one that is stressed in the traditional account of the virtues.

In elaboration of his position, MacIntyre emphasizes the connection between his core account of the virtues and Aristotle's analyses of them (196f.). First, his account, like Aristotle's, is teleological in its emphasis that the virtues are understood as the practices leading to the goal of achieving the goods of the society. This adherence to teleology is not, however, tied to "an allegiance to Aristotle's metaphysical biology." Moreover, MacIntyre's account is not tied to the notion that there is only one *telos*, one ultimate good, for a society. In fact, the account suggests that a society might have a plurality of goals and that such plurality can partially account for conflicts in modern societies. Second, like Aristotle's account of the virtues, MacIntyre's account emphasizes "voluntariness, the distinction between the intellectual virtues and the virtues of character, the relationship of both to natural abilities and to the passions and the structure of practical reasoning" (197). Indeed, *Whose Justice? Which Rationality?* analyzes the relations between various moral traditions and their conceptions of practical reason. Third, MacIntyre's account accommodates an Aristotelian view of pleasure and enjoyment. Achievement of the internal goods of the practices associated with the virtues is pleasurable for the virtuous agent. Such pleasure is not the goal of the activity—the societal goods are instead—but such pleasure makes the performance of the virtues easier and more desirable. Fourth and finally, MacIntyre's account, like Aristotle's, links evaluation and explanation in a special way: Part of the evaluation of any action is to explain to what extent the action achieves or fails to achieve the goals of society (199).

As we have seen, MacIntyre's position contrasts with Aristotle's in accommodating a plurality of societal goods; yet there is a type of unity to the goods of societies MacIntyre allows: "[T]he good life for man is the life spent in seeking for the good life for man" (219). For MacIntyre, the unity of any moral tradition—especially those traditions that embody a plurality of societal goods—is in part constituted by the commitment of participants in the society to try to determine what the good for man is. Although the process may result in very different conceptions of the final good for man, all are united in striving for the conception of the good, which must, of course, be in accord with the moral presuppositions of a society. Aristotle also emphasized the striving for the good of men, but he had a detailed view of what the good was and saw variation only in the ways different men go about achieving this good. MacIntyre allows not only the difference in ways of achieving the goals, but also that there is a plurality of goals.

In a society that is unified in part by the commitment of its members to the quest for what the good of man is, the role of the virtues must be stressed: "The virtues therefore are to be understood as those dispositions which will not only sustain practices and enable us to achieve the goods internal to practices, but which will also sustain us in the relevant kind of quest for the good, by enabling us to overcome the harms, dangers, temptations, and distractions which we encounter, and which will furnish us with increasing self-knowledge and increasing knowledge of the good" (219). So the virtues become the devices by which each person strives toward the goods of society. In themselves, the virtues give the moral agent insight into the good pursued; yet, they also provide, through their internal goods, the skills to pursue the good wherever the opportunity presents itself (220). MacIntyre emphasizes that an individual qua individual is not able to seek the good, and he emphasizes, as we have seen, the absolute need for an individual pursuing a good to be embedded in a moral tradition, but he does not discuss connections between the moral tradition and the role of conscience in preserving it. One searches in vain for a discussion of conscience in *After Virtue*. In *Whose Justice? Which Rationality?* MacIntyre discusses the roles of conscience and synderesis in Aquinas's thought and emphasizes their connection with the virtue of prudence.[12] In his discussion of Hutcheson, the pillar of the Scottish Enlightenment, he identifies conscience with moral sense, which "makes us immediately aware of its particular objects, objects which elicit a specific type of approval or disapproval" (271). Apparently, MacIntyre does not regard conscience as an important part of moral traditions. Needless to say, this is a surprising lacuna because, as we have seen, the formation of conscience is inseparably linked to the moral tradition of a particular society, and the guidance of conscience plays an important role in the activities of moral agents striving toward the perceived goods of a society.

Although it is possible that MacIntyre does not believe that conscience can play such roles in a moral tradition, it is more likely that this is a topic MacIntyre simply does not address. This seems even more likely once one understands that, despite its importance, MacIntyre's discussion of the virtues in his tripartite intellectual project is subordinate to his chief interest: discussion of the incommensurability of moral traditions. His emphasis is displayed most prominently in chapters 18 and 19 of *Whose Justice? Which Rationality?* and in *Three Rival Versions of Moral Enquiry*.

In these works, he is at pains to argue against Donald Davidson that there is a problem about incommensurability among conceptual schemes.[13] This is crucial because he wants to understand the present state of moral discourse as an inheritance of the conflicts between two rival schemes of moral inquiry: the Encyclopedist and the Geneologist. The Encyclopedic tradition, inheritor of the Enlightenment (and especially the Scottish Enlightenment), holds to a universalistic account of humankind and rationality. It holds that there is an unvarying truth that is common to all societies, and the claims of a society must be judged relative to this standard. The Geneologic tradition rejects such universalism as a fiction. There are no eternal truths. Truth is relative to the various societies and their competing systems of rationality.[14]

As a way of resolving the conflict between these two traditions, MacIntyre presents his notion of "Tradition," which is really Thomism. According to MacIntyre, Thomism in the Middle Ages bridged the gap between the incommensurable frameworks of Augustinianism and Aristotelianism. Likewise, in the present, Thomism offers a hoped-for reconciliation between the Encyclopedists and Geneologists:

---

12. *Whose Justice? Which Rationality?* 183f.
13. *Three Rival Theories*, 114f., and *Whose Justice? Which Rationality?* 370f.
14. See MacIntyre's remarks in *After Virtue*, 99f.

Thomism then confronts both the substantive claims of the late nineteenth-century encyclopedists and of its twentieth-century heirs and the subversive claims of geneology with this commitment, one which opens it up to radical judgments of its own success or failure, one by which it exhibits the kinds of intellectual vulnerability which is the mark of all worthwhile theorizing. And since it is with the specifically moral claims of encyclopedists, of geneology, and of Thomistic tradition that I am concerned in these lectures, what is now required is first to specify more precisely how both moral enquiry and the form of the moral life are to be understood within the Thomistic scheme and what the relationship of that understanding to the claims of encyclopaedia and geneology has turned out to be.[15]

But MacIntyre does not really offer a reconciliation between Encyclopedists and Geneologists through Thomism. Rather, in the last chapter of *Three Rival Theories*, he offers a place and a means of reconciliation. The place is the university, reconceived on the lines of the thirteenth-century University of Paris where rival traditions were openly discussed and debated. The means is the lecture, which can be a device to articulate a way of moral inquiry but can also serve as a means for those not in a particular tradition to participate imaginatively in the tradition and bring new lessons to their own traditions. With a place and a means, incommensurable traditions can meet (as they did in the thirteenth century), and a new synthesis that embraces rival traditions and is able to explain the successes and failures of other traditions can emerge. Although the new synthesis may not be Thomism by some other name, it at least shares the historically crucial role MacIntyre attributes to Aquinas. To paraphrase the ending of *After Virtue*, we are not waiting for Godot or even a very different Saint Benedict; we await a new Thomas, master of a truly open university.[16]

Yet, we are far afield of the virtues. To be sure, MacIntyre sees the virtues as especially potent entries into any moral tradition. In fact, to be part of a moral tradition is to have embraced the particular tradition's reading of the virtues. But talk of virtues in MacIntyre's project has been eclipsed by issues of the incommensurability of traditions. It is hardly surprising that MacIntyre pays little attention to conscience and its role in cultivation and preservation of the virtues.

15. *Three Rival Theories*, 125–26.
16. Compare *After Virtue*, 125. For a fuller account of MacIntyre's intellectual project, see Appendix.

Other Virtue Theorists

Even if MacIntyre fails to discuss conscience, it is of course possible that conscience is treated by other virtue ethicists. It is impossible to discuss in detail all the recent work of virtue theorists, but two recent surveys of literature on the virtues provide overviews of what work has been done. As we shall see, it is clear that virtue theorists have neglected issues concerned with conscience.[17]

Gregory E. Pence's "Recent Work on Virtues" offers both a chronological review of significant work on the virtues and a categorization of this literature into work emphasizing that virtues "can be discussed in isolation as individual traits" and work discussing virtues "more broadly as social qualities."[18] Pence focuses on James Wallace and Alasdair MacIntyre as offering a "social sense" view of the virtues. In his discussion of Wallace's work, Pence describes him as a heretic who started out with Foot and MacIntyre, thinking that if he concentrated on character traits, he could dispense with the ideas of moral rules or laws and avoid the familiar problem about the origin, nature, and authority of such rules (282). This issue—whether virtue ethics operates independently of moral rules and laws or in some conjunction with them—is in fact a major concern in the literature on the virtues. Wallace's linking of the virtues with moral rules is by no means the only view among virtue theorists. As we shall see, many virtue theorists offer virtue ethics as an alternative to moral rules and laws.

Pence regards MacIntyre as "the most prominent philosopher of the virtues in a social sense" (283). Yet he criticizes MacIntyre's notion of a 'practice,' which is key to MacIntyre's understanding of the virtues, as "excessively abstract, vague, and different from MacIntyre's previous usage of that term" (283). He also says that *After Virtue does not provide a modern detailed conception of virtues, but it does argue for the possibility of doing so"* (284). As we have seen, there is much to this accusation about the incompleteness of MacIntyre's work.

Pence presents G. H. Von Wright as one of the most significant theorists who emphasize virtues as individual traits. Von Wright's influence extends to many, including Philippa Foot (285). Rejecting the idea that virtues are dispositions toward act-categories, Von Wright defends the view that virtues

---

17. In their very useful bibliography at the end of *The Virtue: Contemporary Essays on Moral Character,* Kruschwitz and Roberts list only ten articles on the relation of conscience to the virtues (263). None of these articles attempts any systematic discussion of the relations to be found.

18. Published in *American Philosophical Quarterly* 21, 4 (1984): 281.

are inward traits depending on knowledge. Overlying Von Wright's analysis of the virtues is his general view that a specific virtue always masters the effects of a specific passion. This view of virtues as principally restraints on the passions has been criticized by many as inadequate, because it fails to account for virtues like prudence that are not tied to one single passion (286). Urmson's somewhat different view, linking specific virtues to the "field" of a specific emotion, also runs afoul of a similar objection that very few virtues are linked to specific emotions (286).

In line with much recent work on virtues, which focuses on the analysis of specific virtues, Pence devotes a considerable part of his discussion to the virtue of courage. He describes it as "a touchstone because: it is a self-regarding virtue; it can be an other-regarding virtue; it is included in all theories of virtues; and it is a virtue in any society or historical period" (287). Geach's and Foot's views of courage (and, by implication, their general view of the virtues) are criticized for adhering strongly to a unity of the virtues view, which results in labeling a virtue like courage when used for evil ends as not a virtue at all. At the root of the difficulty is the circularity of construing virtues in terms of good desires and actions (288). Pence also discusses views on courage offered by Seeskin, Mackie, Wallace, Hunt, Pears, and Dent and ends his comments with the question of whether courage is so connected to overcoming fear that one who does not have fear could not be considered courageous.

Pence goes on to consider recent work on virtues like sympathy, compassion, generosity, tolerance, loyalty, and wisdom. He concludes in this manner:

> Some conclusions: a significant amount of material has been written about virtues, and they've become important topics in contemporary philosophy. Analysis of virtues will likely continue, but at a more sophisticated level. Some early claims about virtues appear to have been exaggerated. The arguments that *virtues* can replace *virtue* have not appeared (this problem is especially acute if justice is considered only as a virtue). Moreover, searching for a master virtue, or an essence of all virtues, appears quixotic. Differing historical origins, as well as differing reasons for valuing traits, preclude a common *eidos* for all virtues. At best, we have a family resemblance here.
>
> There is certainly need for more analysis of traits like loyalty, which have been largely neglected, and which figure importantly in daily life. One might also mention virtues like integrity, veracity

(commonly misnamed "honesty"), self-insight, friendship, and love. Two of the most successful works—MacIntyre (1981) and Wallace (1978)—*systematically* analyzed virtues, and such an approach often has the most power. More work is needed in understanding how different kinds of systems support different kinds of virtues and vices. Finally, understanding the lack or failure of a virtue appears to be a promising method of analysis for all virtues. This is especially helpful in understanding courage, compassion, wisdom, and temperance. (294–95)

There are some significant points to be noticed in this summary. First, there is little emphasis on questions about the development of the virtues, and, specifically, there is no indication of the role conscience might play in the development and functioning of the virtues. Second, emphasis is placed on the need for discussion of specific virtues rather than on the need to clarify general issues about the virtues. Finally, there is an indication that more sophisticated analyses of virtues need to be provided. It is to this need that Gregory Trianosky addresses himself in "What Is Virtue Ethics All About?"[19]

Trianosky characterizes Pence's article as "less systematic and more oriented toward thumbnail sketches of the canonical texts."[20] He tries to offer a much more systematic treatment of recent literature in two different, but related, ways. In the first place, he offers what he takes to be a uniting thread in the literature:

Interestingly, not all those who are engaged in the new investigations of virtue agree in endorsing an *ethics of virtue,* or for that matter any single substantive position. Instead concentration on the virtues has served as a rallying point for many writers opposed in different ways to the main tendencies of post–eighteenth-century thinking in ethics. In particular, what unifies recent work on the virtues is its opposition to various central elements of a view which I will call neo-Kantianism. (335)

Trianosky supports this characterization of recent literature on the virtues as reactive by providing nine central theses of neo-Kantianism, which I sum-

19. Published in *American Philosophical Quarterly* 27, 4 (1990).
20. "What Is Virtue Ethics All About?" 343, note 1.

marize as (1) emphasis on rightness and obligation; (2) emphasis on rightness of actions; (3) emphasis on general rules of right action; (4) emphasis on the universality of moral judgments; (5) rejection of grounding morality in a human good independent of morality; (6) emphasis on moral judgments as categorical imperatives; (7) rejection of the role of desire and emotions in the moral considerations of agents; (8) emphasis that truly virtuous agents must consider the requirements of basic moral judgments in their actions; (9) emphasis that a trait is virtuous in relation to right action (335). Having specified these nine theses, he then looks at the recent literature on the virtues in terms of which of these claims is rejected.

Trianosky also provides a second, related organizing strategy:

> I suggest that we may more perspicuously divide ethical theories along two distinct and orthogonal lines. First, they may be divided into the ethics of virtue and the ethics of duty in the manner indicated at the outset. This distinction divides ethical theories on the question of what sort of *moral* judgments they take to be basic. Next, each of these ethics may take either a teleological or a non-teleological, "deontological," form. This second distinction divides ethical theories on the question of whether they take the basic moral judgments themselves to be autonomous or derivative. Pure *teleological* theories hold that basic moral judgments are to be grounded on some account of the good, where the good is conceived as describable *independently of any reference either to moral rightness or to virtue:* pleasure, the satisfaction of desire, or the obtaining of various intrinsically desirable states of affairs, for example. Pure teleological theories deny that ethics is autonomous because they hold that all judgments about moral value, if I may use this as a generic term for rightness and moral virtue, must ultimately be grounded in this way on judgments about non-moral value. Non-teleological or "deontological" theories disagree, holding instead that basic moral judgments, whether about virtue or about duty, are not grounded on considerations about the (non-moral) good. In this way pure non-teleological theories hold that moral value is autonomous, or not dependent for its philosophical justification on any claims about non-moral value (Scanlon 1982). [Thesis] (5), one of the central propositions of neo-Kantian ethics, embodies the non-teleological claim, albeit in a comparatively weak form. So, as I will indicate below, do the writings of certain virtue theorists. (338)

Of significance for present purposes is Trianosky's division of literature on virtues into "teleological" and "non-teleological" ("deontological"). He goes on to elaborate on nonteleological virtue theories:

> Non-teleological ethics of virtue are theories which maintain against all forms of utilitarianism that the basic judgments about virtuous traits *can* be grounded without appeal to any independently-formulated account of the good. Like the familiar deontological views in the ethics of duty, these theories hold that basic moral judgments, however conceived, may be justified *autonomously*. The most familiar non-teleological theories are perfectionist ones like Aristotle's, on which virtue is a constitutive element (if not the central element) of the human good rather than merely a means, however indispensable, to its attainment (Lamore 1987, 30–36). (338)

Aristotle is a nonteleological (deontological) virtue theorist because *eudaemonia* is just the practice of the virtues; there is not some good over and above their practice that human agents aim toward. Obviously, teleological virtue theorists think that a notion of the good that human agents aim at can be formulated as independent of moral virtue (337). Presumably, teleological virtue theorists see practice of the virtues as leading to some good that is independent of the virtues and certainly does not consist in the practice of the virtues. In fact, Trianosky says, many of the most influential virtue theorists are teleological theorists. A case in point is Von Wright, who looks on virtues as "in the service of the good of man" (338).

Trianosky believes that "despite the great deal of work that remains to be done on them, non-teleological ethics of virtue offer important advantages over any other view" (339). In particular, a nonteleological view can combine the Kantian intuition that "morality is autonomous" and the utilitarian view that "morality is essentially connected with the human good." Although Trianosky does not say this specifically, a nonteleological virtue ethics can combine these two intuitions by seeing the exercise of the virtues as the human good (as did Aristotle). Such a view considers morality as consisting in the cultivation of the virtues (and thus ensures its autonomy) but sees the goal of morality (the human good) as connected with (being identical to) the exercise of the virtues. Trianosky suggests that Anscombe, Geach, Wallace, and MacIntyre should be numbered among the nonteleological virtue theorists.

Perhaps the most important aspect of Trianosky's distinction between teleological and nonteleological virtue ethics is to bring forth the important question of what is the relation between the human good and the virtues. Is the relation one of identity, where the human good is to be seen as identical to the exercise of the virtues, or is it one of means, where possession and exercise of the virtues are means to the attainment of the human good, which does not consist solely in the exercise of the virtues? Of course, the contrast may be great or small depending on how much of the human good consists in the exercise of the virtue. If it constitutes a small part of the human good, the contrast is great. If it constitutes a major portion of the good, the contrast is small.

Despite the care Trianosky takes to contrast virtue ethics with duty ethics, he believes that most virtue ethicists still "operate within a framework of duty" (340). This seems particularly true of the teleological virtue ethicists, who see the virtues as means to either the right or some human good. But it also seems true by reason of the common tendency of recent literature on the virtues to be reactive to neo-Kantianism and its emphases. Most recent literature on the virtues does not provide a pure virtue ethics so much as a correction to duty ethics that emphasizes the importance of the virtues. The usual strategy is to press some failing of duty ethics—its focus on extreme cases; its failure to provide more than simplistic universal rules to determine how to behave in particular situations; its failure to resolve moral dilemmas—and to argue that an ethics of duty must be supplemented by an ethics of virtue (341f.). The extreme here is, of course, to cast virtues as useful in performing one's duties, as did Kant. But most virtue ethicists avoid this position and argue for a fuller role for the virtues. Some authors, MacIntyre for example, want to place issues about the virtues in the context of a morality of rules and laws, but there are various strategies to be found.[21] Needless to say, the relation between the moral rules implicit in an ethics of duty and a virtue ethics is an important issue to explore. It is significant to note, however, that the work done here usually takes a metaethical turn, with emphasis on which areas of moral decision should be the province of duty ethics and which the province of virtue ethics. Little, if any, attention is paid to the development of virtues through the framework of a duty ethics. At best, authorities comment that requisite virtues must be developed to play their role in a mixed virtue-duty ethics. The mechanics are not

---

21. Ibid., 341–42. The work of Pincoffs, Cua, and Moravscik is mentioned.

focused on or are passed on to psychologists or theorists of education for articulation.[22] This is a far cry from the concerns of Plato and Aristotle, who saw education in the virtues as the most important aspect of their ethics of virtue.

Given the neglect of topics about the development of the virtues, it is hardly surprising that little attention is paid to issues of the relation between conscience and the virtues. It probably goes without saying that the general lack of interest in conscience among contemporary philosophers discussed in the previous chapters partially explains the neglect. Indeed, following Ryle, discussions that would link conscience and the virtues are linked to the relation between virtues and conscientiousness. An example here is Wallace's *Virtues and Vices*. Chapter 4 of the work is devoted to 'conscientiousness,' which is defined as "traits of character that focus in a certain way upon the observance of forms of behavior" (90). Examples of such traits are honesty, fairness, truthfulness, and being a person of one's word. Wallace regards these as internal traits, connected to a sense of duty or obligation. His main concerns in the chapter are to describe the traits, balance the seeming paradox that the traits both intrinsically motivate a person and express what is necessary for the person to do, and show how these internal traits play a social role. It is revealing that Wallace quotes a passage from *Bleak House* describing (in his view) a primitive stage of conscientiousness in which the character Sir Leicester Dedlock talks about a man of "strict conscience" (93). Wallace does not mention conscience anywhere else in his discussion of conscientiousness, even though Charles Dickens has made the identification between conscience and the phenomenon Wallace analyzes.

Review of MacIntyre's work and of recent canonical texts on the virtues written in the last twenty years indicates that conscience has been a neglected topic among virtue theorists. Yet, I argue in the next chapter that the topic should not be neglected. To do this, I must turn to a recently published article by Rosalind Hursthouse and to Michael Slote's book *From Morality to Virtue*.

---

22. Michael Slote discusses moral education in his *From Morality to Virtue* (Oxford: Oxford University Press, 1992), 258f.; and William Wallace comments on moral education in his *Virtues and Vices* (Ithaca: Cornell University Press, 1978), 52f.

ELEVEN

CONSCIENCE *and* VIRTUE ETHICS

Authorities have offered numerous criticisms of a pure virtue ethics. Among the most detailed is Robert B. Louden's "On Some Vices of Virtue Ethics."[1] In Louden's eyes, a pure virtue ethics is reductionistic:

> In other words, conceptual reductionism is at work in virtue ethics too. Just as its utilitarian and deontological competitors begin with primitive concepts of the good state of affairs and the intrinsically right action respectively and then derive secondary concepts out of their starting points, so virtue ethics, beginning with a root conception of the morally good person, proceeds to introduce a different set of secondary concepts, which are defined in terms of their relationship to the primitive element. Though the ordering of primitive

1. Published in *American Philosophical Quarterly* 21, 3 (1984).

and derivatives differs in each case, the overall strategy remains the same.[2]

Given this basic orientation, Louden claims that it is clear that the main focus of virtue ethics is on the question of what sort of person one should be. This attitude necessarily emphasizes long-term patterns of action and de-emphasizes particular actions. But this means that in a pure virtue ethics there can be no procedure for making practical decisions. No answer can be provided for a particular person asking what ought to be done in a particular circumstance. At best, advice like "Do what the virtuous person would do" is given, but, because a virtuous person does not typically refer to rules or principles for an action that another might employ in making decisions, the advice is not useful.[3]

According to Louden, there are a number of intrinsic difficulties in making the morally good person the basis of a virtue ethics. First, it is not clear how one identifies a morally good person whom one wants to emulate. Although the close-knit society of Aristotle's Athens might have provided agreed-on paradigms of morally good persons, such agreement is unlikely in pluralistic modern societies, where there is a multiplicity of standards of virtues, which are often at odds. Moreover, must one assume that a morally good person always does what is morally right in every circumstance? If not, then the action of a morally good person in some circumstance might not be what one should do if one wishes to become virtuous. Finally, it appears that even a virtuous person may fail to practice the virtues and may backslide, morally speaking.[4] Even if the previously virtuous person is self-deceived about the loss of virtue, so long as the person is held as an exemplar, there is danger that emulators will be misled in developing virtue.

Rather than dismiss virtue ethics because of these difficulties, Louden argues that an ethical theory combining both the ethics of virtue and the ethics of rules is to be desired. Presumably, the ethics of rules provides the emphasis on acts, which is often the most important practical issue for a moral agent, and the ethics of virtue provides the emphasis on the crucial long-term behavior issues. But Louden gives only a limited sketch of how this can be done.

Rosalind Hursthouse, one of the editors of a collection of essays in honor

2. "On Some Vices of Virtue Ethics," 228.
3. "On Some Vices of Virtue Ethics," 229.
4. "On Some Vices of Virtue Ethics," 231.

of Philippa Foot, has responded to Louden in her essay "Applying Virtue Ethics."[5] Toward the end of her article, Hursthouse comments: "I began this paper with the standard complaint against virtue ethics; that in some sense it cannot answer questions about real moral issues such as abortion or euthanasia. I have granted that in at least two senses that is true—it cannot resolve every dilemma into the right and the wrong, and it cannot render difficult matters of delicate judgement easy and obvious to the adolescent— but claimed in both cases that this is to its credit."[6] Part of her overall strategy in the essay is to argue that a pure virtue ethics answers ethical questions as well as we would want a theory to answer them. We should be suspicious of an ethical theory that produces an algorithm for all decisions in life. There are, after all, disagreements about moral issues among adherents of the same moral theory. Moreover, perplexing moral dilemmas by their nature do not allow one clear decision, and many allow more than one solution. To criticize virtue ethics for its failure to give a definite answer to all questions about behavior is obviously misguided. In fact, virtue ethics does better with situations in which there is no good answer than duty ethics does, according to Hursthouse.

It is also false to say that virtue ethicists do not provide rules of behavior. For example, faced with a particularly difficult issue, a virtue ethicist might well advise a person to "act honestly" or "not act cruelly." These are the general injunctions to cultivate the virtues and avoid vices, which behavior is key to developing into a morally good person. It seems inconsequential to object that these injunctions are too general to be of much use. Much of duty ethics consists of such general rules, after all. Nor is it helpful to point out that such an injunction as "act honestly" does not specify which acts are honest acts. No theory does that. We must rely on standards that are formed by the society we live in.[7] It is perhaps not easy to judge correctly in any particular controversial case, but it should not be a requirement of an ethical theory that it make truly difficult decisions easier.

Much of Hursthouse's article takes this tack of showing that virtue theory is as adequate as any other ethical theory, but she also offers another line of thought. Hursthouse thinks it is false to claim, as does Louden, that "virtue ethics maintains that the concept of the virtuous agent is the only piece of

5. In Rosalind Hursthouse, Gavin Lawrence, and Warren Quinn, eds., *Virtues and Reasons: Philippa Foot and Moral Theory: Essays in Honour of Philippa Foot* (Oxford: Clarendon Press, 1995).
6. In Hursthouse et al., eds., *Virtues and Reasons*, 73–74.
7. In Hursthouse et al., eds., *Virtues and Reasons*, 67–68. This is not precisely Hursthouse's position. She wishes to avoid the apparent relativism in the appeal to societal standards.

conceptual apparatus relevant to moral philosophy and that the theory promises to be able to give a reductive analysis of all our moral concepts in terms of the virtuous or vicious agent."[8] Virtue ethics can draw on such notions as a right, a good, or a benefit. Indeed, Aristotle himself connects the virtues with the good, and criticisms of Foot's virtue ethics that it provides nothing but commonsense observations indicate that virtue ethicists use notions other than the concept of a morally good person to ground their work. In fact, the notion of a morally good agent is connected with such notions: "For built into the theory is the claim that part of the virtuous person's practical wisdom is her knowledge, her correct appreciation, of what is truly good, and, indeed, of what is truly pleasant, truly advantageous, truly worthwhile, truly important, truly serious" (73). This should come as no surprise, Hursthouse offers in a comic vein. Would we, after all, listen to an individual (or a theory) who self-consciously announces that one of her characteristics is that she knows nothing about what is good, worthwhile, and so on and that such notions play no role in her moral advice (74)?

There is much to recommend in Hursthouse's essay, and she goes a considerable distance in showing the viability of a pure virtue ethics. But it is pure in the sense that it does not rely on some version of duty ethics. It is not pure in the sense that it is groundless, for it is obviously dependent on views about the right, the good, and so on. Where do these come from? In the heyday of conscience as a faculty, it surely would have been said that conscience is their source. Hursthouse seems to suggest that the society that an individual lives in plays an important role in agents' intuitions about the good, the right, and so on. But she is reluctant to embrace the cultural relativism that seems implicit in this view (67–68). She wishes to look at specifications of virtue as having no reference to culture and as being instead "a character trait that human beings, given their physical and psychological nature, need to flourish (or to do and fare well)—flourish in this world in which we inevitably find ourselves, not in the particular culture or society we happen to find ourselves in" (68). It seems, however, that the goal Hursthouse aims for might well be unachievable. If MacIntyre's views have merit, there is an inescapable relativism to the virtues if only because the narratives of societies, which are key to determining the goods that human beings in the societies strive for, differ considerably. Yet, if we put this issue about universal traits aside, Hursthouse is still faced with the ques-

---

8. In Hursthouse et al., eds., *Virtues and Reasons*, 72.

tion of how societal notions of the good, the right, and so on become part of the resources moral agents draw on. Because she wishes to divorce a virtue ethics from an ethics of duty, she would not seek the source here. A far better place to seek the source would be conscience as I have presented it in this work. Indeed, as I have presented it, conscience is built in part from societal norms and definitions. And at the stage of the mature conscience, the individual functions in many ways similar to the virtuous agent proposed by virtue ethics. Hursthouse's defense of the viability of virtue ethics would thus be considerably strengthened by an appeal to the importance of conscience in forming morally good agents. A similar conclusion is reached when we look at the recent work of Michael Slote.

According to Michael Slote in *From Morality to Virtue*, what is missing in the contemporary interest in the virtues is "a specific enough foundational or non-derivative account of (the) virtue(s) to enable us to see how such a positive ethical conception fares against the standard conception of ethics— Kantianism, utilitarianism, common-sense moral intuitionism, for example— that represent the most obvious and inevitable competitors of any new and systematic ethics of virtue."[9] He proposes to offer the desired systematic account of the virtues, an account that "will discard specifically moral aretaic concepts in favor of 'neutral' aretaic concepts like admirability and (a) virtue" (p. xvi). Part of his motivation for formulating a virtue ethics is his view that Kantianism and commonsense moral intuitionism fail as moral theories in significant ways. Although both a virtue ethics (as he defines it) and a utilitarian theory avoid the failures of Kantianism and commonsense morality, virtue ethics (as he defines it) is superior to utilitarianism because it is eliminative of certain moral concepts linked to commonsense morality's failures while utilitarianism is only reductive of these concepts (p. xvii).

There are three areas of difficulty for commonsense morality: self-other asymmetries; moral luck; problematic deontological justification.[10] And a

9. *From Morality to Virtue* (Oxford: Oxford University Press, 1992), xiii.
10. Ibid., 4f. To substantiate his claims, Slote first argues that in commonsense morality, there is a bias toward the agent over others in regard to pursuing innocent projects and goods that are not productive of the greatest overall balance of good. Thus, commonsense morality allows an agent to pursue the piano rather than devote energy to becoming a research doctor who specializes in finding cures for infectious diseases. But this bias for the agent is in conflict with the favor displayed to others in agent-sacrificing situations. It is permitted, according to commonsense morality, for an agent to suffer pain or give up his or her life, but it is not permitted for an agent to cause others to suffer pain or give up their lives (4–5). Commonsense morality thus inconsistently treats agent-favoring and agent-sacrificing situations. The peculiar situation of the moral agent is even more emphasized when we call to mind the commonsense view that we have stronger obligations to

similar set of problems confronts Kantianism.[11] Slote concludes, on the basis
of these difficulties with Kantianism and commonsense morality, that neither ethical theory should be accepted. He also claims that a patchwork
combining the two suffers the same fate.[12] What remains as a workable theory, according to Slote, is either a virtue ethics or a utilitarian ethics. He

---

those near to us than to those distantly connected. A father, for example, has stronger obligations to
his family than he does to his neighbor, but stronger obligations to his neighbor than to a citizen of
another country, according to commonsense morality (17). But then it is very puzzling, following
out the logic of closeness relations, why one would have weaker obligations to oneself than to
others, a notion that seems implicit in agent-sacrificing situations.

Moreover, there seems to be an odd tension between rationality and morality in commonsense
morality. It is rational for agents to want to benefit themselves above all others in every situation;
however, commonsense morality suggests that often the morally proper thing to do is to neglect
one's interests for the interests of others. Yet, commonsense morality would in general hold that
morality must be rational (22f.).

Moving beyond issues concerned with self-other asymmetries, Slote goes on to argue that there
are a number of difficulties for commonsense morality in regard to "moral luck." In general, on a
commonsense view, the idea that "judgments of morally better and worse, or greater or less culpability or blameworthiness" are subject to luck or accident is repugnant (35). Yet, in specific cases,
moral luck does seem to temper the degree of praise or blame. That driving on the wrong side of
the road results in no injury is a matter of good luck, which the person who drives into another car
while on the wrong side of the road lacks. That a person accidentally fails to kill another (the gun
jams) is a matter of luck, but we hold an agent more blameworthy when he or she murders than
when he or she is "merely" guilty of attempted murder. (And the penalties under the law reflect this
because punishments also differ for murder and attempted murder.)

Finally, commonsense morality runs into problems of deontological consistency (37f.). Take, for
example, the deontological principle that one should not take an innocent life. Such a principle
does not allow the killing of an innocent to save the lives of five innocent people or to prevent the
killing of five innocent people by some other person, even though doing so will on the whole result
in a better outcome than if one does not kill the innocent. If asked to justify this view, the defenders
of commonsense morality "try to find some feature of violations of the restriction that is 'very bad
or has high disvalue' and that will allow them to say that it is because violations have this objection-
able feature that they are commonsensically forbidden" (38). Examples of violations include someone being used as a mere means or another's innocence being harmed by someone. Trying to
prevent such violations seems to provide a reason for not killing the single innocent when the other
five innocents will be killed as a result of an accident or a disease. But the strategy is unsuccessful
where the five innocents will be killed by some other person(s). The violations—whether someone
is used merely as an instrument or innocence is harmed—occur in such cases if one does not kill the
single innocent. Numerically, in fact, more violations occur if the innocent is not killed, and it is
difficult to see how commonsense morality would approve of allowing more rather than fewer
violations to occur in a moral situation. Commonsense morality requires agents to minimize the
number of violations, and this principle is at odds with the principle that one should not take the
life of an innocent: "So our common-sense thinking in this area is at odds with itself, is incoherent,
because the reasons it tends to offer in its own support actually tend to cast (further) doubt upon it"
(39).

11. *From Morality to Virtue*, 45f. According to Slote, it is most obvious that Kantianism runs into
problems of self-other asymmetry as it pertains to agent sacrifice. According to Kantianism, we are

argues that, finally, utilitarianism is not the best theory—because it is merely reductive and not eliminative of certain problematic moral notions found in commonsense morality and Kantianism—but he acknowledges an important aspect of utilitarianism that causes him to offer a version of virtue ethics based on certain aretaic notions that are not specifically moral. This aspect of utilitarianism is its emphasis on the moral quality of acts in isolation from the moral quality of agents.

According to Slote, "The idea of a virtue ethics is commonly regarded as involving two distinctive or essential elements. A virtue ethics in the fullest sense must treat aretaic notions (like 'good' or 'excellent') rather than deontic notions (like 'morally wrong,' 'ought,' 'right,' and 'obligation') as primary, and it must put a greater emphasis on the ethical assessment of agents and their (inner) motives and character traits than it puts on the evaluation of acts and choices" (89). For Slote, the second element is the most easily misused. Although Aristotle did not do it, virtue ethicists tend to see the ethical status of acts as entirely derivative of the traits and motives of individuals. Thus an act performed by a virtuous person is for that reason virtuous. Plato may have reasoned this way, but Aristotle did not.[13] According to Slote, because Aristotle believes that people who are not themselves virtuous or good can perform good or virtuous acts and the "virtuous person *sees* or *perceives* what is good or right or proper in any given situation," he believes that the ethical status of acts is not solely derived from the ethical

---

permitted (in fact, obligated) to deny ourselves happiness, but we cannot deny happiness to others. In fact, we must seek the happiness of others (11, 45). So in Kantianism, the moral agent is to treat him- or herself differently from the way he or she treats other moral agents. But if morality consists of categorical imperatives that are universal for all moral agents, it is difficult to see how a moral agent can morally treat him- or herself differently from the way he treats others. There is thus a deep inconsistency in Kantianism (46f.).

Kantianism's solution to the problem of moral luck is to allow luck or accident no role in assessing moral merit or culpability. But it does this only by connecting moral values to nonempirical facts of noumenally willing. Yet, according to Slote, the metaphysical presuppositions surrounding the existence of the noumenal and its separation from the phenomenal make this strategy highly suspect (46).

Moreover, it is not at all clear that Kantianism provides answers to the problem of deontological consistency pointed out for commonsense morality (46). For example, a categorical imperative not to take an innocent life seems to conflict with the categorical imperative to act so as to reduce the number of violations of moral worth.

12. *From Morality to Virtue*, 49f.

13. Ibid., 92: "If we leave aside Plato's mystical appeal to the latter [The Form of the Good] as a moral standard, then Plato (like Martineau) is saying (roughly) that whatever the virtuous or healthy person may do, her action will be right because of the kind of person it is done by." (But see a different assessment of Plato on p. 90.)

status of the agent. And Aristotle is right to do this, according to Slote, because it is crucial for an ethical theory that the ethical quality of acts not be derived solely from the ethical status of the agent.

Even though Slote admires Aristotle's virtue ethics, he departs from it principally because it is a moral theory rather than an ethical one. Aristotle's views are based on such moral notions as "the good," and, in his analysis of commonsense morality, Slote believes he has shown that self-other asymmetries are inextricably rooted in moral notions like the good. Any ethical system that is based on moral notions like the good necessarily contain problematic self-other asymmetries (30). Moreover, even Aristotle's notions of self-regarding and other-regarding virtues, which to a certain extent overcome the difficulties caused by self-other asymmetries, are tied too closely to his fundamental notion of the mean, which "seems ill-adapted to helping us understand or justify duties of promise-keeping and truth-telling" (92). Slote departs from Aristotle by avoiding moral notions like "good" and endorsing the ethical notion of "the admirable" (with its negative-assessment partner "the deplorable"). One strives to become admirable, and one performs admirable acts to develop the requisite admirable traits. Admirable acts can, of course, be performed by people who are not admirable because the notion of an admirable act is not derived solely from the ethical qualities of the agent performing it. There is an independent, societal notion of what an admirable act is.

Slote's comments on Aristotle's views are reminiscent of some of Hursthouse's comments about the nonreductive quality of virtue ethics. The morally good agent is not the only resource for determining what one ought to do in a virtue-ethics theory. The virtuous person is made, not born. He or she becomes virtuous by practicing good actions; actions are not good by virtue of the fact that they are performed by the agent (who is only developing into the virtuous person). In Aristotle's virtue ethics, actions are independent of an agent's moral goodness. But it is important to emphasize that Aristotle has two related senses of 'good': "The good" is what is strived for, and a thing "is good" to the extent that it leads to "the good." For human beings, the good aimed at is "living and faring well," and something is regarded as good insofar as it brings the agent to this end. The person of practical wisdom is adept (through upbringing and experience) at knowing what actions are good in the sense of bringing an agent to the good of living well and faring well. Societal norms about what are the best paths to the good help persons of practical wisdom to develop their wisdom, but ultimately they must become their own guide and rely on their practical knowledge even where this diverges from societal norms.

It is not at all clear that Aristotle's moral virtue theory is subject to the self-other asymmetries that Slote thinks are implicit in any moral theory. Clearly, Aristotle's virtue ethics gives primacy to the moral agent's own moral development, and it seems implausible that its morality is in conflict with this rationality. Moreover, given that moral agents morally develop in human communities, it is reasonably clear that any moral agent must be other-regarding, if only to develop his or her own virtues. Indeed, Aristotle's comments on the importance of friendship suggest a strong other-regarding element to his ethics.[14]

Does Slote's ethical—as opposed to moral—virtue theory offer any advantage over Aristotle's views? It is difficult to see how, once one rejects Slote's claim that any moral system must be caught in self-other asymmetries. In fact, there are some distinct disadvantages to Slote's proposal. First, as Slote himself points out,[15] his key notion 'admirable' (and similarly 'deplorable') must be used univocally in all its occurrences. Thus an act is admirable (deplorable) in the same sense that a person or a trait is admirable (deplorable). It is difficult, however, to specify what the univocal sense is. How can the admirability of an act ("it was the perfect thing to do in those difficult circumstances") be the same as the admirability of an agent ("he is someone you would want to be like")? Perhaps one can say that there is an underlying element to all occurrences of 'admirable.' One might say that this element is something like "approved by one's community or society." Thus some act is admirable (for instance, helping an elderly woman across the street) because society approves of it, and a person is regarded as admirable (for example, Mother Teresa) because society approves of the person as someone to be emulated. But is this as far as Slote's view goes? Can we consider a person admirable if the person always does what society considers admirable? Is there room in Slote's ethical theory for the ethical agent to develop a sense of what is admirable that does not strictly rest on society's standards? If it does not allow for this, much of the virtue tradition's emphasis on the autonomy of the virtuous person and the development of internal states associated with virtuous behavior (so evident in Aristotle's views) is lost. But if Slote allows for this development of autonomy, how is it

14. I leave aside the comments about Aristotle's mean because Slote does not develop this point.
15. *From Morality to Virtue*, 123.

to be developed, and what restrictions are placed on its development? These are critical questions, of course, and, I argue that the place to search for their answers is in an investigation of moral education.

In fact, Slote seems to be somewhat sympathetic to such considerations. In his concluding chapter, he talks about the need to develop empirical studies of the development of proper ethical traits and the ways they may be taught in schools. He clearly admires the work of Lawrence Kohlberg, while he acknowledges that his own theory is incomplete in terms of educational and psychological issues.[16] What this suggests is that an emphasis on moral education is crucial for the version of virtue ethics Slote presents. As I have already claimed in relation to Hursthouse's essay, such a view is also true of morality-based virtue ethics. It is suggestive that virtue ethicists who mention moral education at all invariably refer to the work of Lawrence Kohlberg. In fact, Kohlberg's views have been very influential over the last two decades, and connections between his work on moral education and the work of virtue ethicists should not be surprising. What is surprising, perhaps, is that Kohlberg's work on moral education and development can best be understood as talking about the development of conscience in moral agents. To see this, an examination of some of Kohlberg's work is in order.

Kohlberg and Conscience

From the days of his doctoral dissertation, "The Development of Modes of Moral Thinking and Choice in the Years Ten to Sixteen," finished in 1958, to his death, Lawrence Kohlberg was interested in the moral development of human beings.[17] His extensive writings, as well as those of his students, have created an elaborate theory of human development that is widely-accepted in psychological and educational circles.[18]

16. Ibid., 262. See also p. 258 for a reference to Kohlberg.

17. Ph.D. diss., University of Chicago, 1958.

18. See, for example, Lawrence Kohlberg's *Essays on Moral Development, Vol. I: The Philosophy of Moral Development* (San Francisco: Harper & Row, 1981); *Essays on Moral Development, Vol. 2: The Psychology of Moral Development* (San Francisco: Harper & Row, 1984); *Child Psychology and Childhood Education: A Cognitive-Developmental View* (New York: Longman, 1987). For work by his students, see C. M. Beck, B. S. Crittenden, and E. V. Sullivan, eds., *Moral Education: Interdisciplinary Approaches* (Toronto: University of Toronto Press, 1971); F. Clark Power, Ann Higgins, and Lawrence Kohlberg, eds., *Lawrence Kohlberg's Approach to Moral Education* (New York: Columbia University Press, 1989); Thomas Lickona, ed., *Moral Development and Behavior: Theory, Research, and Social Issues* (New York: Holt, Rinehart and Winston, 1976); Sohan Modgil and Celia Modgil, eds., *Lawrence Kohlberg: Consensus and Controversy* (Philadelphia: Falmer Press, 1986).

At the root of Kohlberg's theory is the claim that there are different stages of moral development. In his most widely read formulations of the theory, he argues that there are six stages.[19] In more recent work, he has defended the empirical basis of the first five stages and argued for the need for the sixth stage even if it is not empirically verified.[20] He has also talked about the need for postulating a seventh stage.[21]

The six stages are divided into three groups: the preconventional, the conventional, and the postconventional. Kohlberg briefly explains these groups in this way:

> Piaget's research and theory inspired my own investigations leading to the conclusion that Piaget was incorrect in asserting that clear structural stages in the emergence of moral judgment cannot be identified. We need now to present the theoretical definitions of our moral stages and to report some of the research supporting the idea that they do represent genuine moral stages.
>
> Table 7.2 presents a summary description of the six moral stages grouped into three major levels, the preconventional (Stages 1 and 2), the conventional (Stages 3 and 4), and the postconventional (Stages 5 and 6).
>
> To understand the stages, it is best to start by understanding the three moral levels. The term conventional means conforming to and upholding the rules and expectations and conventions of society or authority just because they are society's rules, expectations, or conventions. The individual at the postconventional level understands and basically accepts society's rules, but this acceptance is derived from formulating and accepting the general moral principles that underlie these rules. These principles in some cases come into conflict with society's rules, in which case the postconventional individual judges by principle rather than by convention. The preconventional moral level is that of most children under 9, some adolescents, and many adolescent and adult criminal offenders. The conventional level is the level of most adolescents and adults in our society and in

---

19. The six stages were offered in a number of essays. See, for example, "The Current Formulation of the Theory," with Charles Levine and Alexandra Hewer, in *Essays in Moral Development*, 2:212–319.

20. *Essays in Moral Development*, 2:224 and 279f.

21. This is postulated, for example, in a reply to criticisms by Habermas in *Essays in Moral Development*, 2:249.

other societies. The postconventional level is reached by a minority of adults and is usually attained only after the age of 20.

One way of understanding the three levels is to think of them as three different types of relationships between the self and society's rules and expectations. From this point of view, the Level I preconventional person is one for whom rules and social expectations are something external to the self. The Level III postconventional person is one who has differentiated his or her values from the rules and expectations of others and defines these values in terms that may sometimes conflict with those of society.

Within each of the three moral levels, two stages exist. The second stage is a more advanced and organized form of the general perspective of each major level. Table 7.2 defines the six stages in terms of: (1) what is right, (2) the reason for upholding the right, and (3) the social perspective behind each stage. This social perspective is a central concept in our definition of moral reasoning.[22]

As this passage indicates, Kohlberg sees Piaget's work as a starting point for his own. He agrees with Piaget's view that there are stages to cognitive development and, in fact, argues that cognitive development is necessary for moral development even though it is not sufficient.[23] In disagreement with Piaget, Kohlberg claims that there are clear and universal stages of moral development. Elaborating on his differences with Piaget, Kohlberg states that Piaget, influenced by Kant, thought that there were two moralities of justice: a heteronomous one of childhood and a more mature, autonomous one.[24] Although his own experimental results did not confirm these two moralities, Kohlberg's theory distinguishes in each of the three stages a Substage A that is more heteronomous and a Substage B that is "more egalitarian and flexible in regard to rules and persons." Besides his debt to Piaget's work, Kohlberg acknowledges a variety of philosophical influences:

Discontented with both the utilitarian view of moral development as a simple accumulation of external or empiricist associations strengthening prudence and sympathy and the Kantian view of an innate rational conscience, and inspired by both the Hegelian philosophy

22. *Child Psychology and Childhood Education*, 283.
23. Ibid., 259–60 and 310.
24. *Essays in Moral Development*, 2:225f.

of stages and the Darwinian conception of evolution, at the end of the nineteenth century the philosopher-psychologists earlier mentioned, like Dewey, Baldwin, and Mead, defined moral stages resulting from the social interaction between a structuring or constructing child and a socially structured world. This tradition, especially as empirically elaborated by Piaget, stands behind my own research and the viewpoint of this book.[25]

In various places, Kohlberg has argued that "there is empirical evidence for the British utilitarian view of the development of moral reason as a natural extension of prudence or practical reason through a sentiment of sympathy or empathy."[26] The position of the empiricists is reflected in Kohlberg's own stages. At Stage 1, individuals have an egocentric point of view.[27] They do not consider the interests of others and confuse the perspective of authority with their own. At Stage 2, although individuals recognize that others have interests that conflict with their own, they see their own interests as paramount. With later stages, there is an increasing understanding of the interests of others as well as an appreciation of a system-perspective that treats everyone equally and impartially. People develop through these stages by means of education and role playing. Role playing is particularly important. Through it, an individual is able to see him- or herself in the role of another and in doing so to understand the perspective of others. When the emotional side of role taking is stressed, empathy or sympathy for another is developed.[28] Kohlberg describes Stage 6 as the stage where there is "the self-conscious operation of moral musical chairs in making just choices."[29] What he means by this is that at Stage 6, an individual is able self-consciously to place him- or herself in all roles in a moral situation (he terms this "reversibility"). This ability enables the individual to make sophisticated moral decisions.

In fact, the ability to place oneself in a variety of roles to make a moral decision is also reflective of a Kantian perspective on morality. By placing oneself in different roles, one can judge which role is most defensible. Kohlberg points out that, in higher stages of morality, there is greater uniformity

25. *Child Psychology and Childhood Education*, 261.
26. Ibid., 260.
27. See Table 7.2 on p. 284 of *Child Psychology and Childhood Education*. See also *Essays in Moral Development*, 2:314–17.
28. *Child Psychology and Childhood Education*, 312.
29. *Essays in Moral Development*, 2:317.

in agents about what choice should be made. So there is a type of universality to the choices made by individuals in Stage 6, the same universality
that Kant thought was part of the moral point of view.

Kohlberg's Kantian assumptions have been the source of many criticisms
of his theory. His claims that morality is at base deontological and that
intentions—as opposed to consequences—provide the most important
component for morally judging a person have been criticized by those with
a behavioral perspective on morality.[30] His view that the moral stages are
transcultural (and thus universal) has been questioned by many who adopt a
relativistic perspective on morality.[31] Most important, Kohlberg's emphasis
on justice-reasoning as the basis for judging moral development has been
criticized as sex based and dismissive of perspectives on morality that emphasize care.[32]

In response to his critics, Kohlberg acknowledges that there is a gap
between talk about moral decisions and actual moral practice. Yet it is clear
from empirical studies that the stages of moral development determined
through the posing of ethical dilemmas correlate with moral behavior.[33]
Moreover, transcultural and longitudinal studies in Turkey and Israel indicate
that his scheme of the stages of moral development is not limited to citizens
of urban, Western civilizations.[34] And, although his original studies were
conducted only with male subjects, subsequent studies of both sexes show
no differences in stages for the sexes.[35] In response to the claim that his
scheme overlooks the perspective of caring, Kohlberg writes:

> My own view is that judgments of justice presuppose "caring" and
> "sympathy"; only if the individual sympathizes with the good of
> others can the justice problem of how the good should be distrib-
> uted become a problem for moral reasoning. Stated in different
> terms, justice (at the higher stages) centers on equal respect for hu-
> man persons, treating others as ends not merely as means. To treat

30. Ibid., 28f. Kohlberg discusses his links to Kantian universality and its relation to reversibility
in his "Conscience as Principled Responsibility: On the Philosophy of Stage Six," in *Conscience: An
Interdisciplinary View* (Dordrecht: D. Reidel, 1987).

31. *Essays in Moral Development*, 2:321f.

32. Carol Gilligan has frequently criticized Kohlberg on this point. See *Essays in Moral Development*, 2:338f.

33. *Child Psychology and Childhood Education*, 305–6.

34. *Essays in Moral Development*, 2:330.

35. *Child Psychology and Childhood Education*, 304.

others as ends means actively to sympathize with their interests and concerns as well as to respect them as persons with rights. (305)

This response may not satisfy his critics, but it is symptomatic of Kohlberg's theory of moral development. The key to moral development is an individual's ability to move beyond his or her own perspective and to understand the perspectives of others. As we have seen, Kohlberg sees role playing as an important instrument for this development. He also holds that participation in diverse groups aids moral development:

> These findings contrast with many sociological notions as to how group memberships determine moral development. It is often thought that children get some of their basic moral values from their families, some from their peer groups, and others from the wider society, and that these basic values tend to conflict with one another. Instead of participation in various groups causing conflicting developmental trends in morality, it appears that participation in various groups converges in stimulating the development of structures of moral reasoning, which are not transmitted by one particular group as opposed to another. The child lives in a total social world in which perceptions of the law, of the peer group, and of parental teachings all influence one another. Various people and groups may make conflicting immediate demands on the child. In the course of "normal" development, however, the conflicts between demands of groups and individuals constitute conditions of cognitive-moral conflict that stimulate the development of structures or stages of moral judgment. (314)

Kohlberg also suggests that moral education plays an important role in moral development (315–17). Although exposing children to moral reasoning of the next higher stage in moral development seems to benefit moral development, a far more successful method is to provide classes with "free discussion and argumentation about moral dilemmas" (316). Kohlberg's speculative explanation of the success of this method is that underlying moral development is the establishment of a cognitive-moral conflict at one level, which requires reintegration at the next level for resolution. Discussion of moral dilemmas highlights the conflicts implicit in lower moral stages. Recognition of such conflicts then requires the individual to reason on a higher moral stage.

As a psychologist, Kohlberg is interested in levels of moral development and how such development takes place. Although he draws on significant philosophical material, his interest is not primarily philosophical nor is his work principally directed to philosophers. When he mentions 'conscience,' he defines it as "the moral element of human personality."[36] Given this very general notion of conscience, Kohlberg is at pains to indicate that he does not view conscience as something that in an a priori (Kantian) fashion intuits rational moral principles. He also points out that 'conscience' does not necessarily mark a distinction between conventional and postconventional morality. Following conscience as opposed to following the law may occur in conventional morality (Stages 3 and 4) as well as in postconventional morality (Stages 5 and 6). But given what Kohlberg means by moral development and its relation to morality, it is plausible to interpret much of what Kohlberg discusses as relevant to conscience. In fact, some of Kohlberg's students have focused on the impact of Kohlberg's views for issues connected with conscience and have identified the notion of conscience with Kohlberg's claims about moral-cognitive development. Justin Aronfreed, for example, writes:

> Some conceptions of the development of conscience assume a developmental sequence of qualitatively distinct stages which transform the mind of the child in an increasingly unifying or integrative manner until he attains (if he is properly nurtured) one or another cognitive structure which identifies him as a creature of a particular moral status. From this point of view, socialization and moral development are essentially synonymous. They move together towards an end state (sometimes defined as "maturity"), and the stage of their evolution is judged from criteria of the form, complexity, and substance of the child's values. This point of view characterizes not only Piaget's (1948) classic formulation of developmental shifts in children's moral judgment, but also the rather more sophisticated description of stages of moral thought in Lawrence Kohlberg's recent work (1963, 1971).[37]

36. *Essays in Moral Development*, 2:313. Interestingly, in his "Conscience as Principled Responsibility," 5, Kohlberg indicates that there is in his work a deep commitment to the importance of conscience: "[W]hen I started my work back in 1958 I took a few rather loose notions and used them for *a definition of the highest stage.* Reference to judgments of conscience was one necessary condition."

37. In *Moral Education: Interdisciplinary Approaches*, 186.

Aronfreed understands Kohlberg this way in part because he works with "an expanded notion of conscience" that claims "moral judgment, in its more traditional sense, is only one sector of the extensive value systems which we now tend to subsume under the concept of conscience" (188). Aronfreed's studies investigate principally conscience as internal control (194). In agreement with Kohlberg, he sees conscience as developing in a stage-like fashion as a result of the child's contact with human society. He notes, however, that there are difficulties with theories that emphasize an evolutionary view of moral development (196–97). Chief among these is the nature of the evidence used to establish stages: children's verbalizations of their evaluative thought processes. For one may wonder whether changes in verbalization are due to the changing complexity of the child as a verbal responder to questions posed by adults or due to changes in values.

Questions about the connection between values and performance, of course, bring to mind the issues about the virtues I raised in earlier chapters. Kohlberg's attitude toward virtues appears puzzling. In his essay "Education for Justice: A Modern Statement of the Socratic View," Kohlberg takes as his point of departure Plato's claims through Socrates that we do not know what virtue is and that virtue cannot be taught.[38] His summary halfway through the essay captures many of his chief points:

> Let me recapitulate my argument so far. I have criticized the "bag of virtues" concept of moral education on the grounds, first, that there are no such things and, second, if there were, they couldn't be taught or at least I don't know how or who could teach them. Like Socrates, I have claimed that ordinary people certainly don't know how to do it, and yet there are no expert teachers of virtue as there are for the other arts. Rather than turning to nihilism, I have pointed to an example of an effective moral educator at the adult social level, Martin Luther King. Since I cannot define moral virtue at the individual level, I tried it at the social level and found it to be justice, and claimed that the central moral value of the school, like that of the society, was justice. Justice, in turn, is a matter of equal and universal human rights. I pointed to the cloud of virtue labels attributed to King and pointed out that only one meant anything. Justice was not just one more fine-sounding word in a eulogy; it was the essence of King's moral leadership. (38–39)

38. In *Essays in Moral Development*, 1:29–48.

Kohlberg's criticisms of the "bag of virtues" view are really criticisms of what Kohlberg takes to be the Aristotelian view of virtues. In the first place, Kohlberg criticizes Aristotle's split between the moral virtues and the intellectual virtues. Not only is this split contrary to the blending of the moral and the cognitive that one finds in Plato (and Kohlberg finds crucial to his own theory of moral-cognitive development), but this split also leads to an incorrect view about the development of the virtues. If moral virtues are not connected to the cognitive order, then one would think they can be developed by mere imitation and repeated performance. But it is clear (as Plato saw) that character development through mere imitation of examples does not work. Much more is needed. Moreover, mere imitation does not provide the necessary development of autonomy so important for moral maturity, and it leaves the agent without a solid moral foundation: "If we, like Charlie Brown, define our moral aims in terms of virtues and vices, we are defining them in terms of the praise and blame of others and are caught in the pull of being all things to all people and end up being wishy-washy" (35). Elsewhere in his writings, Kohlberg indicates that his research does not focus on the moral value of lives or persons or questions that ask about ideals of the good life or the good person.[39] That is, his research does not address issues about virtues. Given his (mis)understanding of the Aristotelian view of the virtues, his silence here is understandable. Because virtue development (on his reading of the Aristotelian tradition) eschews cognitive issues in favor of rote imitation, virtue development has no role in a theory that emphasizes the stages of cognitive-moral development.

Needless to say, Part I above shows that Kohlberg has misunderstood the Aristotelian tradition of virtue ethics.[40] To be sure, imitation of exemplars plays a crucial part in the development of the virtues, but at the beginning stages alone. Only if the individual is transformed in certain ways by the practice of actions can the agent acquire the relevant virtues. This transformation involves not only a change in affections but also the development of practical wisdom. It is the development of practical reason that provides the cognitive changes Kohlberg finds missing in the Aristotelian tradition. In fact, the medieval discussions of practical wisdom in Scotus's and Ockham's work on the virtues, with their emphasis on specific and general rules of prudence, highlight the need for cognitive components to the development of the moral virtues. As it turns out, Kohlberg's views about developing

39. *Essays in Moral Development*, 2:305.
40. Paul J. Philibert has also noted a number of difficulties with Kohlberg's reading of the Aristotelian virtue tradition in his "Lawrence Kohlberg's Use of Virtue in His Theory of Moral Development," in *International Philosophical Quarterly* 15 (1975): 455–79.

cognitive-moral stages fit very well with the virtue tradition of ethics as I have described it in this work.

Another implication of Kohlberg's work fits well with one of the main themes of my book. Once we see Kohlberg's discussion of stages of moral-cognitive development as talk about the maturing of conscience in an individual, a number of points become apparent. First, Kohlberg's arguments that there is a movement from heteronomy to autonomy in the moral individual (also claimed by Piaget) can easily be understood in terms of the movement from the conventional to the mature conscience, discussed in Chapter 9. The type of conscience one finds in Stage 6 in Kohlberg's scheme very closely resembles the mature (or authentic) conscience discussed in the writings of Macquarrie and others. It can function as a positive force moving the individual toward an ideal rather than as a punitive, checking mechanism that drives an individual through indirect means. Conscience as internalized prohibition (Stages 1 and 2) constitutes the beginning of the development of the virtues. Through the internalization of the prohibitions of parents and teachers, one begins to develop a set of internal rules that guide moral practice. Further education (Stages 3 and 4) leads to more general rules and the bases for experiences in society that lead in turn to success or failure in a variety of circumstances. These experiences may, in some individuals, result in the examination of societal rules and a transformation of them in ways suited to achieve their ends. These individuals may then develop new bases for the actions they perform (Stages 5 and 6) through the moral autonomy they have developed. But such transformation does not always take place. In fact, Kohlberg suggests that people who achieve a "post-conventional" stage of moral development are rare.[41] And we have seen a similar lesson for virtue ethics (one Kohlberg seems to have missed). The process of experience, trial and error, and reflection on successes and failures is the only way to develop the virtues; but such activity does not guarantee that one in fact develops the virtues. As Aristotle saw, there is a mystery here that does not promise explanation. But it is the same mystery Kohlberg and others face in trying to understand the movement from the conventional to the postconventional cognitive-moral stage.

Kohlbergian Conscience and Its Critics

In the present culture wars in the United States waged with a strong emphasis on "family-values" (whatever these may be), many criticisms of Kohl-

---

41. *Essays in Moral Development*, 2:172.

berg and variations on his views have been posed, particularly in the name of the virtues. William J. Bennett, former Secretary of Education and former professor of philosophy, has been called a "virtuesmeister" and "virtuecrat" for his emphasis on the virtues in his *The Book of Virtues* and *The Moral Compass*.[42] Bennett, in his forewords to these compilations of stories and verse, emphasizes the need for "moral examples" for children to develop the virtues. He explicitly sets up such examples as a contrast to courses in "moral reasoning."[43] The contrast is infelicitous, and perhaps inadvertent. It is clear that children need moral examples as reference points for decisions and behavior. But Bennett seems to think there is an obvious clarity to the morals of the texts he provides in his books. It seems clear to him that Robert Louis Stevenson's poem "Good and Bad Children" is about self-discipline, the practice of good habits, and the resultant balance of the soul (in a Platonic sense) (21–23). But is it? Would a child learning the first lines— "Children, you are very little, / And your bones are very brittle"—perhaps think of his or her fragility? Or would a child hearing

> Happy hearts and happy faces,
> Happy play in grassy places—
> That was how, in ancient ages,
> Children grew to kings and sages.

think that happiness (in whatever sense children have of it) is the key to a good life? It seems clear that some instruction about how to read the texts is required, and Bennett, of course, tries to do this with his various introductions. But is this enough? Is it sufficient to provide a reading of the virtue exemplified in a text and hold it as a paradigm? Obviously not, and Bennett recognizes this. One must practice the virtues and form the proper habits of the virtues to acquire the virtues—this is why "self-discipline" is so important and emphasized in Bennett's reading of the Stevenson poem. But does this suffice? Can imitation and practice create the internal states that are traditionally associated with the virtues, such that one does, for example, just acts but as the just person does them? To be sure, there is a mystery here that was commented on by both Plato and Aristotle, and it would be unjust to criticize Bennett for not providing a sure means of cultivating the virtues. But it is

---

42. *The Book of Virtues* (New York: Simon and Schuster, 1993); *The Moral Compass* (New York: Simon and Schuster, 1995).
43. *The Book of Virtues*, 12.

precisely the point of Kohlberg's work that "moral reasoning" is a crucial part of the development of the internal states. It is through dilemmas and exposure to other ways of conceiving issues that one develops morally and moves toward the goal of autonomy. Unless moral agents adopt the reasoning (whether explicitly or not) behind a moral rule or exemplar, moral agents cannot make the reasoning their own and internalize it as a state of character. Exemplars are important, but they are not sufficient for the moral development of the virtues. Autonomy and internalization are crucial, too, and they are best achieved through moral reasoning, according to Kohlberg.

Gilbert Meilaender has also criticized Kohlberg's views.[44] He thinks it a myth that there can be such thing as "neutral" moral reasoning, as the practitioners of "values clarification" proclaim.[45] There are subtle and not so subtle displays of values-bias among the proponents of "values clarification." Merely isolating what one calls salient characteristics of examples displays such biases. Given this fact, Meilaender thinks that the important issues in moral education become (1) what values-bias should we endorse?; (2) how can we avoid indoctrination? To the first, he argues that different communities should be allowed to choose the values they want to emphasize. In particular, for Meilaender, Christian communities should be allowed to foster the Christian values they deem all important. To the second, Meilaender's views are somewhat ambiguous. He wants to distinguish two types of indoctrination. The first type, a good type, is the teaching of the values a community wants to foster. We might, in fact, just want to call this "moral education." The second type is pernicious. It is simple brainwashing, and, as such, it is to be avoided. What distinguishes the two types for Meilaender is the willingness of the practitioners of the "indoctrination" to live by what they try to indoctrinate in others. If the practitioners, humbly, see themselves as subject to what they preach to others, this is "moral education." A practitioner's failure to live by what he or she teaches is a sure sign that indoctrination in a pernicious sense is taking place.

Meilaender's distinction is much too simplistic. There are surely deplorable values taught by people who themselves live by what they preach.[46]

---

44. See "Instructing the Conscience," in The Theory and Practice of Virtue (Notre Dame: University of Notre Dame Press, 1988).

45. Meilaender sees Kohlberg as holding that there is a neutral moral reasoning. In fact, Kohlberg does not think this. See, for example, Child Psychology and Childhood Education, 57–58. What is really at issue between Meilaender and Kohlberg is what virtues should be endorsed.

46. The Handmaid's Tale, by Margaret Atwood (Boston: Houghton Mifflin, 1986), is an intriguing story of levels of indoctrination and how pernicious values can be.

Examples like Adolph Eichmann, who apparently lived by the values of ethnic hatred he preached, come readily to mind. So "living by what one teaches" cannot be the sole rule by which one distinguishes "moral education" from "indoctrination" (in the pernicious sense). A better rule, and the one postulated by Kohlberg, is that true "moral education" educates the individual to examine in critical ways the principles taught. Such examination is key to the development of moral autonomy, which should be a primary goal of any moral education. An education that has as a principle the virtue of questioning itself cannot be indoctrination; of its nature, it undermines indoctrination. In fact, such questioning is the purpose behind "values clarification" and education through discussion of moral dilemmas in Kohlberg's theory.

Kohlberg criticized Aristotle as offering "a bag of virtues" approach to moral education. As I have remarked, this is based on a misunderstanding of Aristotle's virtue ethics. But the "bag of virtues" label is appropriately given to the views of critics of Kohlberg like Bennett and Meilaender. In Bennett's case, the fault lies in the view that there are "obvious" stories and that presenting exemplars of virtues is enough for moral education. In Meilaender's case, the fault is that the bag is not self-critical and thus easily becomes indoctrination. Importantly, both critics have failed to see the real import of Kohlberg's views and the importance of moral autonomy. It also is clear that a virtue-based ethics requires a strong notion of conscience combining many of Kohlberg's insights. A virtue ethics that includes a mixture of duty- and virtue-based morality requires the commitment of individuals to the duty-based rules of society. As I have indicated, conscience as I have defined it incorporates societal rules and thus serves as a source for adherence to societal rules. And it is also clear from the discussion of Hursthouse's and Slote's attempts to formulate the bases of a pure virtue ethics that conscience as I have defined it would provide the sense of societal standards a virtuous person must have. Virtue ethicists of whatever stripe should direct their attention to conscience. Properly understood, conscience is a critical part of any complete virtue ethics.

CONSCIENCE *and* OTHER VIRTUES

Influenced by the work of, among others, Butler, Kant, and Freud, many
philosophers in this century accepted the view that conscience is to be
regarded as a faculty. Having done this, they went on to argue that there is
no conscience because there is no such faculty. At best, 'conscience' is shorthand for something else: moral reasoning, a personal monitor, emotive responses. Moreover, the horrific events of the past century have caused many
to question whether there is the moral guiding force that conscience is
thought to provide. This all-too-pervasive dismissal of conscience is unfortunate and displays an ignorance of the history of the notion of conscience. In
the Middle Ages, conscience was not viewed as a faculty; on the contrary, it
was seen as an aspect of practical reasoning. Even more important, in the
years following Aquinas's *Commentary on the Nicomachean Ethics,* such medieval
thinkers as Scotus and Ockham linked conscience with issues associated

with the development and cultivation of the virtues. I have argued that this insight is one contemporary virtue ethicists should take to heart, for virtue ethicists have also neglected to talk about conscience even though it is critical for any ethics of virtue.

I have suggested that conscience be regarded as a relational entity. Such an understanding of conscience allows it to play the multiple roles in a moral agent that a conscience needs to play. As a relational entity, it can be involved in moral reasoning, be a part of the emotive commitment to follow the good determined through moral reasoning, express the positive ego-ideal a moral agent strives to attain, and guide the emotive reactions to the attainment of an ideal or the failure to do so. Yet, it is also convenient to treat conscience as if it were a substantial entity, taking care not to treat it as a faculty. The convenience concerns principally issues connected with the development of conscience. It is far easier to develop a conscience without paying attention to its complexities as a relational entity, especially in the earliest stages of formation. A Jiminy Cricket proclaiming that conscience should be your guide is a better teaching device for the young than a moral expert concerned with fine distinctions between systems and entities.

In its earliest stages, conscience will be centered on the parental and societal rules and assumptions taught to the moral agent. Obviously, these rules and assumptions differ from society to society to the extent that the societies themselves differ. This early training will impress in the moral agent the goals and means to these goals that the parents and the society want to be impressed. This will be achieved through direct moral instruction, the telling of stories, and informal intercourse with other moral agents. Moral exemplars will be pointed to, and moral agents will be encouraged to imitate them. Advice about behavior and demands to follow certain rules will be given in an attempt to move the moral agent in approved directions. Necessarily, the virtues approved by parental figures and the society as a whole will be taught and extolled, for these virtues not only express the desired goods of a society but will be seen as the best means for achieving these goods. Proper training will make these virtues desirable for the agent and specify ways that they can be developed. And the moral agent will use this stock of moral education to perform the first actions leading (with luck) to the formation of good habits. Without a doubt, a great part of successful training of moral agents at this stage will be a molding of emotions like guilt and pride. The moral agent will be trained to regret not achieving desired goals (performing specific actions or developing special habits) and to take pride in achieving them. The deeper the moral agent is trained in the virtues, the stronger the commitment to following conscience will become.

This early stage of conscience—the conventional conscience—must, however, give way to more complex stages. To develop successfully, the moral agent must modify the parental and societal advice to fit his or her particular circumstances. As Aristotle pointed out, what might be a good rule for a person of rash temperament would not be an appropriate rule for the timid. Given the complex nature of societies and the different groups making up any modern society, there will be conflicts among moral principles and even societal virtues. The moral agent must confront these tensions and resolve them in appropriate ways. In fact, such conflicts will be critical for developing a mature conscience. It is only through experience and the successes and failures of plans and actions that a moral agent can test the means chosen for achieving ends. Through such activities, practical wisdom can be developed, and practical wisdom—often called prudence—is necessary for the development of any virtue. The circularity of needing experience to develop practical wisdom and the need to possess practical wisdom to act in appropriate ways to attain goals has often been noted, but the circularity is unavoidable. Conscience, however, provides a point of entry into this circularity by providing moral agents with direction as to what ought to be done to cultivate the virtues.

The development of practical wisdom is an important component of the creation of a mature conscience in a moral agent, and it proceeds hand in glove with moral development in general. As Kohlberg suggests, the ability to see oneself in the position of others (reversibility) is crucial for moral development. Only when one can move beyond an ego-centered view of morality can a moral agent be open to creating moral rules that lead effectively to the goods of society and deal with morally ambiguous situations like dilemmas. Undoubtedly, encountering different cultures and rival sets of moral assumptions will help to develop the ability to see other points of view. And surely reading literature is one way to do this, for imaginatively entering into stories is an important way to examine alternative points of view. Being challenged by moral dilemmas, as Kohlberg advocates, and analyzing decisions made in such situations also increase sensitivity to the viewpoints of others. Paradoxically, one other way to achieve this sensitivity is to stress that one's conscience is not simply a personal monitor. On the contrary, it needs to be stressed that the dictates of one's conscience should be those dictates one would want all moral agents to follow. This is part of the importance of Kant's much-maligned view that moral principles must be universalizable. Simply to universalize one's own perspective and make the fulfillment of one's own wishes the guide to moral behavior is a recipe for moral disaster. Such a strategy inevitably leads to conflict with others and ultimately makes it impossible to achieve one's own goods, let alone the goods of a society. Only by taking into account the perspectives of other moral agents and fashioning rules for oneself that others should obey is there a possibility that the moral rules one adopts will help one to function in a society. Ultimately, the best strategy for a moral individual in a society is to act with regard to others. An important way of doing this is to form one's conscience so that the moral rules one comes to live by are rules that one would want others to live by. In fact, Kohlberg indicates that among people in the high stages of moral development there is little disagreement about how to act. To be sure, the mature conscience of such individuals must be trained so that there is satisfaction in formulating and acting in accord with such moral rules and discomfort in not so acting. So there needs to be the unique tie between aspects of a moral agent's conscience and the moral agent. But this tie must take place in view of the conscience's need to formulate moral rules others should live by.

There is little doubt that virtues like fortitude, temperance, compassion, and steadfastness help the moral agent to formulate moral rules and stick by them. Possession of these virtues also transforms the moral agent in ways Aquinas saw. Because a moral agent possesses the virtues, he or she can evaluate moral situations in morally appropriate ways. Such an agent takes into account long-term effects and goals of actions and sees, for example, adultery not as an instance of desired pleasure but as a forbidden activity. Such skills of moral assessment enable the moral agent to avoid the pitfalls of weakness of will because he or she correctly sizes up situations and sees the best ways to behave. Conscience, of course, plays a role here. By motivating the agent to orient him- or herself toward a positive ego-ideal, conscience moves the agent not only to focus on actions that foster this goal but also to avoid those actions leading away from it.

A developed, mature conscience in general helps a moral agent live by the virtues because it moves the moral agent to adopt behavior that cultivates the virtues and leads the agent to practice actions that reinforce such behavior. Thus, conscience not only allows a moral agent to begin to cultivate the virtues; it helps to sustain the virtues once achieved. Needless to say, the virtues also help the moral agent to develop his or her conscience and live in accord with the dictates of conscience. Because the mature conscience is built from the internalization of socially sanctioned norms, a duty-based ethics ought to give great weight to the role of conscience in the development of a moral agent. This is even more the case for virtue ethics. In fact, it is because there is a strong connection between the virtues and conscience that the emphasis a pure virtue ethics places on the morally good agent avoids the pitfalls attributed to it. The morally good agent is a criterion for moral action not because of some mysterious infallible moral power, but because this agent has cultivated the virtues and the mature conscience essential to their possession. Conscience provides the checks on morally good agents so that their behavior is not at odds with the demands of their societies and prevents the morally good agent from slipping into moral self-delusion. It is because the morally good person has cultivated the virtues and a mature conscience in tandem that this person is a moral expert whose moral views should be recognized. Although conscience as I have defined it emerges as a critical part of any ethical system, virtue ethicists must pay particular attention to conscience as a crucial part of any virtue ethics. It provides the background to the development of a morally good person, which is at the base of any system of virtue ethics.

Once conscience is viewed in the way I have described it, it can again play a prominent role in ethical discussion. Understood in the proper way, conscience can be seen as a useful analytical notion. The recent neglect of conscience, which is tied to its being understood as a psychological faculty, can then be seen as the historical aberration it is.

. . . .

APPENDIX: MACINTYRE'S PROJECT

In reviewing MacIntyre's intellectual project, it is important to note that he self-consciously employs the notion of a "moral tradition" in a way that far exceeds the usual understanding of 'morality.'[1] It is something more akin to Wittgenstein's notion of a form of life or even the more contemporary notion of a conceptual structure. Different societies have different underlying assumptions, goals, and values. These assumptions, goals, and values color judgments made in a particular society; effectively, they set up a standard of rationality for that society. With different societies, there are different standards of rationality, and what may be held as true in one society may not be held as true in another. In fact, what is taken for true in one society may not even be understood in a radically different society, and this problem is labeled incommensurability. As MacIntyre uses the term, *incommensurability* comes in two forms. The first type obtains when one system of thought (a moral tradition or a scientific tradition) evolves out of another. The later tradition (for instance, Newtonian physics) contains notions (inertia, mass) that were not part of the earlier (for example, Aristotelian physics). The second type occurs when two developed traditions—whether historically linked or not—offer rival interpretations of the same phenomena. MacIntyre presents the Encyclopedic tradition and the Geneologic tradition as examples of this later form of incommensurability in *Three Rival Theories*. The Encyclopedic tradition, inheritor of the Enlightenment (and especially the Scottish Enlightenment), holds to a universalistic account of humankind and rationality. There is an unvarying truth that is common to all societies, and the claims of a society must be judged relative to this standard. The Geneological tradition rejects such universalism as a fiction. There are no eternal truths. Truth is relative to the various societies and their competing systems of rationality.[2]

1. See MacIntyre's remarks on "moral enquiry" in *Three Rival Theories*, 2–3.
2. *After MacIntyre: Critical Perspectives on the Work of Alasdair MacIntyre*, ed. John Horton and Susan

MacIntyre is most concerned about the second type of incommensurability, in part because he sees it as part of the moral chaos of the modern period and its advocacy of liberalism. Whereas in *After Virtue* he argues that liberalism is the absence of a tradition, in later writings—including *Which Justice? Whose Rationality?* and *Three Rival Theories*—he sees liberalism as a tradition that incorporates many incommensurable points of view. In fact, this situation of chaos is an almost necessary consequence of the individualism fostered by liberalism. In *Three Rival Theories*, MacIntyre argues against Davidson's attempts to abolish the notion that there can be incommensurability among conceptual schemes, and MacIntyre insists that incommensurability is a serious problem.[3] He also presents a way around the seemingly impossible deadlock between the Encyclopedists and the Geneologists. This is his notion of the third rival tradition of moral enquiry: "Tradition."

"Tradition" as MacIntyre uses the term is really Thomism. In MacIntyre's eyes, its strength is its ability to overcome the divide between incommensurable frameworks by holding onto the ideal of the universalism of the Encyclopedists while acknowledging the historical relativity emphasized by the Geneologists. But there are many difficulties with MacIntyre's position. Not the least of these is that the story of Thomas, as recounted by MacIntyre, is essentially a story about Thomism's role in overcoming certain historical incommensurabilities (the first type of incommensurability mentioned above), and it is unlikely that these historical lessons apply to the incommensurability between the Encyclopedists and the Geneologists. Moreover, it is not even clear that MacIntyre's claims for the success of Thomism in overcoming (historical) incommensurability are justified.

In examining MacIntyre's comments about Thomism, we are immediately faced with a difficulty. In *After Virtue*, MacIntyre sees the Aristotelian tradition (or at least the core notion of virtues deriving from this tradition) as the best candidate for solving the failures of present-day liberalism. He specifically labels Thomas Aquinas a "marginal figure" in the story of this Aristotelian tradition of moral inquiry.[4] Yet, in *Whose Justice? Which Rationality?* Aquinas emerges as the central character in the history of the Aristotelian tradition. His role is even more emphasized in *Three Rival Theories*. Although MacIntyre's *Whose Justice? Which Rationality?* downplays the importance of his

---

Mendus (Notre Dame: University of Notre Dame Press, 1994), presents a number of essays devoted to MacIntyre's thought and his replies. Of particular interest for MacIntyre's discussion of Thomism is John Haldane's essay, "MacIntyre's Thomist Revival: What Next?" (91–107).

3. *Three Rival Theories*, 11f.; *Whose Justice? Which Rationality?* 370f.

4. *After Virtue*, 178.

changed evaluation of Aquinas, it is difficult to see the change as other than an important shift in thinking. Why is there such a shift? The easiest answer is that, as MacIntyre's tripartite intellectual project focused more and more clearly on the problems of incommensurability of traditions and the ways that they can be bridged, MacIntyre became more and more interested in a historical figure who bridged rival conceptual frameworks. Aristotle, as the founder of a tradition of moral inquiry, was more concerned with establishing a tradition than in bridging the gap among incommensurable traditions. Aquinas, on the other hand, was in such a bridging position and in MacIntyre's eyes did, in fact, bridge incommensurable traditions.

The incommensurable traditions Aquinas bridged were the Augustinian and the Aristotelian. According to MacIntyre, "[R]adical inconsistencies between the two standpoints emerged at three different levels," and these inconsistencies make the two standpoints "incommensurable as well as incompatible."[5] The first level concerns central Christian doctrines: "Where Aristotle asserted the eternity of the world, Christianity assigns to it a beginning at the moment of creation; where Aristotle ruled out the separate immaterial existence of the individual soul, and where Averroes' interpretation of the De Anima, although it left room for the resurrection of the dead, reinforced the denial of any survival of the soul apart from the body, Christianity was committed to belief in such survival" (107). The second level concerned the organization of disciplines in universities and, in particular, the relation between theology and philosophy. With the re-emergence of the Aristotelian corpus after 1240, the question of where the Aristotelian philosophical works were to be studied had to be addressed. To assign these works purely to the Arts faculty would be to assign certain issues typically discussed in the Theology faculty to the Arts (and, by implication, to philosophy). And MacIntyre says, "Such a violation of the Augustinian division of intellectual labor in the curriculum seemed to challenge not only the institutional arrangements of the Augustinianism of the University of Paris but the intellectual presuppositions of those arrangements."[6]

It is frankly difficult to assess these two levels of incommensurability MacIntyre posits between the Augustinian and Aristotelian traditions. On

5. *Three Rival Theories*, 107.

6. *Three Rival Theories*, 108. In his discussion of medieval universities, MacIntyre makes considerable use of Stephen C. Ferruolo's *The Origins of the University* (Stanford: Stanford University Press, 1985), but much that he claims is not substantiated by Ferruolo's text. For a different account of university structure, particularly as found in England, see William J. Courtenay's *Schools and Scholars in Fourteenth-Century England* (Princeton: Princeton University Press, 1987).

the doctrinal level, MacIntyre clearly assumes that there is one Augustinian view about the eternity of the world and the separation of the soul and the body. He also assumes that there is a pure Aristotelian view about 'eternity,' the 'eternity of the world,' and a unanimous "Aristotelian" interpretation that Aristotle views the soul—even the intellect, which is part of the soul—as incapable of existence independent of the body. The Pauline view that the soul is not independent of the body, Augustine's various views about time and eternity, and the ambiguous text of the *De Anima* (particularly on the issue of the intellect's independence from the body, leading in some Arab commentators to the positing of the unicity of the Active Intellect) certainly put into doubt MacIntyre's simple dichotomies. Moreover, MacIntyre's remarks about the new challenges to the "Augustinian" setup of the universities assume the dominance of the model of the University of Paris for all universities and a fixed set of distinctions between theology and philosophy. These assumptions are controversial to say the least.

Yet, MacIntyre's argument for the incommensurability of Augustinianism and Aristotelianism does not really rest on the first two "levels of incompatibility." Unless one is willing to think that any two groups that disagree about an issue—whether it be a religious doctrine or the worth of Reserve Officer Training Corps being taught at a college—are participants in incommensurable viewpoints or that rival divisions of disciplines—should history be seen as a discipline in the Humanities or as one in the Social Sciences— constitute incommensurable systems of thought, one is unlikely to see the first two levels as showing the incommensurability MacIntyre is trying to establish. It is really the third level of incommensurability that carries the weight of MacIntyre's argument: "[I]t also became clear that the standards of truth and rationality to which appeal had to be made in order to debate them constructively were not the same for Aristotelians and for Augustinians."[7] This level is itself divided into three claims.

First, there is a disagreement about the objects of knowledge between the Augustinian and Aristotelian traditions. The Aristotelian takes as a central tenet "the mind's potential adequacy to all its objects" (101). Yet, in the Augustinian tradition, a central tenet is the inadequacy of the mind in the face of what it encounters—primarily God, but also created objects insofar as they are what they were created to be—and the mind's discovery of its inabilities and incapacities, which are essential to its progress.

Second, there is a disagreement about the understanding of truth. "Aris-

7. *Three Rival Theories*, 109.

totle locates truth in the relationship of the mind to its objects, Augustine locates it in the source of the relationship of finite objects to that truth which is God" (110).

Third, there is a dispute about the source of error. Augustine places it in the will. "Aristotle, like every other ancient pre-Christian author, had no concept of the will, and there is no conceptual space in his scheme for such an alien notion in the explanations of defect and error" (111).

All three of these claims are highly suspect. First, although there can be no dispute that knowledge of the relationship between finite creatures and their creator is part of what a full knowledge of a creature is in the Christian tradition, the notion of the final cause in Aristotelian thought as one of the four causes necessary for understanding an object and the relation between any final cause and the metaphysical (as opposed to physical) status of the Prime Mover must bring into doubt any radical contrast. Similarly a perusal of Book II of *On Free Choice of the Will* and Augustine's own proof for the existence of God suggest that operating in Augustine's own thought is an Aristotelian notion of truth as the relation of the mind to its object. To be sure, God is the source for truth, but this fact is not seen by Augustine to be in conflict with the "Aristotelian" notion of truth. Finally, many have questioned whether Augustine and the Augustinian tradition before Aquinas have the strong notion of will MacIntyre claims. The nonclassical notion of will, in fact, seems to emerge after 1270, after the death of Aquinas.[8]

Obviously, there are many controversial points in MacIntyre's claims about the incommensurability between Augustinianism and Thomism. Many points MacIntyre takes as established are in fact debatable. The simplistic, static view MacIntyre associates with Augustinianism neglects the variation among Augustinians and the fact that elements of Aristotelianism were present in the Augustinian tradition from its inception. Why, then, does MacIntyre present such a simplistic view of both Augustinianism and Aristotelianism? The answer lies in how MacIntyre sees Aquinas as bridging the gap between the two.

Aquinas bridged Aristotelianism and Augustinianism by creating a synthesis of them, called Thomism. Although Thomism may be seen as containing elements of both traditions, its greatest accomplishment is that through its richer vocabulary and conceptual structure (richer by combining

8. John Boler has questioned the whole notion of will in early medieval thought in recent work. See, for example, his "Will as Power: Some Remarks on Its Explanatory Function," *Vivarium* 36, 1 (1998). See also Risto Saarinen's *Weakness of the Will*.

the two different traditions) it is able to explain both Augustinianism and Aristotelianism and explain how each tradition fails in its own terms to solve problems endemic to each. As MacIntyre puts it in *Three Rival Theories:*

> In this third type of debate, characterized by some large degree of incommensurability, the type of claim which has to be made and then established or refuted is precisely that which Aquinas advanced to Augustinians in respect of his emended and enlarged Augustinianism and to Averroists in respect of his emended and enlarged [Aristotelianism]. It is, as we noticed earlier, the claim to provide a standpoint which suffers from less incoherence, is more comprehensive and more resourceful, but especially resourceful in one particular way. For among those resources, so it is claimed, is an ability not only to identify as limitations, defects, and errors of the opposing view itself, but also to explain in precise and detailed terms what it is about the opposing view which engenders just these particular limitations, defects, and errors and also what it is about that view which must deprive it of the resources required for understanding, overcoming, and correcting them. And at the same time it will be claimed that what is cogent, insightful, and true in that opposing view can be incorporated within one's own view, providing on occasion needed corrections of that view.[9]

The importance of Aquinas is to have begun a moral tradition that unites two incommensurable moral traditions into a more comprehensive one that can explain the successes and failures of the two rival traditions.

Aquinas's success foreshadows for MacIntyre a hoped-for reconciliation between the Encyclopedists and Geneologists that will take place in lectures at universities conceived on the model of the University of Paris in the thirteenth century.

---

9. *Three Rival Theories,* 145–46. I substitute "Aristotelianism" for MacIntyre's "Augustinianism" in the last word of the first sentence of this quotation. I assume there is a typographical error.

BIBLIOGRAPHY

Anscombe, G. E. M. "Modern Moral Philosophy." Originally published in *Philosophy* 33 (January 1958). Reprinted in *The Collected Papers of G. E. M. Anscombe, Vol. I: Ethics, Religion, and Politics*. Minneapolis: University of Minnesota Press, 1981.

Anselm of Canterbury. *The Fall of Satan*. In Jasper Hopkins and Herbert Richardson, eds. and trans., *Anselm of Canterbury*. 4 vols. Toronto: Edwin Mellen Press, 1976.

Aquinas, Thomas. *Commentary on the Nicomachean Ethics*. South Bend: Dumb Ox Press, 1993.

———. *Summa Theologiae*. 60 vols. New York: McGraw-Hill, 1963–. Blackfriars ed.

Baylor, Michael G. *Action and Person: Conscience in Late Scholasticism and the Young Luther*. Studies in Medieval and Reformation Thought, 20. Leiden: E. J. Brill, 1977.

Beck, C. M., B. S. Crittenden, and E. V. Sullivan, eds. *Moral Education: Interdisciplinary Approaches*. Toronto: University of Toronto Press, 1971.

Bier, William C., ed. *Conscience: Its Freedom and Limitations*. New York: Fordham University Press, 1971.

Boler, John. "Will as Power: Some Remarks on Its Explanatory Function." *Vivarium* 36, 1 (1998).

Bonaventure. *Commentary on the Sentences*. In *Opera Theologica Selecta*. Florence: Ad Claras Aquas, 1934.

Bougerol, J. G. *Introduction to the Works of Bonaventure*. New York: Desclee Co., 1964.

Bowers, John M. *The Crisis of Will in Piers Plowman*. Washington, D.C.: Catholic University of America Press, 1986.

Broad, C. D. "Conscience and Conscientious Action." In Donnelly and Lyons, eds., *Conscience*.

Butler, Joseph. *Five Sermons Preached at the Rolls Chapel and a Dissertation upon the Nature of Virtue*. Indianapolis: Hackett, 1983.

Campbell, Robert J. "Superego and Conscience." In Bier, ed., *Conscience: Its Freedom and Limitations*.

Cavanagh, John R. "The Mature Conscience as Seen by a Psychiatrist." In Bier, ed., *Conscience: Its Freedom and Limitations*.

Charlton, W. *Weakness of Will: A Philosophical Introduction*. Oxford: Blackwell's, 1988.

Clarke, Norris. "The Mature Conscience in Philosophical Perspective." In Bier, ed., *Conscience: Its Freedom and Limitations*.

Courtenay, William J. *Schools and Scholars in Fourteenth-Century England*. Princeton: Princeton University Press, 1987.

Cunliffe, Christopher, ed. *Joseph Butler's Moral and Religious Thought*. Oxford: Clarendon Press, 1992.

Curran, Charles. "The Christian Conscience Today." In Nelson, ed., *Conscience*.

———. *The Catholic Moral Tradition Today*. Washington, D.C.: Georgetown University Press, 1999.

Dahl, Norman O. *Practical Reason, Aristotle, and Weakness of Will*. Minneapolis: University of Minnesota Press, 1984.

D'Arcy, Eric. *Conscience and Its Right to Freedom.* New York: Sheed and Ward, 1961.

Davidson, Donald. "How Is Weakness of Will Possible?" In Feinberg, ed., *Moral Concepts.*

Davies, P. C. W., and J. R. Brown, eds. *The Ghost in the Atom.* Cambridge: Cambridge University Press, 1986.

Davis, Scott. "The Structure and Functions of the Virtues." In *Acta Congressa Augustiana, 1986.* Rome: Institutum Patristicum Augustinianum, 1987.

Delhaye, Philippe. *The Christian Conscience,* trans. from the French by Charles Underhill Quinn. New York: Desclee, 1964.

Den Uyl, Douglas J. *The Virtue of Prudence.* Studies in Moral Philosophy, 5, John Kekes, gen. ed. New York: Peter Lang, 1991.

Dolan, Joseph V. "Conscience in the Catholic Theological Tradition." In Bier, ed., *Conscience: Its Freedom and Limitations.*

Donnelly, John, and Leonard Lyons, eds. *Conscience.* Staten Island, N.Y.: Alba House, 1973.

Feinberg, Joel, ed. *Moral Concepts.* Oxford: Oxford University Press, 1969.

Ferruolo, Stephen C. *The Origins of the University.* Stanford: Stanford University Press, 1985.

Flannery, Austin P., ed. *Documents of Vatican II,* vol. 1. 7th printing. Grand Rapids: Wm. B. Eerdmans, 1984.

Freud, Sigmund. *An Outline of Psycho-Analysis.* The Complete Psychological Works of Sigmund Freud, 23. London: Hogarth Press and the Institute of Psycho-Analysis, 1964.

Fuss, Peter. "Conscience." In Donnelly and Lyons, eds., *Conscience.*

Gallagher, Lowell. *Medusa's Gaze: Casuistry and Conscience in the Renaissance.* Stanford: Stanford University Press, 1991.

Hill, Thomas E., Jr. "Four Conceptions of Conscience." In Shapiro and Adams, eds., *Integrity and Conscience.*

Holopainen, Taina M. *William Ockham's Theory of the Foundations of Ethics.* Helsinki: Luther-Agricola-Society, 1991.

Horton, John, and Susan Mendus, eds. *After MacIntyre: Critical Perspectives on the Work of Alasdair MacIntyre.* Notre Dame: University of Notre Dame Press, 1994.

Hursthouse, Rosalind, Gavin Lawrence, and Warren Quinn, eds. *Virtues and Reasons: Philippa Foot and Moral Theory: Essays in Honour of Philippa Foot.* Oxford: Clarendon Press, 1995.

Jones, David H. "Freud's Theory of Moral Conscience." In Donnelly and Lyons, eds., *Conscience.*

Kant, Immanuel. *The Metaphysics of Morals.* Cambridge: Cambridge University Press, 1991. Originally published 1797.

Kent, Bonnie. "Transitory Vice: Thomas Aquinas on Incontinence." *Journal of the History of Philosophy* 27 (1989).

———. *Virtues of the Will: The Transformation of Ethics in the Late Thirteenth Century.* Washington, D.C.: Catholic University of America Press, 1995.

Kohlberg, Lawrence. "The Development of Modes of Moral Thinking and Choice in the Years Ten to Sixteen." Ph.D. diss., University of Chicago, 1958.

———. *Essays on Moral Development, Vol. 1: The Philosophy of Moral Development.* San Francisco: Harper & Row, 1981.

———. *Essays on Moral Development, Vol. 2: The Psychology of Moral Development.* San Francisco: Harper and Row, 1984.

———. *Child Psychology and Childhood Education: A Cognitive-Developmental View.* New York: Longman, 1987.

———. "The Current Formulation of the Theory," with Charles Levine and Alexandra Hewer. In *Essays in Moral Development, Vol. 2.*

————. "Conscience as Principled Responsibility: On the Philosophy of Stage Six." In *Conscience: An Interdisciplinary View*, Gerhard Zecha and Paul Weingartner, eds.

Kosman, L. A. "Being Properly Affected: Virtues and Feelings in Aristotle's Ethics." In Rorty, ed., *Essays on Aristotle's Ethics*.

Kretzmann, N., A. Kenny, and J. Pinborg, eds. *The Cambridge History of Later Medieval Philosophy*. Cambridge: Cambridge University Press, 1980.

Kroy, M. *The Conscience: A Structural Theory*. New York: John Wiley and Sons, 1974.

Kruschwitz, Robert B., and Robert C. Roberts. *The Virtues: Contemporary Essays on Moral Character*. Belmont, Calif.: Wadsworth, 1987.

Langan, John P. "Augustine on the Unity and Interconnection of the Virtues." *Harvard Theological Review* 72 (1979).

Leites, Edmund, ed. *Conscience and Casuistry in Early Modern Europe*. Cambridge: Cambridge University Press, 1988.

————. "Casuistry and Character." In Leites, ed., *Conscience and Casuistry*.

Lickona, Thomas, ed. *Moral Development and Behavior: Theory, Research, and Social Issues*. New York: Holt, Rinehart and Winston, 1976.

Locke, John. *Essay Concerning Human Understanding*.

Long, Edward Leroy, Jr. *Conscience and Compromise*. Philadelphia: Westminster Press, 1954.

Lottin, O. *Psychologie et morale aux XIIe et XIIIe siècles*, vols. 1 and 2. Gembloux: J. Duculot, 1957 (vol. 1, 2d ed.), 1948.

Louden, Robert. "On Some Vices of Virtue Ethics." *American Philosophical Quarterly* 21, 3 (1984).

MacIntyre, Alasdair. *After Virtue*. Notre Dame: University of Notre Dame Press, 1st ed., 1981, 2d ed., 1984.

————. *Whose Justice? Which Rationality?* Notre Dame: University of Notre Dame Press, 1988.

————. *Three Rival Theories of Enquiry: Encyclopedia, Geneology, Tradition*. Notre Dame: University of Notre Dame Press, 1990.

Macquarrie, John. "The Struggle of Conscience for Mature Selfhood." In Bier, ed., *Conscience: Its Freedom and Limitations*.

Mayo, Bernard. *Ethics and the Moral Life*. New York: St. Martin's Press, 1958.

McDowell, John. "Virtue and Reason." *The Monist* 62 (July 1979).

Meilender, Gilbert. "Instructing the Conscience." In Meilaender, *The Theory and Practice of Virtue*.

————. *The Theory and Practice of Virtue*. Notre Dame: University of Notre Dame Press, 1988.

Modgil, Sohan, and Celia Modgil. *Lawrence Kohlberg: Consensus and Controversy*. Philadelphia: Falmer Press, 1986.

Nelson, C. Ellis, ed. *Conscience: Theological and Psychological Perspectives*. New York: Newman Press, 1973.

Nelson, Dan. *The Priority of Prudence*. University Park: The Pennsylvania State University Press, 1988.

Nussbaum, Martha. *The Fragility of Goodness*. Cambridge: Cambridge University Press, 1986.

Ockham, William. *Opera Theologica*. Saint Bonaventure, N.Y.: Franciscan Institute, 1984.

Osterle, Jean, trans. *Treatise on the Virtues*. Notre Dame: University of Notre Dame Press, 1960.

Pence, Gregory E. "Recent Work on Virtues." *American Philosophical Quarterly* 21 (1984).

Penelhum, Terence. *Butler*. London: Routledge and Kegan Paul, 1985.

Perkins, William. *The Works of William Perkins*. Abingdon, England: Sutton Courtenay Press, 1970.

Perreiah, Alan. "Scotus on Human Emotions." *Franciscan Studies* 56 (1998).

Philibert, Paul J. "Lawrence Kohlberg's Use of Virtue in His Theory of Moral Development." *International Philosophical Quarterly* 15 (1975).

Pieper, Josef. *Prudence,* trans. R. Winston and C. Winston. New York: Pantheon, 1959.

Pincoffs, Edmund L. *Quandaries and Virtues: Against Reductivism in Ethics.* Lawrence: University Press of Kansas, 1986.

Potts Timothy C. *Conscience in Medieval Philosophy.* Cambridge: Cambridge University Press, 1980.

———. "Conscience." In Kretzmann et. al., eds., *The Cambridge History of Later Medieval Philosophy.*

Power, F. Clark, Ann Higgins, and Lawrence Kohlberg, eds. *Lawrence Kohlberg's Approach to Moral Education.* New York: Columbia University Press, 1989.

Prichard, H. H. "Does Moral Philosophy Rest on a Mistake?" *Mind* (1912).

Rashdall, Hastings. *Is Conscience an Emotion?* Boston: Houghton Mifflin, 1914.

Regan, Richard J. "Conscience in the Documents of Vatican II." In Bier, ed., *Conscience: Its Freedom and Limitations.*

Rorty, Amelie, ed. *Essays on Aristotle's Ethics.* Berkeley and Los Angeles: University of California Press, 1980.

Ryle, Gilbert. "Conscience and Moral Convictions." In Donnelly and Lyons, eds., *Conscience.*

———. *The Concept of Mind.* New York: Barnes and Noble, 1949.

Saarinen, Risto. *Weakness of the Will in Medieval Thought from Augustine to Buridan.* Leiden: E. J. Brill, 1994.

Scotus, John Duns. *Opera Omnia.* Rome: Vatican City Press, 1950.

Shapiro, Ian, and Robert Adams, eds. *Integrity and Conscience.* New York: New York University Press, 1998.

Shklar, Judith. *Ordinary Vices.* Cambridge, Mass.: Belknap Press of Harvard University Press, 1984.

Slote, Michael. *From Morality to Virtue.* New York: Oxford University Press, 1992.

———. *Goods and Virtues.* New York: Oxford University Press, 1983.

Smith, Robert J. *Conscience and Catholicism.* New York: University Press of America, 1998.

Vicetia, Mariae A., and Joannis A. Rubino, eds. *Lexicon Bonaventurianum Philosophico-Theologicum.* Venice: Aemiliana, 1880.

Vlastos, Gregory. "The Unity of the Virtues in the *Protagoras.*" In Vlastos, *Platonic Studies.* Princeton: Princeton University Press, 1981.

Von Wright, George Henrik *The Varieties of Goodness.* London: Routledge and Kegan Paul, 1963.

Wallace, James D. *Virtues and Vices.* Ithaca: Cornell University Press, 1978.

Walsh, James J. *Aristotle's Conception of Moral Weakness.* New York: Columbia University Press, 1963.

Wand, Bernard. "The Content and Form of Conscience." In Donnelly and Lyons, eds., *Conscience.*

Wiesel, Elie. *Night/Dawn/Day.* Northvale, N.J.: Jason Aronson, 1985.

Wolter, Allan B. *Duns Scotus on the Will and Morality.* Washington, D.C.: Catholic University of America Press, 1986.

Wood, Rega. *Ockham on the Virtues.* West Lafayette: Purdue University Press, 1997.

Zachman, Randall C. *The Assurance of Faith: Conscience in the Theology of Martin Luther and John Calvin.* Minneapolis: Augsburg Fortress Press, 1993.

Zecha, Gerhard, and Paul Weingartner, eds. *Conscience: An Interdisciplinary View.* Dordrecht: D. Reidel, 1987.

Zilboorg, G. "Superego and Conscience." In Nelson, ed., *Conscience.*

INDEX

Anscombe, Elizabeth, 136, 148
Aquinas, Thomas, 9, 23, 28 n. 16, 39–51, 54,
    57, 59, 69, 76, 78, 110–14, 125, 128,
    131–32, 141, 142, 173, 180–84
aretaic concepts, 155–57
Aristotle, 9, 13–20, 37, 44–46, 61, 63, 66,
    78, 106, 111, 137, 140, 142, 148, 150,
    152, 154, 157–59, 168, 169, 175,
    180–84
Aronfreed, Justin, 166–67
Augustine, 21–23, 41, 41 n. 9, 44, 46, 46 n.
    23, 66, 78, 125, 142, 181

Barlow, Thomas, 80
Baxter, Richard, 80
Bennett, William J., 170–72
Biel, Gabriel, 73, 75, 76
Bonaventure, 9, 25–37, 39, 40, 54, 56–57, 59,
    69, 100, 110, 113, 114, 128
Broad, C. D., 99 n. 1, 104, 126–27
Butler, Joseph, 80–82, 91, 92 n. 2, 100–101,
    108, 123, 173

Calvin, Jean, 71, 78
casuistry, 77–80, 84
Cavanagh, John R., 116–17
choice, 46
circularity of moral virtues, 17, 58, 140,
    175
Clarke, Norris, 114, 118–19
conscience
    acting against conscience, 27, 74, 96, 110,
        129–31
    as an affective quality, 99–102
    antecedent conscience, 73, 114–15
    applied conscience, 26, 57
    Aquinas's view of, 43–51

authentic conscience, 116, 128
authority of conscience, 27, 74, 81, 98, 101,
    129–31
    Bonaventure's view of, 25–37
    Butler's view of, 80–82
    Catholic Church's definition of, 109
    cognitive view of, 99–101
    as a conative disposition, 103–7
    consequent conscience, 73, 114–15
    content of conscience, 98, 175
    conventional conscience, 116, 131, 169, 175
    dynamic view of, 28–29, 69
    as a faculty, 8, 77–84, 100–107, 119, 121–
        28, 173–77
    freedom of, 110–12, 119
    Freud's view, 88–91
    Fuss's view, 102–8
    as internal representative of God, 27, 40, 74,
        82, 111
    as judge, 7, 8, 77, 82, 84, 89–91, 96, 123
    Kant's view, 82–86
    Kohlberg's definition of, 166
    Luther's view of, 71–77
    MacIntyre's view of, 141
    mature conscience, 116–19, 127, 130, 155,
        169, 175
    medieval view of, 8
    mistaken conscience, 27–28, 40, 43, 53, 62,
        110
    modern view of, 7
    moral conscience, 113–14
    nonexistence of conscience, 107–8
    Ockham's view of, 61–69
    as a personal monitor, 8, 91–98, 131, 175
    potential conscience, 26, 57
    and practical reason, 8, 111
    psychological conscience, 112

as a relational entity, 126–32, 174–77
Ryle's view of, 91–98
Scotus's view of, 54–61
as superego, 89
traditional conscience, 130
Wand's view of, 103–8
continent man, 44–48
courage, 145
Cousins, Ewert, 117, 131
Cricket, Jiminy, 174
cultivation of the virtues, 17, 20, 50–51, 68, 82, 111, 153, 174
Curran, Charles, 110 n. 2, 113–15

darkness of blindness, 31–32
Delhaye, Philippe, 112–14
deontological theories of virtue ethics, 147–49
Dulles, Avery, 119

ego, 88–89
ego-ideal, 115–16, 176
electron as a relational entity, 123–26
Encyclopedic Tradition, 142–44, 179–84
ethics of rules, 152
eubulia, 48–51

faculties in general, 8, 36
Foot, Philippa, 144, 145, 154
formal distinction, 62
Freud, Sigmund, 84, 87–91, 96, 99 n. 2, 101, 102, 115–16, 119, 123, 173
Fuss, Peter, 102–7

Geach, Peter T., 145, 148
geneological tradition, 142–44, 179–84
Gerson, Jean, 74–75
the good, for human beings, 15, 56, 140, 148, 158
goods, internal and external, 139

habit, 14, 15, 42, 57, 79, 84, 131–32, 174
happiness, 13–15
hardness of obstinacy, 32–34
Henry of Ghent, 53–54, 58, 63
Hunter, J. F. M., 107–8
Hursthouse, Rosalind, 152–55, 158, 172

id, 88–91
incommensurability, 142, 179–84

incontinent man, 44–49
indoctrination, 171–72
intemperate (self-indulgent) man, 44–48
invincible ignorance, 74

Jerome, 9, 23

Kant, Immanuel, 82–84, 91, 99 n. 2, 123, 149, 153–54, 162–66, 173, 176
Kent, Bonnie, 44–48
Kohlberg, Lawrence, 160–72, 175–77

Locke, John, 125
Lombard, Peter, 9, 25
Louden, Robert B., 151–53
Luther, Martin, 62 n. 13, 71–77, 81, 91, 119

MacIntyre, Alasdair, 129 n. 10, 136–44, 148, 149, 179–84
Macquarrie, John, 116, 127–28, 169
Mayo, Bernard, 122–23
Meilander, Gilbert, 171–72
Meno, 11–13
Mill, John Stuart, 101–2
moral convictions, 92–98
moral knowledge, 63–67
moral tradition, 139–43, 179–84
moral worth of actions, 62, 73, 78
morally good man, 151–55, 177
Mover, Prime, 183

narrative, 137–38
Nicomachean Ethics, 13–20, 22, 44–46, 51

Ockham, William, 9, 53, 61–69, 76, 78, 168, 173
opinion, true (right), 12–13

Pascal, 78
Pence, Gregory, 144–46
perception (moral) of objects, 20, 42, 43, 51, 132, 176
perfect, virtuous person, 61
Perkins, William, 80, 82
person of practical wisdom, 16, 158
perversity, moral, 32–34
Philip the Chancellor, 23–25, 53
Piaget, Jean, 161–63
Plato, 9–13, 106, 150, 157, 167
pleasure, 55–56, 60, 83–84, 141

practical reason, 9, 43, 48–51, 59, 73, 76, 114, 123, 140, 168, 173, 175
practical wisdom, 13, 15–20, 37, 168, 175
practice, 138, 144
pre-conscious, 90
Protagoras, 9–11, 32 n. 22, 106
Protestant Reformation, 8, 62
Protestant turn, 77
prudence, 41–51, 59, 62, 64, 66–69, 111, 113, 119, 142, 163, 175
  actual prudence, 65
  and conscience, 43–51
  and practical knowledge, 43–51
  proper prudence, 57–60, 65–68
psychoanalysis, 87–91

rationality of traditions, 137, 179–84
relational entities, 122–32
reversibility, 163, 175
role-playing, 163
Ryle, Gilbert, 91–98, 99 n. 2, 100, 104, 127, 150

Saarinen, Risto, 47–48
Scotus, John Duns, 9, 53–69, 76, 78, 125, 168, 173
scrupulousness, 93–98
Slote, Michael, 155–60, 172
Socrates, 9–13, 95
sophists, 12
stages of moral development, 161–69
suneidesis (syneidesis), 7, 92, 116
superego, 88–91, 115–16

synderesis (synteresis), 9, 23–25, 30 n. 20, 31–35, 39–43, 54–59, 68 n. 21, 73–77, 91, 110, 113
synesis, 48–51

Taylor, Jeremy, 80
teleological views of virtue ethics, 147–50
theology of the cross, 72
Tradition (Thomism), 142, 180–84
Trianosky, Gregory, 146–50

unicity of the active intellect, 182
unity of the virtues, 10–17, 22, 60, 62, 66
University of Paris, 181–84
Urmson, J. O., 145
utilitarianism, 157–60

virtue ethics, 136–50, 151–60, 174–77
virtues, 9, 12–13, 15, 22, 29, 35, 50–9, 62–66, 76, 81, 83, 111, 119, 131–33, 137–38, 141, 144–45, 149, 167, 174
  bag of virtues, 167–72
  cardinal virtues, 22
  moral virtues, 14, 15–18, 57, 168
  intellectual virtues, 14, 42, 168
  theological virtues, 67
Von Wright, G. H., 136, 144, 148

Wallace, James, 144, 148, 150
Wand, Bernard, 103–7, 109
wantonness of pleasure, 32–33
weakness of will (*akrasia, incontinentia*), 9, 18–20, 22–23, 42, 44–51, 97, 128, 176
will, 54–57, 59, 125–26

Made in the USA
Middletown, DE
16 November 2023

42898746R00120